W9-BRR-262

Shattering the Myth

PRINCETON STUDIES IN MUSLIM POLITICS

Dale F. Eickelman and James Piscatori, Editors

Shattering the Myth

ISLAM

BEYOND VIOLENCE

Bruce B. Lawrence

PRINCETON UNIVERSITY PRESS

PRINCETON, NEW JERSEY

Third printing, and first paperback printing, 2000
Paperback ISBN 0-691-00487-0

*The Library of Congress has cataloged the cloth edition
of this book as follows*

Lawrence, Bruce B.
Shattering the myth : Islam beyond violence /
Bruce B. Lawrence.
p.   cm. — (Comparative studies in Muslim politics)
Includes bibliographical references and index.
ISBN 0-691-05769-9 (cloth : alk. paper)
1. Islam—20th century. 2. Violence—Religious aspects—
Islam. I. Title. II. Series.
BP163.L34 1998
297′.09′04—dc21
97–38776

This book has been composed in Sabon typeface

The paper used in this publication meets the
minimum requirements of ANSI/NISO Z39.48-1992
(R 1997) (*Permanence of Paper*)

http://pup.princeton.edu

Printed in the United States of America

10   9   8   7   6

TO MIRIAM

COMPANION, CATALYST, CRITIC, AND,
ABOVE ALL, FRIEND

Islam's middle position can be recognized by the fact that Islam has always been attacked from two opposite directions: from the side of religion that it is too natural, actual, and tuned to the world; and from the side of science that it contains religious and mystical elements. There is only one Islam, but like man, it has both soul and body. . . . For the future and man's practical activity, Islam means the call to create a man harmonious in his soul and body, and [the call to create] a society whose laws and socio-political institutions will maintain—and not violate—this harmony.
—ʿAlija ʿAli Izetbegovic, Islam between East and West

Jihad means "to insure that the real-world struggles of Muslims for social justice and peace may bear fruit. The ultimate goal of every Muslim is Islam, the state of peace, of submission in the certainty and power of Allah."
—Digital Jihad, an entry for the Activist Resource Center of the Dunya and Cyber Muslim Information host line of the World Wide Web, 26 February 1996

Contents

CONTENTS

Illustrations

Foreword

VIOLENCE is never far from popular assumptions of Muslim politics. Islamists, or Muslim "fundamentalists," are thought to be single-mindedly pitted against the secular state; suicide bombings and hostage-taking are viewed as a critical, if not the decisive, component of the modern Muslim-Western encounter; and the subordination of women in Muslim societies has acquired the normative status of a cliché. As with all received understandings, there are elements of truth in these formulations, but adequate analysis requires a fuller exploration of the contexts in which Muslim societies have evolved and of the ways they interact with larger economic and political orders. Bruce Lawrence has provided just such an informed interpretation of the contemporary Muslim experience.

For Muslim societies from the eighteenth century onward, as for countless other peoples, the defining event has been the imperialist intrusion of the West and the advent of colonial dependency. The consequences have been manifold: the distortion of economic development and subordination to "global"—that is, Western—trade, investment, and production requirements; the emergence of local bureaucratic elites that, in the name of independence, replicate the nationalist ideological superstructure of the colonizers; the reaction of counterelites that seek to affirm their own claims to power and legitimacy by contesting the bases of political and cultural "authenticity." This course of history is scarcely unique to Muslims, and to the extent that they, like others, are buffeted by larger currents, explanations for Muslim political conduct based on such categorizations as "Muslim rage" seem not only reductionist, but also parochial.

If Muslims have been subjected to structural violence like others, the common victims of economic and political hegemonies, they have not, however, lost control over their destinies. Indeed, to grant that they possess agency, the means to respond to the challenges and dilemmas of modern life, is to recognize the analytical and policy significance of what is evocatively called the "Islamic difference." Although ideologically determined explanations may well end in unhelpful caricatures, Muslim symbols and values have a place in our examination of Muslim politics for they often shape discourse and influence conduct. Muslims do more than simply react; motivated by their own norms and ideas, they routinely reshape their world—and Islam—even as they reshape through interaction the worlds of the postcolonial or, generally, non-Muslim "Others."

This process, described in the pages to follow, is complex. On the one hand, although the term "Muslim politics" may at first glance appear to suggest uniformity of intent or practice, it is grounded in the assumption of variability and change. Circumstances affect the contours of that politics, and Lawrence's explanations for the particular states of affairs in Egypt, Iran, Pakistan, and Malaysia, among other cases, are compelling. Yet, on the other hand, there are broadly shared characteristics, notably the manipulation of symbolic resources and the permeability, even volatility, of boundaries. Women, to a large extent, have emerged at the core of politics in Muslim societies because they have been invested, or have invested themselves, with the representation of "Islam." They become the bearers of cultural orthodoxy, the very symbol of the faith and purity of the community. However, the production and maintenance of this symbol, like others, is an intensely political act that speaks directly to—at times sustaining but often subverting—established hierarchies and approved codes of social conduct. Thus, contention over the status, legal and otherwise, of women in Muslim societies both delineates and challenges the boundaries of public morality.

Negotiations are a constant feature of the Muslim landscape, but a more visible aspect is protest, whether it be against colonial or neocolonial power, the dominant local state apparatus, the religious establishment, or the prevailing economic system. In a sense, this focus on negotiation almost naturally flows from the fragmentation of authority that marks Muslim societies today. Political and religious bureaucracies, officially sanctioned 'ulama or religious authorities, Islamist movements, urban intellectuals, Sufi orders—all present in Lawrence's study—represent the range of competitors for the mantle of defender of the faith. Their very competition spurs a sense of discontent with the status quo and the search for alternative futures. But Professor Lawrence refines our understanding of the dynamics of protest by noting the importance of timing and sequence, placing protest into a historical framework that distinguishes among revivalist, reformist, and fundamentalist phases.

Revivalists were preindustrial and overwhelmingly Sunni, responding to a potent combination of direct European intervention, disruptions to traditional trade, demographic shifts, and agricultural decline and finding a cushion of sorts in the reaffirmation of Islamic identity and values. Reformers, who formed an intellectual elite and were the product of the colonial presence, adapted to the nationalist and ideological legacies of the West and saw them as compatible with Islam. Whether they acknowledged it or not, they found in these Western ideas a rival standard to that of the divine text. It is thus no surprise that, from the 1970s, fundamentalists have sought to right the imbalance and to wrest power, and therefore the control of authenticity, away from the "modernists." Structural realignments of global economic, political, and military power provide the context in which these protest movements hope to overcome the interconnected senses of vulnerability and cultural outrage and to achieve empowerment.

We come full circle, then, to the specter and reality of violence. Although not all fundamentalists have the same goals and adopt the same strategies, it is obvious that many deploy directly confrontational means in their assault on the mighty state or what they regard as the neoimperialist West. But, as Lawrence acutely observes, other voices, whether from Bosnia or from Malaysia, are beginning to be heard as well, and basic concepts are being redefined in the direction of pluralism. The current debate over whether Islam is compatible with democracy turns in large part on whether Islamic values and symbols are seen as evolving and flexible or as definitive and unyielding. Lawrence's argument in this regard is subtle and penetrating. Muslims, particularly Muslim women of course, face economic underdevelopment within their own societies and marginalization in the high-technology global economy; even the oil-rich Gulf states are disadvantaged in their reliance on Western technology and science. However, just as economic and political need provided the engine for change in the past, so too now the concept of *jihad*, long reviled in the West as a sign of Muslim aggressiveness, has emerged in some quarters as an internal challenge to Muslim societies. Despite what fundamentalists may say, the real struggle of the modern world is against economic dependence, and rather than seeing neocapitalist corporate culture as a sterile conformity with, or capitulation to, the global hegemon, some recognize that striving toward that culture—*jihad*—is consistent with evolving Islamic norms of economic responsibility and social justice. As Muslims accept that accommodationism of this kind is both necessary and desirable, space may well be created for tolerance between Muslims and others—but, perhaps more importantly, among Muslims themselves—and the cause of pluralism advanced.

The challenge in evaluating the manifold dimensions of contemporary Islam is to accord analytical respect to the evolving normative code while avoiding the overdeterminism sometimes implicit in notions of religious politics. Muslims, we often forget, do not always act as Muslims or as members of a religious community; rather, they respond to economic, social, and political needs that may direct conduct more than ideological signposts do. Yet, at the same time, the "world view" or imagination of Muslims remains a renewing source of guidance in a world undergoing bewildering transformations. Bruce Lawrence's distinguished contribution is to demonstrate a balance of perspectives that is instructive, and to alert us to the salutary effects that an Islamic difference can make.

James Piscatori
Dale F. Eickelman

Acknowledgments

IT IS IMPOSSIBLE to thank everyone in a project such as this, but foremost recognition belongs to the Harry Frank Guggenheim Foundation, which funded the research and writing of much of this book in the early 1990s. Karen Colvard, the senior program officer at the Harry Frank Guggenheim Foundation, not only helped me to conceptualize the project but also organized a seminar to provide valuable feedback on the manuscript after it had been accepted for publication by Princeton University Press. Karen was as generous with her imagination as with her time, and I am glad to acknowledge my indebtedness to her on both counts. I also benefited from the interventions of several scholars who attended the March 1997 seminar at the Harry Frank Guggenheim Foundation: Janet Abu-Lughod, Pinar Batur Vanderlippe, Miriam Cooke, Hamid Dabashi, Ainslie Embree, Abdullah Hammoudi, Robert Hefner, Arlene MacLeod, and John Vanderlippe. Joel Wallman, another program officer of the Harry Frank Guggenehim Foundation, helped facilitate the March seminar, quietly but effectively assisting in this as in other dimensions of my work with the foundation; I acknowledge with gratitude his role as well in the making of this book.

The Fundamentalism Project of the University of Chicago gave me both programmatic and financial incentive to craft an earlier essay on the Shah Bano case, which appears as chapter 5 below and was first published in slightly different form in *The Journal of Religious Ethics* 22.1 (Spring 1994). In their complementary roles, Martin Marty and F. Scott Appleby of the Fundamentalism Project have been consistent, helpful supporters of my work, and I thank them for including me in several useful workshops in Cambridge and Hyde Park. I also thank *The Journal of Religious Ethics* for permission to reprint the Shah Bano essay.

The United States Information Agency funded trips to Pakistan in the 1980s and to Malaysia in the 1990s, trips which permitted me to give lectures, make contacts and, above all, develop an onsite acquaintance with fluctuating, often unpredictable developments.

I also benefited from a trip to Iran in early 1996. At the invitation of the Ministry of Culture and Islamic Guidance, I traveled to Tehran to give a plenary paper on the significance of Persian culture in the study of Islamic civilization. A side benefit of the trip was the possibility that it afforded me to observe firsthand the latest phase of the Islamic Republic of Iran. I am especially indebted to Dr. Nasrollah Pourjavady, director of Tehran University Press, for facilitating that trip, and for making every aspect of the conference a pleasurable reintroduction to present-day Iran.

I have also benefited from colleagues who have read and responded to versions of this book in earlier drafts. I want to acknowledge Vincent Cornell and Carl Ernst, in particular, for thoughtful comments that exceed collegial responsibility, even as they reinforce the meaning—and value—of friendship.

Graduate students at Duke University, whether in seminars or in library stacks, have devoted time, expended energy, and shown creativity in helping me to think through some of the issues addressed throughout this book. I would like especially to thank Mark Lynch, Charles Wilkins, Maddie Adelman, Kelly Jarrett, Randy Styers, Scott Kugel, Ann Burlein, Munis Faruqi, and Eric Boyd.

One staff person at Duke University has also assisted me immeasurably: Connie Blackmore, administrative coordinator for Comparative Area Studies, not only gave me feedback on the form of earlier versions but actually typed the entire manuscript prior to its submission to Princeton University Press. She has been a spectacular example of quiet efficiency and unfailing good humor, even when tested, as indeed she was, by gaps and inconsistencies in my text. More recently, both Lynda Harrison and Lillian Spiller of the Department of Religion have aided me in putting the revised manuscript into publishable form, and I would be remiss in not acknowledging their support as well.

As this project has moved through the manuscript stage to the book stage, I have become increasingly indebted to Ann Wald. First as religion editor then as editor-in-chief at Princeton University Press, Ann has encouraged me to pursue submission, review, and preparation of this book for Princeton University Press. Without her creative advice I still would have written and published this book, but it is no exaggeration to say that it has become a far better book because of her oversight.

Few persons are as lucky as I am in my academic labor; I share travels abroad as well as writing at home with one who also shares almost all other aspects of my life yet never stints from offering me fresh perspectives and occasional goads. If I have read nearly everything she has written and published, she has read all of mine. We work together, but I consider myself the one more profited. It is to my wife, Miriam Cooke, whom I dedicate this book.

Yet neither Miriam nor anyone else is responsible for the use to which I have put their generous gifts of time and thought. For over twenty years I have continued to reflect on the complexity of contemporary Muslim life. I remain perplexed at its diverse norms, but I also remain in awe of its persistent values. This book mirrors my ongoing engagement with Islam and with Muslims. Its errors, like its judgments, remain mine; both are but the latest way station in a lifelong journey.

Shattering the Myth

Islam across Time and Cultures

MY MAIN argument is simple, yet it is at odds with most popular and academic understandings of Islam. I argue that Islam cannot be understood except as a major and complex religious system, shaped as much by its own metaphysical postulates and ethical demands as by the circumstances of Muslim polities in the modern world. The last two hundred years have witnessed challenge upon challenge, from colonial subjugation to sporadic revivalism to elitist reform movements to, most recently, pervasive struggles with fundamentalism or Islamism. During each phase, Muslims have had to address internal tensions as well as external threats. The success of anticolonial struggles was followed by the disappointment of indigenous neocolonialisms. More recently, postcolonial Muslims—some Arab, most non-Arab—have been playing ever greater roles in economic changes, both regional and global. As the impact of these changes has become evident on societies everywhere, they have propelled new actors into public view. The most remarkable new presence is that of Muslim women.

In what follows I argue that the experience of Muslim women, above all, calls for a more nuanced approach to Islam and global change. It is time to counter negative stereotypes about Muslim women with knowledge about their newly constituted roles.

Yet few books attempt to synthesize data from regionally separate and geographically discrete countries with a majority Muslim population. Where such an effort has been made, it is usually through multiauthored or edited volumes that belie the very coherence suggested by their titles. While I do offer an in-depth study of one pivotal judicial saga, from India, I have otherwise drawn together data provided by others in order to demonstrate (a) that Islam is not inherently violent and (b) that the longer view of Muslim societies offers hope, rather than despair, about the role of Islam in the next century.

This book offers three convergent foci: the crystallization of Islamic sociopolitical movements, women as the key index of

3

Muslim identity, and finally the staging of new global economic developments that bode an unexpected Muslim difference in world affairs.

The Muslim difference will remain hidden, its force unacknowledged, unless the dominant stereotype is exposed: Islam is not violence, nor are Muslims intrinsically prone to violence. The stereotype amounts to a slur, and it must be addressed at the outset if the emerging profile of postcolonial Muslims is to be understood.

ISLAM BEYOND VIOLENCE

Islam is . . . Islam is . . . Islam is . . . Islam is many things. Just as there is no single America or Europe or the West, a seamless caption etching diverse groups and persons with the same values and meanings, so there is no single place or uniform culture called Islam. There is no monolithic Islam. There is a Muslim world spanning Africa and Asia. It is as pluralistic as the West, outstripping both Europe and America in the numerous regions, races, languages, and cultures that it encompasses. The Afro-Asian Muslim world is also internally pluralistic, containing multiple groups who might be said to represent Islamic norms in each Muslim country. And Muslims themselves are aware of how necessary, and how difficult, it is to specify differing notions of Islam. An Indonesian friend of mine once quipped: "There are three Islams: the popular Islam which anthropologists are fond of studying, mostly as curious spectators; the public Islam with which political scientists, journalists, and policy makers identify, mostly as adversaries; and the academic Islam in which Orientalists delight, whether as art historians, linguists, or religion scholars, each studying artifacts esteemed by their guild. In Indonesia we try to provide our visitors with all three."[1]

If Islam is so diverse and Muslims so accommodating, then why has Islam so often been viewed by non-Muslims as alien at best and violent at worst? I suggest that the principal reason for the negative view of Islam is the predominance in popular thinking of the second view: public Islam. In that view, Islam emanates from a hostile, "Arab" Middle East. Most journalists, and many policy makers, continue to discount any but Arab Islam, or what is conjured up as Arab Islam in projecting the orthodox face of puritanism and militancy. In the 1990s most Euro-American journalists continue to echo the sentiments that drove European kings and their subjects to launch their crusades almost a millennium ago, crusades whose enemy was Arab Muslims. In the aftermath of the Cold War the enemy, once again, has become the one Islam, the militant, unyielding, violent face of "Arab" Islam. Whether one picks up a popular book claiming to represent "Western cultures and values" under attack from Islam,[2] or lead articles of *The New York Times*, such as the recent "Seeing Green: The Red Menace Is Gone. But Here's Islam,"[3] the message is the same: Islam is one, and Islam is dangerous.

The Muslim enemy is invariably male, whether a foreign warrior conjured from the past or a potential terrorist stalking modern America. The fierce Kurdish anti-Crusader Salah ad-din Ayyubi, known popularly as Saladin, seems to have multiple contemporary look-alikes. Whether it is Ayatollah Khomeini denouncing the United States as the Great Satan or the Egyptian Sheikh Omar Abdel Rahman plotting to bomb the World Trade Center and other New York public buildings, Muslim leaders continue to be newsworthy principally for their adversarial words and deeds.

Behind the hostile Muslim men, Americans imagine the faces of Muslim women, homebound creatures marked alike by seclusion from the outside world and apparent oppression by their tyrannical husbands. The reality of Muslim women's active participation in their societies is glossed, covered, as it were, by a veil that projects the violence of male "Arab" Muslims everywhere. They hate the West and abuse their women.

Both images depend on singularizing Islam and then describing it as both different and violent. That stereotype remains remote from Islam as lived experience. Popular Islam is more than just the remote village or exotic domain of anthropologists. It is also the shared notion of a world view and a pattern of living that characterizes most Muslims in Asia and Africa. It provides enormous challenges and hopes and satisfactions for Muslim women and for Muslim men. Islam offers all Muslims no fewer possibilities than every major religious tradition offers the women and the men who identify with it.

Because gender imbalance pervades both popular understanding and Muslim historiography, I will call attention to the places where women have been excluded. I will also draw out the implica-

5

tions of their exclusion. How best to weave the multiple levels of women's history and their interests into a narrative that also takes account of macropolitical changes has not been an easy task. I have decided to do a separate section on women's history for three countries—Iran, Pakistan, and Egypt—in order to show how different that history looks from the "standard" history I provide in the earlier analyses of these same countries. While the preponderance of dates given in country chapters highlights male actors, it is the significant dates for women that highlight chapter 5, where I explore the double bind of Muslim women in the current period of Islamic fundamentalism. In chapter 6 I limit analysis to one non-Muslim country and one famous court case, that of Shah Bano in India. The Shah Bano case is important for India but also for its Muslim majoritarian neighbors, Pakistan and Bangladesh. Since these three polities govern the largest number of Muslims in the world, I have tried to demonstrate how the Shah Bano case discloses the juridical structures that define, and also restrict, the public opportunities for Muslim women throughout the Asian subcontinent.

To some, the arrangement of chapters might seem to perpetuate the perverse axiom "equal but separate" as applied to women in general and Muslim women in particular. My intent has been the opposite: to argue for the inclusion of a perspective on Muslim women that complicates the standard interpretation of Muslim norms and values, at the same time that it does not obscure the prevalence of violence as a condition that affects both Muslim men and Muslim women, in much of Asia and Africa but also in Europe and America.

Why do I begin with violence? Because violence is where most non-Muslims begin to think about Islam, especially if they live in a society where Muslim citizens are either silent or absent. In some cases, Muslims are too few to be properly viewed as multiple rather than singular in their outlook. Such is the case with America in the mid-1990s, where popular attention focuses on Louis Farrakhan and his message of hatred as if that messenger speaks for most Muslims as well as many African American males.[4]

Though there are episodes in which Muslims, like members of any contemporary religious community, do commit violence, and though there are other Farrakhans in the world outside the United States, violence remains an aberration rather than the norm. Violence is no more intrinsic to Islam than to Judaism, Christianity, Hinduism, Buddhism, or Sikhism. The distorted link of Islam to violence has to be brought into the full light of critical enquiry.

It is to restore balance to the popular Euro-American understanding of Islam and Muslims that I begin my foray into recent Muslim history by focusing on violence. Violence fully exposed can illumine how Islamic rhetoric and symbol function for Muslim leaders and institutions. If violence pervades Muslim public life throughout this century, it is because violence pervades the world order, old and new. It affects all Muslims indirectly, but it has a direct and immediate impact on those who are marked as Muslim political figures.

Take, for example, ʿAlija Izetbegovic. The president of Bosnia-Herzegovina, Izetbegovic provides the first epigraph for this book. "Islam," in his view, "means the call to create a person harmonious in body and soul, and [the call to create] a society whose laws and socio-political institutions will maintain—and not violate—that harmony." Why Izetbegovic? Because he has lived during a period of unprecedented turmoil for himself and for his countrymen. The Cold War ended abruptly in 1989, yet the promised new world order did not emerge, at least not in Bosnia. Izetbegovic, however, continues to struggle as an East European Muslim who refuses to parochialize Islam or to advocate a defensive Islam against an offensive West. Izetbegovic exemplifies the crucial, transregional scope of impulses to locate Islam within rather than against global processes.

Who is Izetbegovic? Except for his dour countenance flashed from time to time on CNN, he remains little known to most Americans or Europeans. Yet he is an intellectual turned activist. Neither Arab nor Asian nor African, he is fully European. His being European calls into question the standard set of equivalents attached to religious affiliations that tend to frame Islam as Afro-Asian, Christianity as Euro-American. A lawyer and a philosopher, Izetbegovic is conversant with the major intellectual and social challenges of this century that originate from the so-called West, that is, the nation-states of Europe (and America) located to the west of Bosnia.[5]

To some Izetbegovic might well be dubbed a "violent" Muslim, since violence forms part of his world view and he does not flinch from its consideration in his writings. But he views physical vio-

7

lence, including military confrontation, as a last resort only, a counterforce to others' violence. What he advocates is a defensive, not an offensive, resort to violence: violence to achieve a more harmonious political-social order. In Bosnia, and elsewhere, Izetbegovic seeks a pluralist polity where Islam becomes not the preemptive religion but the pragmatic middle way, a modus vivendi between remnants of the formerly Communist East and the emerging European Union, with its global allies.

Yet violence of another kind does loom large, casting its dark shadow over Izetbegovic's Bosnian homeland, as it does over the destiny of most Muslims in most parts of the globe at the end of the twentieth century. It is a structural violence that reduces the range of choice for European, as for African and Asian, Muslims. It is a structural violence that restricts the options for Muslim nation-states in a post–Cold War world, but it also does something far more subtle and consequential: it victimizes Muslim intellectuals by imposing limits on discourse about Islam at the end of this century. It talks *about* some other, in this case Muslim others, but never talks *from* a perspective that is self-critical about location (Euro-American) and time (end of a century).

But which century is ending? It seems obvious, almost banal, to state "the twentieth century" because we take it for granted as *our* century. We presume the Christian century as a universal time gradient, though there is also a new Muslim century (the fifteenth) that is only in its second decade. Most persons calculate "real" time only by the Christian calendar, and that is fitting since the century that is coming to an end in the year 2000/2001 is a supremely Christian century. The common calendar reflects the axis of global power: the twentieth century belongs to Christian nations or to "secular" nations with a residual Christian ethos or a majority of Christian citizens. Muslim players have been few and peripheral. This century, more than any that preceded it, will be remembered and portrayed as the Euro-American century. And it is against that backdrop of taken-for-granted hegemony, a kind of blind structural violence writ large, that the relationship of Islam to violence needs to be reconsidered.

Izetbegovic, alert to French science, British history, and Russian literature, able to cite Freud, Marx, Engels, and Buber with equal ease, should be in the so-called Western camp: both by training and by disposition he is a Muslim modernist. The first of two epigraphs for this book was taken from his major theoretical writing published in 1984, long before the debacle of 1991 in ex-Yugoslavia. Yet already Izetbegovic felt himself beset by enemies. Despite being an eclectic pluralist broadly engaged in the scholarly tradition of modern Europe, he asserts (a) that Islam is under attack and (b) that Islam under attack is always split into two Islams, one etherialized as religion, the other demonized as politics.

Izetbegovic rejects the dichotomization, which amounts to the demonizations, of Islam. He acknowledges the link between Islamic rhetoric and *some* acts of political violence, but he stops short of making Islam either the primary cause or the principal motivation for violence. Instead he tries to project and preserve the Islamic middle ground or middle way. He also tries to restore Muslim intellectuals to a role of mediation in charting the future for Muslim polities and the Muslim world as a whole.

In what follows I will try to chart my own middle way, steering between the twin minefields of apologetics and polemics. While no one can deny that some Muslims perpetrate acts of violence, I will attempt to show how the variability of Islam permits not one but several Muslim responses to violence: loyalty to Islam may be invoked as easily to avert cyclical violence (as in the case of Izetbegovic) as to pursue violent confrontation in the name of Allah. Nor is such variability unique to Islam; it is shared by other religious traditions—Hindu, Buddhist, or Sikh—that also share with Islam the experience of being shaped by a Christian century, one stamped by "the West" in its colonial and now postcolonial configurations of public space and institutions.

To disconnect the equation of Islam with violence, I will employ a double stratagem. The first stratagem will be definitional: I will explore how Islam is more than what is commonly presupposed as religion. In the deepest sense, Islam remains a religion, since those who profess belief in Allah and in Muhammad as His final prophet are marked with a distinctive set of rituals and laws. Yet Islam is also a modern ideology subordinated to the dominant ideology of this century, nationalism, and it is the relationship of Islam to nationalism that is at once pivotal and understudied.

It is fashionable in some circles to debunk nationalism, and to project either the "end of history"—in Francis Fukuyama's misguided slogan—or a "coming clash of civilizations"—in Samuel Huntington's vaporous restaging of postnational, global conflict.[6]

A close look at day-to-day affairs, however, suggests both that nationalism is alive in the mid-1990s and that the nation-state is far from obsolete as an instrument of power. As one shrewd observer has lamented, the nation-state remains "the politics of the first person plural." It coalesces ideological forces precisely because "the sense of being 'we' . . . is the necessary foundation for any durable political system" and "only the nation-state possesses this necessary sense of identity." "The nation-state will last longer than most people had thought."[7] And because most Muslims exist within postcolonial Muslim nation-states, the ubiquitous character of nationalism has to be acknowledged in any discussion of contemporary Islam. At the same time, one must be alert to recall, as Bruce Kapferer has reminded us, that nationalism itself is far from a unitary movement; it reflects much more than European norms, First World values, or elitist experiences.[8]

If my first stratagem is to revisit and redefine basic categories, my second stratagem will be discursive: I will focus on how European colonial powers have used religion in the service of ideology to divide and control major segments of the world, from West Africa to Southeast Asia. The record does not permit blanket condemnation of all legacies from the colonial period, for the modern sector of Muslim societies has produced creative advocates and notable benefits. Yet fifty years after the founding of the United Nations and the near elimination of European control over much of Asia and Africa, one must remain wary of how postcolonial independence has been shaped by the immediate past. The British may have gone home, and the French mission to civilize (*la mission civilisatrice*) declared a failure, but British and French, as also Dutch and Russian, legacies persist in the Muslim world. Part 2 will explore the durable influence of postcolonialism in specific Muslim nation-states.

I approach this task conscious that I am limited as well as enabled by who I am. I am male. I am Anglo. I am upper middle class. European in ancestry, I was born in America. Raised non-Muslim, I remain non-Muslim. Yet after studying both the Arabic language and Middle Eastern history from an early age, I remain deeply attracted to Islam as a life force: it animates many Muslims with whom I have lived and worked and whom I count among my closest friends.

While these are ascriptive limits shaping my viewpoint, I am further limited by what I embrace: I choose to be both an intellectual and an unabashed humanist. Despite the many assaults on the humanities from within and beyond the academy, I remain not only a humanist but a late modern humanist.

I am not a *post*modernist humanist, however. I continue to scan metanarratives in the pursuit of local histories. I seek patterns that interconnect numerous Muslim histories, whether local, national, or regional, and also link them collectively to global forces. At the same time, I reject the judgment that none but the persons invoked can talk about themselves. In that case, only the words of informants count, and they must be cited as the trump authority, or if one does not cite their exact words, goes the argument, then at the least one must use terms that these same informants would be comfortable having others use.[9]

The Syrian philosopher Sadik al-Azm has exposed the foolhardiness of embracing rank nominalism as a benchmark of scholarship. Rhetorically, he asks: "Were I to take seriously the subjectivist advice of those who ask us never to 'apply words to describe people that they would not accept and apply to themselves,' would I ever be able to say that such and such a Middle Eastern ruler is 'a brutal military dictator,' considering that he never applies such words and descriptions either to himself or to his regime?"[10]

The evident answer is "NO!" But too often it is a muted or defensive "No!" It needs to be announced again and again as a "NO!" "NO" to relativism, "NO" to delusionary escapism from the interlocking character of late capitalist culture and social movements that relate to it even when they claim to be independent of its influence.

At the same time, I do not advocate the total neglect of other people's self-presentation. It *does* matter what people say about themselves, the categories they use, the arguments they construct, or the goals they advocate. It does matter what people say, yet as the American religious critic Robert Segal deftly put it, "there is a difference between *starting* with the actor's point of view and *ending* with it. . . . The actor may be right, but the assumption that the actor automatically is right is dogmatic."[11]

Beyond trying to make comparisons through explicit and interdisciplinary categories, I espouse cross-cultural enquiry as a genu-

11

ine form of academic labor. It is not reducible to the new Orientalism that the feminist critic Gayatri Spivak claims it to be. In
Spivak's view, cross-culturalism serves only to perpetuate banality
in a postcolonial world,[12] but it can do more: it can also become a
pathway to exploratory dialogue that is both interdisciplinary and
international.

But cross-culturalism, if it is to generate useful dialogue, must
first accept "open appraisal, the typical plausibility tests, the bar-
gaining adjustments regnant in an open pluralist market of ideas."
The criteria are set forth by the sociologist Jose Casanova.[13] I advocate the same criteria, and I advocate them as a humanist who is at
the same time a perspectivist. In an open pluralist market of ideas,
I set out self-consciously what beliefs, attitudes, and assumptions
inform my approach to the social reality of the Muslim world.[14]
And it is from the perspective of the humanities that I challenge
both humanists and social scientists to rethink how their own prior
convictions—religious, political, and social—have shaped their
approach to contemporary Islam. What units of analysis are suitable to assessing Muslim thought and Muslim societies? What pre-
sumptions do some of the taken-for-granted categories carry? How
do we account for the difference that they convey from a context
that is predominantly Christian and secular to one that is Muslim
and often nonsecular?

I begin with the category religion.

ISLAM AS RELIGION AND ALSO NOT RELIGION

> The history of the twentieth century has confirmed
> something well known to all the historians of the
> past, something our ideologies have stubbornly ig-
> nored: the strongest, fiercest, most enduring politi-
> cal passions are nationalism and religion.
> —*Octavio Paz*, One Earth, Four or Five Worlds

To unhinge the reflexive stereotyping that plagues too much scholarship on modern-day Muslims, I begin at a point of reference outside the Muslim world but within the so-called Third World. I take
as my starting point Octavio Paz, the Mexican Nobel Laureate in
Literature. Like many contemporary Euro-American intellectuals,

Paz implies not only that religion and nationalism are equivalent passions but also that religion, like nationalism, is an undifferentiated whole that evokes deep-seated *political* passions. He concurs with the cultural historian Daniel Pick that nationalism is a form of mimetic religion, "involving a kind of faith, indeed something of the aura of 'religion' which it arguably both displaces and substitutes."[15] In that sense, religion can be both opposed to nationalism and allied with it. Yet religion is more than political and it is other than passion; it also entails language, values, and institutions. One cannot begin to compare religion and nationalism without recognizing at the outset that they are very different categories of individual expression and collective experience. While they have been engaged, each with the other, since at least the sixteenth century, Paz argues that it is in the present century that their interrelationship has become most explicit and most dangerous. Why? Because only in the twentieth century did historians for the first time recognize nationalism as evoking a passion equivalent to religion; only then did both become enduring passions—not just enduring, but "the strongest, fiercest, most enduring."

While religion can be and should be conjoined with nationalism, there remains a deeper, crucial question: Is religion privileged or diluted by being paired with nationalism? The question cannot be avoided, and Paz does give an implicit answer: in the twentieth century religion has been superseded by nationalism. Its influence, defensive and residual, becomes felt to the extent that its advocates can couple their goals with nationalist aspirations, their structures with the administrative, political, and commercial apparatus of the state. In short, for Paz religion can succeed, but it can succeed only when it becomes part of the nationalist agenda.

Yet Paz's notion of religion, never stated, seems restricted to Christianity and at the same time divested of the early modern history of Christian missions. He ignores the role and influence of "colonialism" as the vanguard and often the partner of Christian missions.[16] His notion of religion needs to be expanded beyond its most immediate referent group, Euro-American Christian elites living in the postcolonial era. Few Muslim intellectuals, still facing the legacy of colonialism, juxtapose religion to nationalism as equivalent categories, for Islam still retains a symbolic force independent of nationalism, just as it projects a pragmatic function that can, and often does, challenge nationalist ideologies.

13

Consider the Muslim intellectual with whom we began this book: Izetbegovic. Religion as a category remains problematic for Izetbegovic precisely because it projects belief as Christian belief unaffected by the historical process that led to European control over much of Asia and Africa. Yet Christian missions and missionaries were married to the colonial project in much of Asia and Africa, even when, as in the case of India, British officials attempted to limit missionary activity in order to curtail civil unrest. Religion can never be neutral when it is controlling or linked to structures that control.

At the same time, religion should have, and does have, political valence apart from the state. The Islamic "difference," in Izetbegovic's view, is to project a holistic world view that invokes religious norms as a corrective to political practices. Religion becomes a vehicle for the redress of public life, not its betrayal, since Islam advocates control—of mind, of body, of space—as an *explicit* dimension of religion.

Whereas Paz links religion with nationalism, Izetbegovic contrasts religion with worldly gain. Islam, in Izetbegovic's view, escapes the too Christian/European dialectic of religion and nationalism because pure Islam, ideal Islam, is not mere religion: it applies alike to the inner and outer life; it couples belief with action in a single, equal accent. The most palpable site of belief enacted is the mosque. It functions as a place of worship and education. "That is why schools in the Islamic world cannot be classified according to the European criterion: secular-spiritual."[17] They are both spiritual and secular, even as Islam is both other-worldly and this-worldly. The stress is double rather than staged; to believe in the next world is to be engaged in this world.

Yet engagement with this life entails more than educational pursuits; it also requires attention to the pivotal role of politics. Ideal politics are channeled to a higher vision than narrow self-interest. Islam, according to Izetbegovic, should be invoked not for expedient political ends but rather for justice: How then does one serve justice?

> In principle, force has nothing to do with morality. But in real life, there is no justice without force. Justice is the unity of the idea of equity and power . . . the impotence of religion[18] to carry out in practice even a part of the great ideals it preaches, compromises its demands before the humble and the repressed. Violence and politics, on the contrary,

have been justified to a certain extent, for they created the means needed for realizing the great ideas which religion had discovered or inspired but could not manage to translate into reality.[19]

Though Izetbegovic's view is that of an idealist, his views very closely match those of the Cyber Muslim host line citation that appears, along with his, at the outset of this book: the goal of lived Islam is "to insure that the real-world struggles of Muslims for social justice and peace may bear fruit." In pursuit of his ideals, Izetbegovic went to jail under Tito. Later he was maligned by both Serbs and Croats for his commitment to a pluralist polity in Bosnia-Herzegovina. He remains a committed exponent of Muslim universalism, seeing Muslims as one group among many, not Islam as a socioreligious orientation superseding others in the civil domain.

Yet, in trying to make Islam more than an exclusionary religion, Izetbegovic overlooks the challenge that nationalism has posed to the autonomy of religious language, religious values, and, above all, religious institutions. Especially in this century nationalism has become a quasi-religion, displacing prior religions. There are several instrumental reasons, such as the emergence of print-capitalism,[20] that help to explain the success of nationalism. But still more important has been the ability of nationalism to provide an alternative vocabulary to religion. Nationalists preempted the public authority of religious leaders and institutions. Beyond the instrumental force of language, one must also calculate the *values* of nationalist leaders. These values, as I have argued elsewhere,[21] often clashed with those of religious leaders, at the same time that nationalists either undercut or co-opted the resources of religious institutions for their own ends.[22]

Islam—no less than Christianity or Judaism, Hinduism or Buddhism—is shaped by its world historical context, in which nationalism occupies center stage. However much religious symbols may be invoked or religious leaders coopted, or religious buildings sprinkled on the landscape, nationalist fervor remains at heart a rival to the universalist claim of religious fervor. In the twentieth century nationalism and ethnic/regional markings have superseded religion as the hallmark of collective identity. Nationalism does for the modern era what religion did, or tried to do, in the premodern era: to direct the hopes of the majority toward its norms while also engaging their energies in its public life.

The displacement of religion by nationalism on these grounds needs to be closely examined if we are to understand the shifting valence of Islam in the high-tech era. Can religion become an adjunct of the state and still function as religion, or does co-optive nationalism amount to little more than a thinly disguised variant of the secularization hypothesis?

These questions are crucial to any reconsideration of post-colonial Muslim hopes, for behind all the arguments about Islam and politics remains the twinfold assumption that (a) Christianity defines "true" religion, and Islam as religion must, or should, resemble Christian models, and (b) all religion is premodern and antirational while the state is both modern and rational. Assumptions die hard, and the most closely held resist even sympathetic exposure. Underlying the critique of religion in general and Christianity in particular is an evolutionary bias. Religion, whether Christianity or Islam, could not stand the light of scientific truth. When the modern era fully dawned, the superstitious and backward nature of antecedent myths (scriptural dicta, creedal formulae, local magic) became evident, their hold on believers gradually eroded or disappeared. And in those instances where religion did not vanish, it was at least revalued and consigned to its proper domain, which is to say, private spaces of individual choice, far from the public realm of scientific progress and rational pursuits. To the extent that civil society was independent of political society and the state, it provided a haven for belief in, and pursuit of, prescientific myths.[23]

Such is the assumption of evolutionary "believers." Seldom exposed, their convictions permeate much so-called neutral or objective scholarship on religion. A corollary of evolutionism is also claimed with equal conviction, namely, that societies where religion lingers as something other than a gnostic symbiosis between self and other[24] remain suspect. In the new order heralded by all modernists (and not just liberals), public loyalty to religious precepts connotes what Laroui once called historical retardation. That is to say, religion comes to symbolize a willful resistance to the tidal wave of change that must move the premodern (religion) off center stage in order to propel the modern (nationalism) onto it.[25]

By this approach, there can be good and bad nationalisms but no religious nationalisms since the very phrase "religious nationalism" embodies a logical impossibility, an illusion, an oxymoron.

16

Major First World nationalisms, according to one widely cited sociological study, can be deduced from the review of five nation-states, all of which have forged more or less adequate roads to modernity. All are roads to the modern, which is to say, industrial, high-tech era. The dominant trope, the goal to which these and other nationalist polities aspires, is liberal democracy; no other candidate of social organization can be admitted. Religious structures, like religious actors, are omitted, or else defeated, in the great venture of nation-building.[26]

Just as nationalism is deemed to be the exclusive carrier of secular modernity, so is it further presumed that the reason only some countries succeeded in the high-tech era is that only some were able to modernize. Nationalism becomes but one more way of differentiating the modern West from all its precursors, which in the post–Cold War era have also now become its dreaded nemeses. Nationalism cannot be ascribed to any premodern point in the preindustrial past.[27] With nationalism, as with industrialism, all those groups who have not already succeeded can succeed only by mimesis. Nationalism occurred in one place, among those groups prefiguring the high-tech era. They clustered as the nations of Western Europe and North America. All other nations came later. They were compelled by events beyond their control to imitate antecedent Euro-American models. In Richard Falk's haunting phrase, all the non-West was transformed into state-nations hoping to become nation-states,[28] yet destined to flounder and fail.[29] Economic inequality led to despair and often violence, causing the have-nots to drift still farther to the margins of global exchange.

There have been some who question this view of nationalism, but they choose to make their's a rearguard protest. They resist from the margins, as those who acknowledge their powerlessness even while voicing their opposition to the dominant view. The 1980s witnessed the emergence within critical theory of a new generation of Asian and African intellectuals. They challenged extant paradigms of nationalism. In particular, they "opposed much of the prevailing academic practice in historiography and the social sciences because it failed to acknowledge the subaltern (i.e., the indigenous non-elite) as the maker of his [or her] own destiny."[30] Despite excesses and shortcomings, a group of scholars linked to the Asian subcontinent, known as the Subaltern School, has made evident the problem of social scientific assertions about what nationalism means and how it can best be studied. To the centrist, top-down gaze of Ernest Gellner and Benedict Anderson, subaltern scholars counterpose views from the margins or from the bottom up. To complicate a public-sector, masculine view that excludes women actors or voices, they highlight a private domain where women, along with elders and minors, contribute to postcolonial developments.[31]

Yet even those who oppose a hegemonic, Eurocentric view of nationalism have not thought to restore religion to a place of distinction compatible with other ideological options. The ideal nationalism remains one that enshrines Profit, Progress, and Peace. (The other P's—Poverty, Population, Pollution, and Proliferation—are usually ignored, or else treated as problems that will be solved along the way.[32]) Where is religion in this forward gaze? Religion might relate to Peace: insofar as it either protects or threatens peace, it can be included in the nationalist project, but it is deemed out of bounds on the major subjects of Profit and Progress. Mark Juergensmeyer,[33] for instance, not only has given new life to the term "religious nationalism," he has also argued that religious sensibilities should be conjoined to the nationalist project, where they would serve as a valuable counterweight or deterrent to violent outcomes.

Religion in the national interest? That suggests a return to theocracy, and a nationalist theocracy would attempt to transform history, not merely recuperate and validate a golden past. As Juergensmeyer himself notes about the Iranian revolution, "it was not simply a revival of an earlier form of Muslim rule, but a new form of Islamic politics. In a curious way, it was the shah's vision of an Iranian nationalism come true."[34]

Despite the clarity of Juergensmeyer's thesis, late twentieth-century theocracy frightens most analysts of religion and nationalism. It conjures up particular fear when applied to the case of Islam because ideal Islam, like the premodern Catholic Church, functions as the comprehensive defining code for public as well as private pursuit. While every religion, from a modernist viewpoint, is "bad," to be minimized or better excluded, there remain degrees of exclusion. Islam remains the worst religion, the spoiler for a nationalist utopia. It remains the worst because many scholars argue that no Muslim nation-state, including Turkey and Tunisia, has ever experienced social modernity. Social modernity is linked to the formation of an urban middle class. Turkey since the 1920s may have come close to generating an indigenous secular bourgeoisie, but even Turkey is said to have failed, just as Tunisia appears to have been stymied by an overgrown urban bureaucracy. Other newer Muslim nations, like Malaysia and Indonesia, are excluded because the general public and even many academics deem them too remote from the Middle East heartland to be considered "real" Muslims.[35]

Yet the historical "failure" of Turkey and Tunisia is minor compared to the ongoing "threat" of Iran. For among all those premodern nations that cling to Islam as arbiter of public norms, Iran stands out as the most glaring culprit. While official Turkey in the 1920s distanced itself from Islamic symbols in trying to emulate European/secular norms, the Iranian revolution of the 1970s threatened to bring Islam from offstage to center stage in the realm of global politics. It posed a twin threat, making Islam central and the West villain. It was against this twin threat of the Iranian revolution—its perceived impossibility, its geopolitical unacceptability—that the dread of Islam's antiquarian status as antimodern was rekindled. In its most distinctive religious guise, Islamic "fundamentalism" was seen to be inseparable from the undiluted opposition of Muslims to Christian or pluralist influence. In vain could an Izetbegovic try to demonstrate that Islam is already modern, and that a middle class is not the analytical key to its character, for from Iran came a flood of literature suggesting the opposite: Islam can never become modern, not because Muslim countries lack a bourgeoisie, but because Muslims—in this case, Iranian Muslims—themselves invoke religion to perpetuate the continuing, unremitting primitiveness of Islam. The renowned Iranian essayist Jalal Al-i Ahmad speaks for numerous others when he lauds an "Islamic totality":

> India reminds one of Africa as a linguistic Tower of Babel and agglomeration of races and religions. Think of South America becoming Christianized with one sweep of the Spanish sword or of Oceania, a collection of islands and thus ideal for stirring up dissensions. Thus only we in our *Islamic totality*, formal and real, obstructed the spread (through colonialism, effectively equivalent to Christianity) of European civilization, that is, the opening of new markets to the West's industries. The halt of Ottoman artillery before the gates of Vienna

19

concluded a process that began in 732 C.E. in Andalusia. How are we to regard these twelve centuries of struggle of East against West if not as the struggle of Islam against Christianity? . . . In the present age, I, as an Asian, as a remnant of that *Islamic totality*, represent just what that African or that Australian represented as a remnant of primitiveness and savagery. . . . I, as an Asian or an African, am supposed to preserve my manners, culture, music, religion and so forth untouched, like an unearthed relic, so that the gentlemen can find and excavate them, so they can display them in a museum and say, "Yes, another example of primitive life."[36]

Al-i Ahmad cannot escape the contradiction embedded in his eloquent lament. Though he decries the reification of a Muslim mindset as unchanging, at once anti-Christian, anti-Western, and now antimodern, he, unlike Izetbegovic, perpetuates the mindset that he opposes. He offers no alternative to what he opposes and, by invoking an Islamic totality, confirms the stereotype of European observers, and now their American successors. Al-i Ahmad demonstrates that Islamic obscurantism is not solely the whimsical distortion of colonial administrators and political commentators; it also becomes the project of certain Muslim advocates insofar as they repeat, without modifying, the profile of a primitive and unchanging, a defiant and challenging Islam.

To offset the dialectic of self-other, progressive-primitive that pervades Muslim and anti-Muslim rhetoric alike, we must reveal its tenuous, recent origins; we must not only cite the alternative, modern view of Izetbegovic, which announces a dialectic of accommodation, we must also examine the many faces of Islam that, though less evident, are as real as its one face, the face of bloclike antagonism, whether to Christians, to the Christian West, or to the post-Christian modern world.

THE MANY FACES OF ISLAM

Though Izetbegovic is right about the ambivalent status of Islam in the late twentieth century—it is too often seen as either sociopolitical or religious but seldom both—his argument still needs to be extended. While Islam is not "mere" religion, it is also more than "mere" religious politics. Islam can be as well a kind of symbolic resource or world view that invites accommodation to other world views, not confrontation with them. Islam as religion, Islam as politics, Islam as world view—all three, and not merely the first two, need to be explored.

Such categorization emerges out of critical reflections on the role of imagination in defining and projecting identity. Imagination is both collective and individual. Collectively imagination is nourished by the institutions of a society; individually it is shaped and reshaped by members of that society. In religious discourse, it is imagination—the ability to play with the material world and its limits, including the too evident limits of love and death—that sustains the conscious advocacy of a range of beliefs and practices deemed to be inseparable from the "real" force of life. Names abound for the Object/Subject of imagination: Yahweh, God, Allah, Other. Let us call it Other. Other is always a transtemporal force; exceeding time, it also exceeds all other human limits. Yet Other also must always be mediated in human discourse and through social institutions. In its most intellectual form it becomes theology, in its most pervasive expression popular religion, and in still another form ideology.[37]

Numerous Muslim apologists who assert that Islam is, above all, religion mean that Islam as religion concerns itself with the practice of imagining the Other, also known as divine revelation. Whether systematic or pragmatic, theological, popular, or ideological, Islam, in their view, is always religion. Even when it assumes a political dimension, Islam expresses a religious impulse. It is the impulse to align the human imagination with the divine imagination, so that social norms and individual conduct are always directed toward a path already specified. While obstacles on the path may vary, the contours of the path, as also the requirements it imposes on those who would tread it, have not changed. This is the message, for instance, of Muhammad Qutb in his diatribe, *Islam: The Misunderstood Religion* (1977). Examining all the facets of modern science and European civilization, he summarizes them as embodiments of an age-old pattern of slavery. Islam rejects slavery, slavery of men and women, slavery of whole nations and classes. Since both capitalism and communism, the two ideologies of the modern West, continue age-old patterns of slavery, they must be opposed in the name of Islam. It is only Islam as the "third" way that can provide guidance on the path that will help humankind "get out of the darkness it has long since been plunged in."[38]

While Muhammad Qutb's writings do have a political message, the message is implicit rather than explicit: he does not advocate a specific political system nor a set of political reforms. Others do. More than a few modern-day Muslim writers see Islam as preeminently an ideology, that is, "an organized and polarized formulation" of a system that must be equally secular and sacred, encompassing the instrumentalities of politics as well as the pieties of mosque, court, and home. Among those who argue for political Islam is Muhammad Qutb's older brother, Sayyid Qutb. He is the oft-cited ideologue of Islamic extremism or fundamentalism. A founding figure of the Muslim Brethren in prerevolutionary Egypt, he opposed Nasser when the latter came to power. His opposition led to jail and eventually to the gallows: he was hanged, along with two other Brethren leaders, in August 1966.

But it was not just Nasser whom Sayyid Qutb opposed. Sayyid Qutb opposed Nasser as the advocate and embodiment of Arab nationalism. The true evil was nationalism—whether Arab, Iranian, Turkish, or Pakistani—nationalism as an ideology rivaling Islam. Qutb's numerous writings gradually came to stress a Manichaean divide: on one side was justice, rule according to the precepts of the Qur'an and Islam, that was the sign of *hakimiyya*, or divine lordship. On the other side was *jahiliyya* or opposition to *hakimiyya*, the willful persistence in ignorance, perversity, and error. It consisted of glorifying any -ism, whether communism or capitalism, scientism or humanism, instead of God. Nationalism became one more Godlessism. Loyalty to it, like loyalty to any other -ism, was false. It was a sign of *jahiliyya*. The difference between *hakimiyya* and *jahiliyya* was epitomized by Sayyid Qutb in a famous set of slogans that subverts the nationalist agenda. In true Islam, when *hakimiyya* prevails, according to Qutb, "nationalism will be recognized as belief, homeland as Dar al-Islam, the ruler as God, and the constitution as the Qur'an."[39]

Yet those who advocate Islam either as an oppositional religion (Muhmmad Qutb) or as religious politics (Sayyid Qutb) reduce Islam to a single platform of protest against the dominant forces of the modern world system. Despite the urgent, impassioned, and often impatient tone of their writings, they do not advance arguments that integrate Islam either with its own past history or with the issues that commonly confront humankind. They too easily elide human imagination with the divine imagination read as divine will. As one shrewd observer of Islamic movements wrote, their advocates make political philosophy shoulder the role of metaphysics: "God's relevance can only be seen in a political context."[40]

"Divine" politics is a meaningless concept unless related to history. Raimundo Panikkar, a seasoned cultural critic, was only half-right when he declared that in the modern period "religion without politics becomes uninteresting, just as politics without religion turns irrelevant."[41] The crucial factor remains historical location, and for contemporary Muslims the most significant dimension of their history is marked by European colonial expansion and consequent anticolonial nationalist movements. *One cannot talk about modern Islam without paying attention to the world-transforming activity of the eighteenth, nineteenth, and early twentieth centuries.* It was only in the colonial period that nationalist movements involving Muslims first emerged, and the subsequent history of Islam is inseparable from nationalisms both European and indigenous. There are specific turning points in this history that merit recapitulation, if we are to understand why Islam is more often the victim than the agent of violence.

1. Colonial rule gave birth to national movements organized in *secular* terms with mythical appeals, structural features, and institutional mechanisms that reflected, even when they did not imitate or replicate, the same instruments characteristic of the colonizers' country of origin. Ethnic nationalism became the primary organizing principle or symbolic engine to liberation from overseas rule. This was so even when religious symbols were invoked, or religious movements, such as Pan-Islamism, drew sizable numbers of followers. It is crucial not to accept at face value the assertions of Muslim revivalist leaders. For instance, one scholar, after charting the Pan-Islam movement in massive detail from primary sources, concluded that in the 1990s "Pan-Islamists (along with other consociational groups) may well turn a 120-years' old dream from what seemed a utopia into a political reality."[42] Yet another scholar, taking a functional view of this same movement, chose to look not at what Pan-Islamists say, but rather at the impact their movement had on subsequent nationalist endeavors. In so doing, he reached a conclusion opposite to the first scholar: not only is

23

there no future to Pan-Islamism, but "the rise of Pan-Islamic sentiments helped to establish the credentials of particularized nationalisms."[43] Why? Because Pan-Islamic ideologues posed, albeit indirectly, the question of permeable boundaries and drew attention to
both ethnic nationalism (*qawmiyya*) and region-specific nationalism (*wataniyya*) as alternative polities—alternative not only to European rule but also, more importantly, to the universal Muslim
community (*umma*). Pan-Islamism may conjure the "fear of Islam"
yet it itself proved to be a restricted, short-lived movement. The
antidote to fear is to look beyond slogans and examine the historical development of a protest movement. Pan-Islamism relies more
on ideological accents than on pragmatic strategies. Throughout
the twentieth century links among Muslims of different races, regions, and languages remain more rhetorical than pragmatic, signaling a loose affinity of faith, not an actual alliance of forces,
whether military or political or both.

2. Islam as a pragmatic referent in organizing social or economic
life was denied autonomy under colonial rule, even when certain
farsighted elites attempted to forge a link between Muslim and national identity, as did Muhammad Abduh, for instance, in British
Egypt. "What had begun as an attempt to protect Islam by reinter-
preting it tended to end as a discussion of the possibility of creating
a secular society with nationalism as its animating principle, and
with Islam as its inherited culture rather than a guide to social
action."[44] The subordination of Islamic ideals and values to political pragmatism continued in postcolonial polities. As a result,
Islam remained a reservoir of symbolic dissent, often couched in
violent terms, available to marginalized, aggrieved groups.

During the postcolonial period, as political independence was
achieved by more and more newly formed Muslim polities, appeals
to Islam were slow to garner attention. Whether hidden from European eyes or ignored by indigenous elites, it was not until the late
1960s and early 1970s that Islamic rhetoric and Islamic loyalty
were brought to the forefront of domestic, regional, and international issues. Nationalism did not provide the panacea for a host of
ills and inequities, and Muslim spokespersons began to contend
not only with external non-Muslims but also, just as often, with
internal, "impure" Muslim others.

Again, there is no uniform view of the "Islamic difference."
Even within the ranks of social science, the lack of consensus is

evident. Two social scientists concerned with Egypt disagree on how Egyptian elites viewed the ideal postcolonial polity. One German-based political theorist argues that nationalism, like modernization, rules out religion. He cites as proof of this maxim the stance of the nineteenth-century Egyptian Rifa'a al-Tahtawi, for whom "the social was more important than the religious." Al-Tahtawi's neologism *hubb al-watan*, "love of country," was thoroughly secular, since it conveyed the sense of *wataniyya*, the Arab(ic) equivalent of patriotism, a concept divorced from religion.[45] But in the view of an American political scientist, it is not al-Tahtawi but another twentieth-century Egyptian theorist, Tariq al-Bishri, who augurs the future stance for his country: neither a secularist nor a fundamentalist but a liberal (of sorts), al-Bishri argues that Arab nationalism cannot omit Islam, while at the same time admitting that Islam cannot be made the sole basis for Arab/Egyptian nationalism. What should be the modus operandi then for Muslims and the state? Islam, according to al-Bishri, should play an instrumental role in fostering what are the primary goals, namely, "independence, cultural authenticity, and political integration."[46] While al-Bishri does not offer his own prescription for an ideal Muslim state, his engagement with Islam is a far cry from al-Tahtawi's vision of a secular state.

3. It is the presence of colonialism that linked all Muslim collectivities, throughout the Afro-Eurasian *oikumene*, especially in that heavily populated cosmopolitan area south and east of the Mediterranean. There has been an attempt from time to time to isolate Saudi Arabia, as though what happened on the peninsula was immune from events around it. But it was not, for as Marilyn Waldman has pointed out: "though not all Muslim territories were colonized, nearly all experienced some kind of dependency, be it psychological, political, technological, cultural, or economic. . . . Even in Saudi Arabia oil exploration, begun in the 1930s, brought European (and then American) interference."[47]

If the colonial experience has a crucial mediating role in the development of the present-day Muslim world, it is a role that commands attention in order to avoid a double myopia. One is the myopia of indigenous elites who claim to be exponents of "true" Islam. To the extent that they ignore the colonial period, except as a reminder of the "defeated" enemy, such elites tend to project their own polities as homogeneous associations, at once natural and voluntary. The other myopia is that of dissidents who claim, on behalf of Pan-Islamic ideology, that there has always been a borderless Muslim nation, that all nation-states are fictive, post-colonial inventions, their leaders impeding the reemergence of the pristine Muslim collectivity, the *umma*.

The misfortune of recent scholarship is to perpetuate, rather than correct, these reinforcing myopic readings of the Muslim past. There are two dominant social scientific approaches to Islam and nationalism. One offers a straightforward narration of Muslim polities, linking them to each other and not to neighboring or similar non-Muslim polities, as if the mere label "Islam" were sufficient to merit their clustering as a discrete group separate from all other groups.[48] The other approach traces how Muslim polities took on relevance *only* with reference to an invasive colonial administration, whether Dutch or Russian, French or British. This blindness is much more serious than the first, because it erases the Islamic "difference" and freezes all Muslims into the role of defensive opponents of an emergent global order. Its proponents claim that Muslim elites, in competing with one another under the same non-Muslim aegis, became redefined: they came to differ as much from their precolonial Muslim ancestors as they did from their contemporary non-Muslim compatriots. The cultural marking of Islam, if not irrelevant, was at best residual, while the temporal marking of modernity became all-important. From the premise that the European/Christian West as colonial overlord provided the crucial dimension is drawn the conclusion that only attention to the colonizing process will generate analytical insights into the relationship of Muslim polities to nationalism.[49]

While the first approach oversimplifies the emergence of Muslim polities from a common colonial past, the second overloads the significance of the colonial experience. Its advocates deny the agency of their Muslim subjects, dismissing urban intellectuals, in particular, as little more than hapless purveyors of an ossified or retarded civilizational legacy.

The truth is more complex. If Europe transformed the Muslim world, it did not itself remain immune from change. The direction of influence between Europe and the Muslim world was never uni-linear; it was always interactive. Those European colonial powers that extended their influence, whether by direct or by indirect rule,[50] were themselves reshaped by the experience of their colonial subjects. But they seldom acknowledged their own reshaping as a direct experience of the other. Instead, colonial history, when not luxuriating in the romance and mystique of the Orient, masked its own change as economic gain, commercial profit, overseas investment, or civilizational uplift. Implicit in the exercise of massive military and political power was the denial of agency anywhere in Africa or Asia, including countries with major Muslim populations.

Yet not all Europeans acted with the same motivation or the same set of interests: in the early phase of British colonial rule in India, for instance, not only administrators but also often linguists identified with their subjects, as Richard Fox has shown in his critique of the Orientalism thesis.[51] And when the imperialists did succeed the colonialists, as happened in most cases after the 1870s, there was a heightened degree of intra-European rivalry—from French-British in the Sudan to British-Dutch in the Asian archipelago—that shaped the regional outcome of colonial projects.[52]

Often wrapped into social scientific analysis of Islam is a variant of the economic determinist argument: capitalist forces are placed in the foreground and credited with changing the colonial and postcolonial Muslim world. Particular emphasis is placed on the dismemberment of the central premodern Muslim polity, the Ottoman Empire.[53] Modern-day Turkey becomes the chief negative case representing all Muslim polities stumbling into the twentieth century: its leaders could neither reverse outdated modes of production nor generate a viable middle class.[54] Absent in the Turkish case as elsewhere, we are told, were mechanisms of exchange. Without either accountability or obligation, how could one produce either a viable democracy or a modified authoritarianism? One could not, according to these theorists, and so most African/Asian polities were doomed to be undemocratic; oil merely worsened their economic malaise in the late twentieth century.[55]

Perhaps the most negative assessment of oil production/export and its impact on Arab/Muslim state formation has been set forth by the Lebanese political commentator Georges Corm. Corm offers an intensely detailed, closely argued variation of Delacroix's thesis about the evils of a distributive economy and rentier state. Corm is especially bitter about the petromania unleashed since the early 1970s. "In the deserts of the Arabian Peninsula, . . . the oil-exporting countries of the Gulf barely had sufficient manpower,

27

managerial staff, technicians, employees and teachers to meet the needs and projects this new oil wealth gave rise to. Other Arab countries (and also Pakistan and Bangladesh) were suddenly drained of the most dynamic among their active populations, which further undermined their already eroding social structures."[56] In the case of Pahlavi Iran, petromania did not cause an influx of Muslim outsiders, but it did create a too rapid immigration of rural Iranians to Tehran, leading to structural asymmetries that have persisted in post-Pahlavi Iran.[57]

To place the colonial period and the determinist interpretations of Islam in a broader perspective, one must move beyond both politics and religion to the contingencies of history. The best place to begin is with the boldly revisionist thesis of the world historian and American Islamicist Marshall Hodgson. As Hodgson explained, Islamic loyalties relate above all to a larger, complex process that he labels the Great Western Transmutation. The Great Western Transmutation was "great" because it was *global*: European norms of political rule and social and economic exchange were introduced throughout Asia and Africa. It remained "Western" not only because it was European in origin but also because it reflected changes going on in the New World, especially North America. But finally it remained a transmutation because it depended on a variety of factors rather than a single, predictable response to European events and actors; it was not inevitable to one region or one culture or one time; it was not even a transformation but rather, following biological models, a transmutation.

The Great Western Transmutation was *local* as well as global, since the process it spurred was framed within indigenous contexts and limited by indigenous responses, in our case Muslim responses to European norms. To the extent that we can depict a composite Muslim profile, it emerged only after World War I and did not achieve widespread prominence till after World War II.[58] What it revealed was a world turned inside out.[59] Neither Muslim collectivities nor individual Afro-Asian Muslims could any longer operate from a position of parity in the world-system.[60] All Muslim elites—whether by choice or compulsion, whether explicitly adjusting or implicitly demurring—were reshaped by European norms and expectations.[61] Precisely because their lives were under constant stress, their identities remained in flux, and Islam became a symbolic resource both shared and debated. Colonial and postcolonial reverberations were most evident in urban metropolitan centers, yet their impact also extended to rural or peripheral groups, even when these groups seem not to be affected or represented by the momentous events occurring at the center.[62]

To understand the difficulty of this circumstance, but also to locate the kernel of hope within it, one must revisit the colonial period and attempt to analyze its internal shifts, or successive phases, reflecting the views of Muslim "others" as well as European overlords. One must recognize that not all colonizers had the same agenda nor did all periods yield the same record of brutal conquest and systematic negation of Africans and Asians who happened to be Muslim. Instead, one must look at three major periods that overlap but still need to be distinguished each from the other: revivalist, reformist, and fundamentalist.[63]

PART ONE

EUROPEAN COLONIALISM AND ITS SEQUELS

The Three Phases of Modern-Day Islam

EACH BROAD-SCALE Islamic movement—revivalism, reform, and fundamentalism— belongs to a pattern of interaction between Europe and the Muslim world. The latest chapter of that interaction begins with European colonial expansion in the eighteenth and nineteenth centuries. The initial response was revivalism. When revivalism failed to achieve long-term results, it was replaced by efforts at Islamic reform that worked in tandem with nationalist movements. It was only with the failure of the latter that Islamic fundamentalism emerged.

As a preamble to considering each of these movements one must note, and then repeat, and repeat again, that the Muslim world is at once very large and very diverse. The more than 800 million believers in Allah and His prophet Muhammad are as diverse as any comparable community would be. They exhibit marks of ethnic, linguistic, and cultural diversity, and while no single graph can encompass the range of this diversity, it is hoped that figure 1 will suggest at least the broad contours of what coheres as the Muslim world.

Muslims total between one-quarter and one-third of the world's population. More Muslims are Asian than African, more African than Arab. The numbers are startling: perhaps 200 million Middle Easterners are Muslim, but that is only if you include Turkey's 50 million plus Iran's 55 million. In other words, less than 90 million Middle Eastern Muslims are Arabs. About the same number are Turks if you add to Turkey's 50 million plus the 30 million Muslims of Turkish descent who live in the Commonwealth of Independent States, formerly known as Soviet Central Asia. There are more Arabs living in the two North African countries, Morocco and Algeria, than in the whole of the Middle East outside of Egypt. In sub-Saharan Africa, Nigeria alone has more Muslims than any Arab country: its closest rival would be Egypt, with 40 million Muslims, yet it is hardly a close rivalry since Nigeria, the most

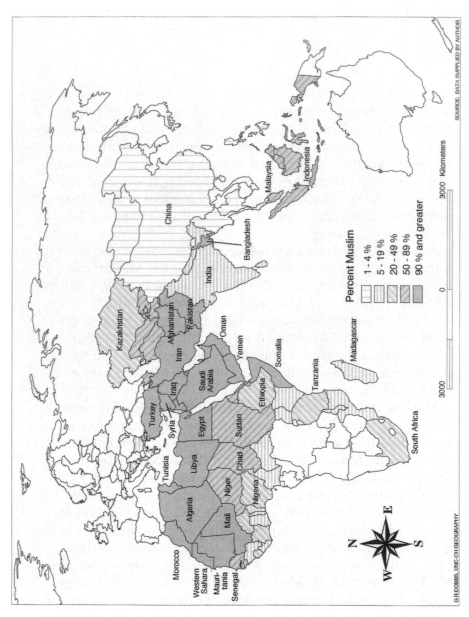

Percent Muslim

1 - 4 %
5 - 19 %
20 - 49 %
50 - 89 %
90 % and greater

3000 0 3000 Kilometers

China

Kazakhstan

Afghanistan

Pakistan

Bangladesh

India

Malaysia

Indonesia

Iran

Oman

Yemen

Saudi Arabia

Somalia

Madagascar

Tanzania

South Africa

Ethiopia

Sudan

Chad

Nigeria

Niger

Mali

Algeria

Libya

Egypt

Syria

Iraq

Turkey

Tunisia

Morocco

Western Sahara

Mauri-tania

Senegal

N E S W

G R DOBBS, UNC-CH GEOGRAPHY

Figure 1. The Muslim world (Africa and Asia).

populous country in Africa, has a population approaching 110 million, of whom about 60 million are Muslim.

However, it is South and Southeast Asia that outstrip all other claimants to majoritarian representation in the Muslim world. Until 1947 South Asia, which includes Pakistan, India, and Bangladesh as its principal polities, formed a single administrative unit under British rule. Today they are home to at least 300 million Muslim inhabitants. Farther east, Indonesia, with more than 13,000 islands and a population exceeding 170 million, can boast that it is, and will remain for some time to come, the largest Muslim country in the world: 150 million Indonesians profess faith in Allah and His prophet Muhammad.

In the face of such numbers it is nonsensical to speak of Muslims and Middle Eastern Arabs as if the two were interchangeable. A recent book outlining major Western misconceptions of Islam listed as number one the notion that "Muslims are mainly Arabs, and Islam is the exclusive religion of the 'Middle East.'"[1] Even more shortsighted is attention to the Arab-Israeli struggle as the epitome of Muslim global concerns.

What matters most for Muslims lies beyond Palestine. It is an economic rather than a territorial nightmare. It relates to the present uneven distribution of global resources; above all, to the grinding calculus that not only sorts out the world into haves and have-nots but makes the division between the advanced industrialized bloc and all others wider and wider, year after year. Although economic constraints are not the only way to understand Islam and the Muslim world,[2] it would be foolhardy to speak of cultural norms and societal options without taking into account economic indices. Where then can one find a neutral benchmark to address economic disparities? The best seems to be the OECD, an acronym for the transnational Organization for Economic Cooperation and Development. In 1979 the OECD published its decadal report, *Facing the Future*. Its authors concluded that the Third World is "defined in relation to the developed countries more than in relation to itself; it comprises all the human societies which could not or did not want to adapt to the shock imparted by Georgian England and which, as a result, now display common characteristics both as to their present reality and (future) dynamics." In other words, countries of the Third World, including all majority Islamic nations, are willy-nilly out of step with their First World contemporaries. There are exceptions, such as Turkey, Egypt, Iran, Pakistan, and Malaysia, yet most lack deep-rooted democratic traditions even more than did Second World or Communist countries before 1989. Enjoying neither economic nor social parity with Euro-America, they have been branded inferior in every other category.

The recent ascendancy of the Pacific Rim countries has only served to give the Islamic difference a stronger negative accent. Over a decade ago Eric Hoffer, author of *The True Believer,* declared: "No Islamic country has mastered industrial production or achieved anything remotely comparable to what was accomplished in Japan, Taiwan, South Korea, Singapore, Hong Kong and (also) India."[3] Hoffer's characterization must now be modified because of dramatic strides taken by Malaysia and Indonesia in the past decade. Both are Muslim countries, if not Islamic states, and both have recently generated high-tech, rapid-growth economies that compete on a global scale. Is it pure accident that both are also part of the Pacific Rim prosperity zone?

As bright as the future looks for both Malaysia and Indonesia, their exceptionalism brings up a further dilemma of perception for the U.S. public. Ever since the gasoline shortages of 1973, most Americans have tended to scapegoat the Muslim as Saudi Arabian, accepting the frequent cartoons that depict a wealthy Muslim sheik depriving cowed motorists at the gasoline pumps. The blanket ascription of wealth is as much in need of correction as the monochrome Islamic identity. The oil-rich Arab states, such as Saudi Arabia, Libya, the Gulf states, and also Iraq, are the least populous, and also the least professionally inclined. The resource-poor Arab states, particularly Egypt and Sudan, are overpopulated, though with an excess of trained but underemployed professionals in every branch of the modern sector, from medicine to engineering to business.

So great are the disparities within the Arab world that the gift of black gold, as oil is often called, has not been an unmixed blessing. Counterintuitive though it may seem, the tyranny of oil burdened the rich as well as the poor Middle Eastern countries between 1945 and 1973. For the Kingdom of Saudi Arabia as for many of its oil-rich Arab neighbors, an avalanche of petro-dollars produced neither an immediate release from poverty nor the emergence of a kind of modern-day version of capitalist utopia in desert sands. Rather, it created a panic of spending. In Georges Corm's view:

> Not since the fall of the Abbasid empire (in the 13th century) has the Arab world seen population movements on such a scale. Like Libya, the oil-exporting countries of the Gulf barely have sufficient manpower, managerial staff, technicians, employees and teachers to meet the needs and projects this new oil wealth has spurred. Other Arab countries have been suddenly drained of the most dynamic among their active populations, which has further undermined their already eroding social structures. Expatriates earning high salaries have remitted savings to their home countries, increasing not only the flow of capital but also the craving for consumption and subsequent inflationary pressures.[4]

Nor has religion been exempt from this same gold rush mentality. For it was due to the sudden flush of extraordinary wealth, produced by the quadrupling of oil prices in 1973, that Saudi Arabia and other oil-rich Muslim nations were able to sponsor the unprecedented World of Islam Festival. Convened in London in 1976, it was the most lavish display of Muslim art and architecture, replete with replications of Bedouin life and extraordinary coffee table picture books, that the non-Muslim world had ever seen. It marked not the end but the beginning of Saudi, Libyan, and Gulf funding for a variety of Islam-related activities. Might not Islamic fundamentalism turn out to be nothing more than "an enormous malaise brought on by poorly assimilated and badly shared-out oil wealth clogging up the scrawny frames of these societies, still historically deprived of real industrialization"?[5]

Corm's rhetorical question begs for qualification. It denies Muslims agency for their own future. It smacks of economic determinism ratcheted to the highest level. Yet Corm's cynicism serves as a healthy antidote to the flood tide of journalism and scholarship that parrots Muslim assertions about Islamic revolution as if such revolution were at once self-evident and inevitable.

No real revolution has succeeded, either in Iran or elsewhere in the Muslim world. The real litmus test for success remains the global socioeconomic order. No revolution can be deemed successful unless it challenges, and attempts to level, socioeconomic disparities. One need not be a Marxist or a capitalist to apply the standard of distributive justice, nor does one have to accept the judgment of modernization theorists, that Muslims must accommodate to the values as well as the structures of modernity, and to the extent that they do, they will inevitably abandon Islam.[6] Muslims can be modern and democratic as well as loyal to the tenets of Islam, but their options for self-expression are nonetheless limited by the current criteria of economic privilege. One cannot ignore what is happening throughout the so-called Third World, at every level among all groups, advantaged and disadvantaged. Those who have been excluded from the front rank of technicalizing societies suffer stark structural inequities. The list of handicaps is grim: political limitations, reflected by the prevalence of military dictatorships or clan rulership permitting only restricted popular participation; economic disparities, situating a few landed or mercantile rich above masses of urban and rural poor, precluding the emergence of a middle class; educational restrictions, especially at the top, where overcrowding in too few universities and the absence of high-tech institutions force elites to send their children abroad while others are denied training in essential skills; and, of course, gender asymmetry, characterized by the invocation of tradition as the reason for excluding women from the public sphere, which conceals the real issue: job scarcity for unemployed or underemployed men.

Faced with these structural constraints, Muslim nation-states are as stymied by the presence of oil revenue as they were deprived by its absence. Islamic societies cannot escape the hierarchical gradient that privileges the advanced nations of Western Europe, North America, and the Pacific Rim while precluding others from competition except in subordinate relations of implicit or outright dependency.

This observation is directed to external criteria and to the global economy. Within the so-called advanced technicalistic nations there exist major groups who also suffer from their positioning at the lower end of the spectrum of educational access and economic privilege, whether they be the urban poor of London and Manchester or Los Angeles and Detroit. Yet the presence of marginalized others in the West merely tempers, it does not refute, our basic contention, namely, that Asian-African Muslims experience wholesale marginality not because Islam is at base defective but because they are located within imposed, and still contested, nation-state borders. Due to the arbitrary construction of these borders, tribal rather than constitutional processes prevail, and authoritarianism is the norm, even when socioeconomic success at some level can be claimed.[7] One need not be surprised that many members of ex-colonial states have come forward to challenge the process by which they were constituted as "self-evident" states. Saddam Hussein became merely the latest, and most extreme, of those who hoped to remake their national boundaries. We must revisit the process itself if we are to understand why Muslim groups have been at such a disadvantage in making their newly formed, postindependence governments work. It is this large-scale process that demands more attention than the specific form by which some groups were placed within a certain state and others displaced from that state or denied their own identity altogether.

Islamic Revivalism: Anti-Colonial Revolt

IT IS within such a global frame of reference that the story of Islamic revivalism needs to be retold. All blanket words such as revivalism, reformism, or fundamentalism are arbitrary invocations of the English language; they do not, and cannot, describe the varying degrees of Islamic loyalty and protest.

Why, then, do I continue to use these terms? Three guidelines inform my choice of nomenclature.[1] One comes from a comment made by Ihab Hassan in another context. Trying to justify the far-flung use of the term "postmodernism," he noted that "There is a will to power in nomenclature, as well as in people or texts. A new term opens for its proponents a space in language."[2] Because fundamentalism has assumed a new connotation since 1979, when for the first time it was consistently applied to evidence outside Protestant American Christianity, it has in effect become a new term, *global* fundamentalism, with the potential to "open for its proponents [who are its academic analysts] a space in language." Second, as Norma Salem observed in her perceptive essay on Islamic fundamentalism in Tunisia, if one surrenders to local, in-group usage and relies on indigenous terms to the exclusion of all others, the resulting "cultural relativism leads to a dead end . . . since it cannot distinguish between 'etic' categories, referring to the perception of the informant, and 'emic' categories, referring to epistemological concepts developed beyond the limits of the culture involved." In her view, which is also mine, "we cannot avoid using cross-cultural concepts in order to forge links between the informant and the observer."[3] Third, clustering the concepts revivalism, reformism, and fundamentalism together helps us to understand the limits of each in the contemporary Muslim world. But first they must be situated historically within a frame of reference that takes account of how all three have been shaped as defensive reactions to European colonial expansion. The novelty here is to suggest that these three terms, taken together, provide a unique function, helping us to understand why we have reached the point when fundamentalism, and not revivalism or reformism, looms large on the political horizon of Muslim nations.

There is no generic category of religious protest that applies to the past three centuries of Islamic history. Instead, there are three distinct phases of protest. In each phase certain Muslim groups revolted against the ascendant world order. Linked to Western Europe, the ascendant world order in time became the dominant order, but not without resistance, protest, and rebellion. Not all protestors were Muslim, nor did all Muslims protest, but the nature of the religiously valorized Muslim protest merits careful consideration. Only the first phase is properly speaking revivalist. It is succeeded by a second that should be termed reformist, and it is only after the revivalist and reformist phases, and in large part due to their failures, that there emerged recently what can be termed Islamic fundamentalism.

All three—revivalism, reformism, and fundamentalism—are historically specific socioreligious movements propelling a few male leaders into public view as they attempt to reclaim the space that was challenged and reduced, then impoverished and redefined, by European expansion (first through sea power, but later through land power supported by naval control of sea trade). From the eighteenth century to the present, all the major Muslim polities experienced financial crises, demographic disruption, and agricultural stagnation. Some of their malaise resulted from indigenous challenges. Provincial Arabs chafed under Ottoman Turkish rule, Afghans protested when Qajar control in Iran was extended to them, Marattas rebelled against Mughal hegemony in South Asia. In each instance, however, the situation of ruling elites was complicated and worsened by (1) the external diversion of commodity trade from the Mediterranean and Indian Ocean routes to the Atlantic Ocean following discovery and exploitation of the New World; and (2) the internal infiltration of European trade through a nexus of foreign merchants and local middlemen or compradores cooperating to establish new products, new markets, new communication networks, and new sources of profit and reinvestment. To speak of Islamic revivalism is to recognize the ideological reaction of particular Muslim interest groups to the losses that they experienced. Islam became an emblem of protest against the gradual contraction of internal and external trade, brought about by the mercantile activities of European maritime nations,

41

specifically, the Portuguese, the Spanish, the Dutch, the British, and the French. What was contested in the name of Islam by Islamic revivalists was control over vital commodities—textiles, slaves, coffee, tea, spices—gold—all trafficked along the major trade routes from the Atlantic coast of West Africa to the Indonesian archipelago.

The major Muslim revivalist movements were without exception preindustrial. Their leaders mobilized followers in response to the European redirection of global trade, even when they did not acknowledge the extent to which European advances were reshaping their lives. Not all the revivalists directly confronted Europeans; some challenged weakened local elites seen as mediators between Europeans and indigenous groups.

One of the earliest instances of European influence concerns the rebellious Wahhabis. In western Arabia the Wahhabis aligned with a Najdi chief named Ibn Sa'ud. That combination in time produced what is now regarded as a legitimate government, though it remains the only Muslim polity named after a tribal group: the present-day Kingdom of Saudi Arabia. Both Ibn Sa'ud and his appointed ideologue, Ibn 'Abd al-Wahhab, benefited from the loss of revenues suffered by their chief rival, the Sharif of Mecca, who in the eighteenth century reigned as the legitimate ruler of the Hijaz. Dependent as he was on the lucrative Indian trade, primarily in textiles, indigo, and spices, the Sharif could not sustain its diversion away from the Arabian peninsula by the British. Weakened economically, he also became militarily vulnerable. His Najdi rivals rallied to their side other groups who had been deprived by the British ascendancy in trade, and toward the end of the eighteenth century they were able to dislodge and replace the Sharif of Mecca. Although the Wahhabis had other battles to wage, with the Turks and with Muslim loyalists from rival tribes who did not accept their leadership, their initial success was a byproduct of incipient European colonialism.

The pattern evident in Arabia had numerous analogues elsewhere on the seams of commercial activity that came increasingly under the flag of the Union Jack. In Northwest India, the Barelvis, sometimes confused with the Wahhabis because of their intensely Islamic profile, tried to wage war against indigenous groups, Sikhs and Hindus, but the latter were better positioned than the Barelvis vis-à-vis British commercial interests. The Barelvis were strategically isolated before being defeated on the battlefield by Sikhs. Elsewhere, in Northeast India, the Faraidis also resorted to Islamic symbols and tried to mobilize fellow Muslims when they perceived the shift to a moneyed, international economy as advantageous to Hindu landlords while impoverishing Muslim peasant laborers. The Faraidis, under Hajji Shari'atallah, did attract widespread support, at first in local protests and later in regionwide acts of defiance; yet neither succeeded in reversing the tide of change.[4]

It was the same story, with different actors but a similar outcome, in Africa. The best documented of the revivalist movements, the Fulani-Qadiris in Nigeria, pitted Muslim herdsmen and traders against British markets and middlemen, the middlemen often being recruited from rival Muslim tribes. Though the revivalists enjoyed superb Islamic credentials, they were eventually defeated on the battlefield. There were temporary successes: the Sanusis prevailed in the Cyrenaica region near the Ottoman province of Libya, strengthening Islamic identity for over fifty years till the Italian invasion of 1911. A Somali chieftain, too, was able to mobilize interior tribes against British, Italian, and French forces in the coastal areas near Mogadishu. He won several battles and continued to rule for over twenty years, only to have the British bomb and machine-gun their way to victory in 1920. Finally, on the other side of the Muslim world, in Southeast Asia, there emerged a puritanical movement, also linked to the Wahhabis and known as the Padris.[5] The Padris galvanized Sumatran Muslims dispossessed by the shift from gold and pepper trade to a new cash crop, coffee. During the course of the nineteenth century the Padris, after causing much initial concern among local elites and their foreign allies, were harassed and coerced by better organized opponents. They endured defeat after defeat in bloody encounters before finally succumbing to the Dutch authorities.

All these revivalist movements occurred at crucial seams in the expanding imperium of maritime Europe. All were Sunni Muslim movements. The single parallel within Shi'i Islam were the Bahais, a group still despised by Twelver Shi'i clergy. The vilification masks a deeper fear: the first Bahais embodied and then projected the latent messianic impulse of Twelver Shi'ism. They were Shi'i revivalists. Yet Bahaism would have been crushed and ignored, as have been many other protest movements, had its adherents not benefited from the communication networks attendant on the economic penetration of European capitalism into both Iran and Turkey. The newly emergent world order provided havens of refuge for those Bahais who survived persecution in their native Iran. They shifted first to nearby Turkey and then, by the third generation, to the New World. Today they proselytize not for Shi'i Islam but for a doctrine of world peace and universal prophethood, and they proselytize from Wilmette, Illinois, at the same time as they continue to protest the treatment of their coreligionists who remain in Iran. The history of the Bahais is therefore doubly instructive: they offer an early success story of global capitalism, and they also attest to the power of Islamic revivalism as a form of symbolic capital beyond the Afro-Asian Muslim world.

Islamic Reform: Secular Nationalism

THOSE ISLAMIC revivalist groups who, unlike the Bahais, remained in their country of origin were succeeded by Islamic reformers. Islamic reformers were closely linked to nationalist movements, and indeed in retrospect it can be seen that despite their universalist rhetoric, almost all the Islamic reformers were shaped by the influences of the colonial period. Especially keen is the emphasis on science and technology in education, on constitutional structures and parliamentary democracy in politics, and on the revised role of women in social life. If Muslim nationalism became mimetic, it should be no surprise that movements that claimed a loyalty to Islam were also mimetic, picking up elements from Europe that they hoped could be transformed into an Islamic system. There is no spontaneous Islamic movement after the colonial period; all are reacting to some force, or series of forces, that emanates from the Western world, which is to say, first from Northern Europe and then from the United States. Even within Northern Europe, however, the cast of characters is limited: with the exception of the Italians in Libya and the Horn of Africa, the major players in the Islamic world till World War II were Britain, France, and Holland.

It is important to note both the size and the outlook of the reformers. They were very few in number, and their elite character has often been overlooked by outside scholars who feel kinship for the reformers as Muslim thinkers not unlike themselves in outlook and ambition. Despite their small numbers or perhaps because of them, the reformers recognized the power of the institutions that were propelling certain European nations to a unique position of global prestige. The reformers came from those countries whose Muslim elites were most engaged by the specter of European commercial and military penetration—Egypt and India, Iran and Turkey before World War I, but then following the war, also Tunisia, Algeria, and Morocco. The North African reformers coalesced into a movement known as *Salafiya*, or Islamic advocacy. In their own terms, they saw the generation of the Prophet Muhammad as

45

a group to be commended for its energy, vision, and dedication, but also as a model to be re-created in the modern era. Their opponents turned their zeal against them, criticizing the *Salafiya* for their unwitting promotion of historical retardation. Since the *Salafiya* seemed to hark back to a golden age that never existed, or at least could never be reconstructed, their passionate pleas were seen to be draining energies away from the crucial task at hand: to accommodate to the new reality of a European world order.[1]

Yet most of the reformers did act in good faith, as committed Muslims conflicted by the gap between Europe's pragmatic success and what seemed to be its spiritual vapidity. It was as though they were witnesses to a novel and "unholy" revelation. As the European presence shifted from trade to government to social services to ideology, its challenge moved to the deepest register of self-reflection; it became religious. For Muslim reformers, "the arbiter of truth and knowledge suddenly ceased to be enclosed in the revealed word of God. Another text, with no specific author or format, had made a permanent intrusion. It was the West with its political systems, military presence and economic domination which now appeared in the background as an authoritative code of practice."[2]

But the authoritative code was not uniform. As they intervened, the European powers quarreled with one another. Some Muslim polities, such as the Sharifian Kingdom of Morocco, benefited from these quarrels, able to resist direct rule because no Mediterranean power wanted its rivals to control the prize of the Arab/Muslim West. But all polities were affected by the two world wars, sometimes known as the Christian wars, of the twentieth century. It was due to the enormous expenditures and consequent destruction of these wars, and also the personal participation of colonized Muslims in these same wars, that Islamic protest movements were able to cohere and emerge into national liberation movements. Gradually, as the smoke cleared from the second of these horrific Christian wars, most Muslim ruling elites succeeded in grasping the laurel of independence.

Even so, not all were marked by the same opportunities or the same political order. A glaring anachronism was the persistence of monarchs, dynastic rulers who compel allegiance to themselves, their values, and, above all, their interests. Almost one-fifth of all Arab Muslims still owe allegiance to a total of three kings (Hassan

II of Morocco, Hussein of Jordan, and Fahd of Saudi Arabia), one sultan (Qabus of Oman), and nine emirs (all from the Persian Gulf, including the Emir of Kuwait).

In those nations where monarchs have not survived, they have often been replaced by quasi-monarchs embracing a top-down, closed system of governance, enabled by *mukhabarat* or citizen surveillance that often produces a national security state.[3] As long as colonial patterns persist, democracy will remain a challenge. Even countries that were not colonized directly, such as Saudi Arabia and Iran, did not escape the effects of European economic penetration into the eastern Mediterranean and Indian Ocean, and the structures that arose after independence reflect this influence, above all in the sphere of bureaucracy, centrist politics, and commercial law.

It was because the nature of self-rule was shaped more by European than by indigenous models that one must speak of "mimetic nationalism." Though nationalism was embraced by Arab, as by non-Arab, Muslim leaders to chart the path to independence, the models of governance were derived from the departing colonials. Whether one looks to constitutional charters or to the adoption of separate executive and legislative bodies, the impress of European precedents is evident. At the same time the boundaries of new nations reflected a patchwork of compromise implementing the wishes of European powers rather than the preferences of their Muslim subjects. Saddam Hussein's attempt to readjust Iraq's borders with Kuwait in fall 1990 was at once justified and spurious: justified because the borders of *all* African and Asian countries were set in the colonial period or its immediate aftermath; spurious because many countries benefited as well as lost from such manipulation. Without the addition of parts of Kurdistan, especially the oil-rich region around Mosul, Iraq, for instance, would not have had the geopolitical resources that make it potentially the economic giant among all Arab states.

The truth about the process by which postcolonial borders were decided may be simpler, though no prettier, than conspiracy theories allow: disparate communities of Asia and Africa had been welded together as parts of the British or French or Dutch empires. They could not be dissolved and reconstituted in their precolonial form with independence. Often the very conditions of self-rule had to be set by colonial authorities and imperial administration be-

47

cause consent could not have been secured on any other basis. Yet the end result was to make the entire process of Arab/Muslim nationalism seem imitative. It appealed only to a limited stratum of elites. Military control had been a wing of colonial administration—not just a wing but the foundation. With independence, mechanisms to curb military intervention and to spur the emergence of a civil society were never set in place.

It is important to note how most theorists of nationalism stress a few distinct traits as crucial for the coherence of a national ethos and the moblization of a nationalist movement. Religion is not among them. Homogeneity, literacy, and professionalism are the crucial traits, according to Ernest Gellner, the late British sociologist.[4] Each nationalist movement finally seeks to create a world in its own image, a world of theoretically independent and equal nation-states. Hence, in Gellner's view, twentieth-century European nationalism "is revealed as an optimistic, secular and practical ideology." Even when it incorporates elements from prenationalist religious cultures, nationalism transforms them to its own ends. Religion is usually suppressed or collapsed into a personal sphere, defined by its exclusion from the state-dominated public sphere into which it continually threatens to erupt.

What Gellner does not discuss but what becomes evident from his trait analysis is the deep fear that most European nationalists had of theocracy. Not only did they want to prevent religious institutions and leaders from reclaiming a public space they had once dominated, but they also hoped to provide the social cohesion that would make the state an effective instrument of power against both internal and external challenges to its authority. It has been the retention of political power, not the assertion of religious truth, that has loomed as the ultimate goal of European nationalists.

While most Europeans and Americans have lived within "secure" national borders for several generations and see themselves as beneficiaries of the tradition of nation-state loyalty, many Third World citizens, and Afro-Asian Muslims in particular, do not share either their experience or their trust. For most Muslims, it is hard to applaud the arbitrary, top-down process, imposed from outside, by which almost all Afro-Asian polities came to assume their present form.

And not only the external boundaries of territory but also the internal boundaries of identity are open to challenge and reformulation. In thinking about Islamic protest, it is especially important to note how the clash at the core of all other clashes between nationalists and fundamentalists is the totalizing impulse guiding each. As Kenneth Cragg once noted, in the Muslim world the state functions as an obedience context.[5] The majority of Muslim states are praetorian or, in Richard Bulliet's apt phrase, neo-Mamluk dictatorships: the form of military bureaucracy on which they depend imitates the Mamluks, though in fact it derives from the legacy of colonial rule.[6] Each demands total compliance with a vision of state control in which Islam is projected as a legitimating factor, even though no open debate about what constitutes "true" Islam is tolerated. Tacitly it recognizes that the norms it imposes are not universally shared by all Muslims, yet publicly it arrogates to itself and to its custodians the right to decide which elements of Islamic belief and practice are to be supported. The memory of other Islams is too strong, however, to be erased. In each instance Muslims have to decide how to preserve their symbolic identity within a public order that is antireligious at worst, as in the former Soviet Union, China, Indonesia, and Turkey, or pseudoreligious at best, as in most Arab states, Iran, Pakistan, and Bangladesh.

The greatest failure of mimetic nationalism is that it left each of the colonized countries, many of them in Africa and Asia, many of them majoritarian Muslim, with the illusion that they could reclaim both identity and purity as nation-states. The nationalist leaders of Muslim states played to these hopes. Having ended foreign domination, they could claim to have banished the hated foreigner. Yet the foreigner did not go away. Frantz Fanon made prophetic warnings about the danger of independence, namely, that colonial values might persist even after the colonizers had left.[7] As a result, twentieth-century nationalism produced for the entire Muslim world a cleavage of enormous magnitude. The most evident cleavage was between Muslims and the dominant culture of Western Europe. But an equally great cleavage was among Muslim reformers, between those who were attracted to European achievements, seeking to appropriate their benefits but packaged in an indigenous idiom, and those others who sought to oppose them, arguing that no accommodation was possible without loss of authenticity. The danger for reformers was their apparent affinity with that which they admired but did not embrace. Even when colonialism finally yielded to independence movements, they as well as nationalist leaders were seen to be tainted by neocoloni-alism, representing, as Fanon put it, black/brown skins wearing white masks.

If the final legacy of colonialism was to reshape the Muslim world into truncated territories and contested borders, capitalism left it with economies that could only function on the margins. Capitalism benefited its captains, the major powers of the high-tech era. These powers are the technologically advanced, profes-sionally differentiated, and economically privileged societies of Western Europe, North America, and now East Asia. Even before the rubric of First, Second, and Third Worlds was invented in the 1950s,[8] there existed a proto-Third World. It embraced *all* Muslim societies, even those that were to benefit from the petro-dollar infu-sion begun in the 1950s and 1960s but then accelerated through the 1970s and 1980s before flattening out in the 1990s. It is this economic gradient that undergirds, or should undergird, all at-tempts to explain Islamic fundamentalism.

Islamic Fundamentalism:
Religious Nationalism

THE SUDDEN dramatic increase of oil revenues in the 1970s did not produce, but it did catalyze, the eruption of an uncoordinated set of protests against Muslim rulers who seemed to accept the dominant and un-Islamic global order. That chain reaction has been dubbed Islamic radicalism, Islamic fundamentalism, or just plain Islamism. Even as Islamic revivalism cannot be separated from the introduction of European commerce in the early modern period at a certain moment in time, so Islamism or Islamic fundamentalism cannot be divorced from the structural realignment of global power—economic and social as well as political and military—that preceded the rise of the Organization of Petroleum Exporting Countries (OPEC). There might have been Islamic fundamentalism without OPEC, and economic factors alone do not explain its myriad expressions, yet the global context is crucial to understanding how Islamic fundamentalism has appeared and reappeared during the last quarter of this century.

While petromania was contagious in the 1970s, the tyranny of oil, in Georges Corm's apt phrase, had begun much earlier. It culminated in the 1970s due to the coincidence of political frustration after the bitter Arab-Israeli War of October 1973 with the overdue readjustment of oil prices leveraged through the newly founded union of oil-producing states named OPEC. OPEC was a union rather than a cartel, as is often supposed. By any standard of proportionality, its members were more than justified in seeking a fairer share of profits for *their* extraction of a nonrenewable resource.

But proportionality, and with it higher profits for OPEC members, did not pave the way to higher status in the international community, nor did it ensure independence from the skills and ambitions of others. The new wealth was monetary. It had to be invested or distributed in a way that would allow these preindustrial societies to enter the postindustrial or high-tech era. The way was never found, in part because financial resources could not be transformed into social restructuring without reliance on the techno-industrial complexes of Europe and America that pioneered modernization even while projecting an "alien" civilization. Genuine independence proved impossible, and in its stead emerged a self-destructive frenzy. Drawn into an economic order where they remain marginal, the principal members of OPEC can only function with the assistance of other, more advanced and more powerful countries. They require foreign assistance in everything from agricultural goods to military weapons to construction projects to transport vehicles. They employ an enormous number of expatriate workers to help them try to keep up with the modern world. Some do recognize the irony of sudden riches. As a Saudi official once lamented, "We Saudis are rich while you Americans are wealthy. I'd rather be wealthy." By this he meant that the true criterion of national prosperity is not export-import surpluses or per capita income but rather the potential to construct and maintain an economic infrastructure that is globally competitive *without* foreign assistance. By that criterion, Saudi Arabia, like every OPEC country, including Iran, remains underdeveloped and therefore dependent on others for what it needs to exist and to compete as a modern nation.

As long as the greatest field of play in the high-tech era remains science—scientific discovery, technological adaptation, commercial deployment—Muslim countries will remain disadvantaged, and Islamic fundamentalism will function as a spoiler. Its ideological appeal is strengthened by the failure—the inevitable failure—of other ideologies, namely, nationalism, socialism, pan-Arabism, or even pan-Islamism. Yet the state against which the fundamentalists rail is a durative institution. Not only have governments proven their ability to survive insurgency, with the solitary exception of Iran, but the state, in the words of a Lebanese observer, "has become the strongest dominant shadow over the lives of the individual and society."[1] From control of the army and secret police to ownership of major industries to recruitment in administrative bureaucracies, the new postcolonial state exercises centripetal pressures unimaginable in the pre–World War II era. Fundamentalists can challenge the state. They can even kill the pharaoh, as some Egyptians did when they assassinated Sadat in 1981, but there will be other pharaohs and other centrist deployments of power.

There is more, much more, to Islamic fundamentalism than can be gleaned from the "great man" approach to history, an approach that in this case would conjure a list of fundamentalist heroes, from the Pakistani Mawdudi to the Egyptian Qutb to the Tunisian Ghannouchi, and then show how they have influenced the way alienated Muslims come to express their grievance with global patterns of economic and cultural exchange. Instead of offering biographical snapshots of fundamentalist heroes, I will look at the socioeconomic as well as the cultural profiles of particular countries that have experienced a series of postcolonial crises. I begin with Pakistan and Egypt in order to gauge the extent of fundamentalist protest in former British colonies. I then turn to Tunisia and Syria to illustrate parallel protests in the ex-French colonial sphere. I conclude by focusing on Saudi Arabia and Iran because their intrinsic rivalry is even more important than their evident and explicit policy differences. Each polity claims Islamic credentials and yet each has responded to the threat of exogenous control in opposite ways, the Saudis by allying with Western capitalism while suppressing the fundamentalists in their midst, the Iranians by pursuing a form of theocratic capitalism that permits limited but real internal dissent.

ANTINATIONALIST DISCOURSE

If one can locate a substantive kernel of Islamic fundamentalist thinking, it comes from the subtle religious response to the limits of secular-style Arab nationalism. It is well illustrated in two statements by Jordanian Islamic spokesmen. They reflect the antinationalist mood of Sunni Arab Islamists or fundamentalists, as experienced in Jordan but also in many countries caught between the ascendant West and their own memory of a glorious Muslim past. A leading jurist who has authored over forty books, 'Abd al-'Aziz Khayyat once summed up the five divinely mandated preservations that were at the heart of Muslim law (shariʿa). They are:

1. Self-preservation, enjoining what is proper to eat and drink, while prohibiting indulgence in prolonged fasting
2. Preservation of the mind, or mental health, encouraging literacy and education while prohibiting alcohol, hashish, or drugs

53

3. Preserving the species, requiring marriage while also limiting the number of wives to four, and making even that option remote by mandating conjugal parity

4. Preserving wealth and property, by honoring labor and investment of money while also prohibiting unfair interest or usury or excessive accumulation of wealth

5. Preserving belief since belief in God as One, in Muhammad as His final prophet, and in the Qur'an as His perfect revelation are enjoined on Muslims, while superstition and idolatry in all forms, including the elevation of country above God (nationalism), are prohibited[2]

Note the order in which these preservations are cited. The two most specific preservations, concerning food and marriage, are first and third. Both are traditional. Both are modern. The first inveighs against Sufi brotherhoods that deem fasting to be a meritorious way of encouraging dependence on God alone (*tawakkul*). The third acknowledges the option of four wives but also, following the Qur'an, makes clear that each wife must be treated equally. Since most modern-day nations support monogamy, this implicit compromise is an effective way of being both modern and Muslim.

What is most curious, however, is the reiteration of the most basic creed of Islam as the fifth preservation. At first this seems to be out of proportion to its operative importance, but in fact its intent is not merely to reinforce monotheism but to suggest that true compliance with Oneness may supersede other loyalties. Many Jordanians, especially those of Palestinian origin, would read this as a rationale for demurral from honoring King Hussein too highly, but at the same time it could be seen as a not-so-veiled message to the Palestinians that they should honor their own commitment to a Palestinian homeland less intently than their devotion to God!

The very fact that this ethical digest could allow for alternative readings illustrates its appropriateness as a list of fundamentals. They are all terms which most observant Muslims would generally accept. They do not incite violence or even active resistance to political authorities, yet they project as a seamless program norms on which there is not a consensus, leaving open how various Muslims would apply them as directives to their own lives.

Equally adept at couching emotive language in abstractly displaced referents is Dr. Mohamed Sakr, an economics professor at the University of Amman and a member of the Jordanian branch of the Muslim Brothers. In a magazine interview Dr. Sakr, who earned a Ph.D. degree in economics from Harvard University, blasts the West. Without once mentioning a specific Western country as the culprit or villain, he is adamant that "the West is against us." Having lived in the United States, he claims to know it as "a civilization stricken by forces from within." The alternative to the West, he suggests, is a united Muslim world, one that would allow countries to share their resources in a complementary fashion. "Some countries like Saudi Arabia and Qatar have money, and others like Jordan and Egypt have the labor force. Unity would bring greater benefits for all." Unity would allow benefits of oil extraction to be shared because "today the wealth of the region is in the hands of a few sheiks, and the majority of the people are poor." In the end, the masses will take decisions into their own hands, he warns. What, then, should the West do? Two things: first, it should take note that "we have millions of people who have U.S. educations and who are not slaves of the West"; and second, Euro-American firms should stop squeezing profits out of the region, instead allowing its citizens to govern themselves "without dictation from Washington, Paris or Bonn."[3]

Though admittedly fragmentary because it was gleaned from an interview, the above captures the tone of the discourse common to Islamic fundamentalists. The finger of accusation points with equal pique to enemies at home and abroad. Those who are the real Muslim culprits are "the few sheikhs" who take money from the West for oil. Yet, in the same breath, these Sheikhs are asked to join an Islamic unity movement that would provide their countries labor from Jordan and Egypt in return for "fair" wages. It is a plea for distributive justice likely to fall on deaf ears in Riyadh and Kuwait City.

Should one then ignore the appeal of this argument? No, for despite its seeming incoherence, it exactly mirrors the dilemma of Islamic fundamentalists in the 1990s: to have the best of the West—its education, its technology, and its dollars—and yet to evolve into a separate, Islamically renewed, world order. In the words of Roy Mottahedeh, "Islamic government is for many Muslims what the old but recently revived phrase 'civil society' is for many liberals: a repository of collective hope and an aspiration that the fundamentally good values at the roots of their traditions can be recovered and strengthened." That is the goal but, as Mottahedeh goes on to note, "the actual agreed-upon content of Islamic government remains very limited and, more often than not, severely disputed."[4]

EXAMPLES OF ISLAMIC FUNDAMENTALISM

No appeal works unless it matches the mood and the options for change in particular countries. The sameness and the difference of Islamist movements can best be grasped by looking at specific Muslim nation-states. The following six cases are selective, but they are not random. While they show the limits of fundamentalist movements, they also represent different aspects of the colonial experience. Two—Pakistan and Egypt—suffered British rule. Two others—Syria and Tunisia—became victims of *la mission civilisatrice* or French rule, while the final two—Saudi Arabia and Iran— operated only within spheres of influence, escaping direct rule from a European capital. Each of these six countries signals changes within its own sociopolitical sphere at the same time that it portends trends of broad significance for postcolonial Islamic identity. Though I draw attention to the arch rivalry between Saudi Arabia and Iran, I also highlight Iran as the most significant symbolic site for understanding, and misunderstanding, contemporary Islam. Without the Islamic Republic of Iran, there would be no Islamic fundamentalism, nor would the "menace of Islam" ever have become a siren call for both Euro-American policy makers and the public at large. It is because of its singular importance that I conclude the country-by-country analysis with Iran.

Pakistan

Principal key dates,[5] including major leaders since independence:

1858	Beginning of direct British rule of India
1906	Founding of the Muslim League separate from the Indian National Congress
1941	Founding of Jamaʿat-i Islami in East Punjab
1947	Formation of East and West Pakistan, independent of both Britain and the Republic of India

1947–50	Muhammad ʿAli Jinnah
1956	Pakistan proclaimed an Islamic republic
1958–69	Ayub Khan
1969–71	Yahya Khan
1971	Revolt of East Pakistan, formation of Bangladesh
1971–77	Zulfikar ʿAli Bhutto
1973	Promulgation of constitution officially declaring Pakistan to be an Islamic republic
1978–88	Zia al-Haq
1988–90	Benazir Bhutto
1990–93	Nawaz Sharif
1993–96	Benazir Bhutto
1997–	Nawaz Sharif

After an experiment with parliamentary democracy, Ayub Khan, a general, assumed direct rule through a coup in 1958. Field Marshal Yahya Khan and General Zia al-Haq also invoked martial law, with the Bhuttos (father and daughter) and Nawaz Sharif being the only duly elected, nonmilitary leaders of Pakistan during the past three decades.

Pakistani Islamic fundamentalism cannot be understood apart from Pakistani history, which is also a function of geography. A part of the Asian subcontinent, Pakistan is linked by historical development to India, by faith orientation to Central and West Asia (i.e., the Middle East). Its hundred-million-plus inhabitants are predominantly Muslim. Three hundred years of Mughal rule provided Muslim elites in North India with a sense of their continuity to Central Asian forebears. Yet it was British colonialism that shaped the profile of present-day Pakistan: Lord Mountbatten presided over the partition of a vast region along communal lines, religiously defined. His goal was to ensure maximum political influence and future economic opportunity in England's "crown jewel," even after independence was granted. His was a fatal error, resulting in the death of millions but also destroying the dreams of other millions.

Some of those dreams were Muslim dreams of a *united* postcolonial Indian state. I can remember discussing Partition with a distinguished Indian Muslim scholar from Delhi in the mid-1980s. I asked him which side he chose at the end of British rule. "Both," he answered calmly, and then, his voice cracking, he explained.

57

"Both. I wanted to be both Indian and Muslim. I still want to be both Indian and Muslim. There was no destiny to create this division of brothers. An Islamic state? It was a human error, not the divine will. An Islamic state is where Muslims live together in peace with their neighbors. Bharat [the Sanskrit name for the subcontinent] is an Islamic state, not this *bid'a* [innovation] called Pakistan. What an error! What a havoc!"[6]

Though many Indian Muslims did favor a separate Muslim polity, not all wanted to be joined together in the same Islamic state. The subsequent rift between East and West Pakistan resulted in the formation of Bangladesh in 1971, again with much bloodshed. Two incompatible parts came unbound from the mold into which they had been cast in 1947. The result was three separate nation-states that held in common only a constitution as their norm of governance, but even the constitutions differed in what they specified as the basis for the state: one, dominated by Hindus, was constitutionally secular (India); another, with a Muslim plurality, had an avowedly Islamic constitution (Pakistan); while the third (Bangladesh), though dominated by Muslims, remained constitutionally secular till 1987.

The great dilemma for Pakistan was how to be an Islamic state while also accommodating diverse ethnic/linguistic groups within its Western and Eastern wings. No figure from East Pakistan ever attained consensus support from West Pakistan as a national leader. All the political, juridical, economic, and social structures of the new state were shaped in West Pakistan. The national language also was Urdu, not Bengali, and all those Bengali leaders who had to fly to Islamabad for parliamentary meetings had to speak Urdu once they boarded the Pakistani International Airlines plane in Dhaka.

Among those who stood forth as religious nationalists from West Pakistan was Mawlana Abu'l-'Ala Mawdudi. Every history of Islam in Pakistan cites his name prominently, and it is with reference to him that the tale of Islamic fundamentalism is told, the claim of its prestige in the subcontinent advanced.

A trained journalist rather than a religious professional or *'alim*, Mawdudi experienced a powerful second conversion to Islam in his twenties and thereafter became a prolific pamphleteer, spokesman, and activist on behalf of Islamic causes. Especially because he was a skilled wordsmith, it is important to distinguish what he said from what he did: he was able to articulate ideals that in practice neither he nor others could uphold.

In 1941 Mawdudi founded the Jama'at-i Islami, an organization dedicated to promoting Islamic norms within India. He was opposed to the Pakistan movement and to the Muslim League, arguing that the Muslims of India were effectively irreligious and that the creation of a separate state would not help them any more than it had helped the irreligious Muslims of Iran and Turkey (even though neither Iran nor Turkey had been founded as self-consciously Islamic states). Yet when Pakistan came into being in 1947, Mawdudi ignored his disagreement with Muhammad Ali Jinnah and, despite the secular tone of the Muslim League, migrated to Lahore. Through the Jama'at-i Islami he played the role of religious gadfly, repeatedly challenging the government's claims to be Islamic, risking imprisonment and even the death penalty (in 1953). After being freed from prison, he came to terms with the military regime of Ayub Khan, and from 1962 till his death in 1979, with few interruptions, he continued his work on behalf of the Jama'at-i Islami.

Mawdudi confronted the traditional religious professionals, the *ulama*, as well as the successive governments of Pakistan. His was an inclusive, consistent critique of human failure to come to terms with the radical message of true, which is to say originary, Islam. He so simplified that message that it seemed to be accessible to all. From his initial publication of a book on *jihad* through his subsequent essays on virtually every domain of contemporary Muslim life, Mawdudi applied twin hermeneutical principles, both related to the Qur'an: (1) God's word provides the supreme yardstick for human conduct; and (2) it is possible to derive a single, correct interpretation of its meaning for the present age. It is as if he took upon himself the enormous task of "proving Islam's ability to supersede modern secular ideologies."[7]

Mawdudi did live under very secular governments, none more so than the martial rule of Ayub Khan. In 1970, after Ayub had resigned, Mawdudi lamented that "it was the leftists who had really controlled his government. All religious elements were crushed and the administration went into the hands of the leftists. Press, news agencies, radio and television—in fact all the organs of the mass media—were used by leftist forces [while] Jamaʿat-i Islami had very little opportunity to work."[8]

Despite the passion of Mawdudi's protest, his posture was compromised on two fronts, or at least so his opponents have argued. One weakness in his lament derives from the nature of the state he was attacking; the other, from his own engagement with representatives of that state. It is important to understand both positions to see how precarious, and fragile, is the future of Islamic fundamentalism in Pakistan. Mawdudi waged a kind of internal *jihad* against the Pakistani government: though its leaders claimed to be "good" Muslims, Mawdudi criticized their policies as un-Islamic. Most heads of state were military rulers with little engagement in religious subjects, but when they claimed to act on behalf of some ideal higher than self-interest, that ideal was invariably Islam. Even a nonmilitary ruler, such as the socialist Zulfikar ʿAli Bhutto, attempted to legitimize his tenuous authority with reference to Islam. What other ideology could compete with Islam? Could socialism or capitalism or democracy? No. Islam was the cement holding together the diverse elements within Pakistani society, and every leader wrapped himself (or herself) in the mantle of Islamic legitimacy. There was the liberal-modernist Islam of the early parliamentary phase. Ayub sponsored a developmentalist Islam; his successor Yahya Khan, a nationalist Islam; and the secular Zulfikar ʿAli Bhutto, a socialist-populist Islam. The successor to Bhutto, who also proved to be his fatal nemesis, Zia al-Haq, claimed that his was a revivalist (though it was actually a fundamentalist) Islam. In the aftermath of his 1988 death, Bhutto's daughter Benazir perpetuated a socialist-populist Islam, while her successor, Nawaz Sharif, advocated a capitalist Islam that she did not entirely abandon after replacing him, and to which he reverted when becoming prime minister for the second time in 1997.[9]

And so Mawdudi had to compete with variant notions of Islamic identity *within* the government. At the same time, he had to placate other Islamic activists *outside* the government. One such was Dr. Israr Ahmad, a fellow member of the Jamaʿat-i Islami. According to Dr. Israr, as he likes to be known, Mawdudi changed after his release from prison in the 1950s. He retreated "from his fundamentalist position and instead sought allegiance, first with the religious groups and then with avowedly secular political parties." Mawdudi, in other words, tacitly cooperated with the very government that he openly criticized; he only appeared to be remaking Pakistan in the image of true Islam. As a result of this shortfall between words and actions, Dr. Israr resigned from the Jamaʿat in 1957. Later, in 1974, he formed his own organization, Tanzim-i Islam. His project in many ways resembles Mawdudi's, as Vali Nasr has pointed out.[10] Yet there are two major differences. First, Dr. Israr adamantly excluded women from the public work force, stressing the need to "honor" them for their unique domestic roles. (Mawdudi had also advocated the seclusion of women, until the 1964 elections, when he did an about-face and supported, albeit half-heartedly, the candidacy of a woman who was running for president against Ayub Khan!) Second, Dr. Israr understood that a religious movement, to succeed in the late twentieth century, required modern media. Skillfully he used both television and overseas travel to project the image of a worldwide organization: reaching beyond Pakistan, he reinforced his local, regional, and national standing as the bellwether of Islamic ideals. He often seemed to use media professionals, whether journalists, radio commentators, or television program planners, to his own ends. Once, during a 1982 visit to Pakistan, I picked up the English evening newspaper, The *Leader*, only to find the headline: PAKISTAN ON THE VERGE OF ISRARIZATION. The lead article went on to highlight how the growing influence of Tanzim-i Islam was feared in many quarters, not least among professional women.

The worse did not come to pass, however, because the Zia al-Haq regime realized that its own fundamentalist image was not served by this headstrong Punjabi activist. Since the Pakistani media is government controlled, Dr. Israr could be, and was, denied access to the airwaves and also to the headlines. His star faded, as the nation-state in Pakistan made clear that *it* was the decisive forum for shaping acceptable Islamic ideology. When Benazir Bhutto came to power in the fall of 1988, Dr. Israr suffered a further setback: female domesticity could no longer be flaunted as the sole appropriate model of Islamic womanhood.

Other expressions of fundamentalism have also been undercut by the lack of popular support for either the Jamaʿat-i Islami or its competitors, many of which are advocates of local ethnic nationalisms. Muhajirs are the Urdu-speaking refugees from India who settled in the Sind region of Pakistan, especially in the large cities of Karachi and Hyderabad. They have become Sindhis by default: though at first some were drawn to the Jama'at-i Islami, they now embrace a variant of Sindhi nationalism and advocate refugees' rights, rather than religious norms, through secular political parties.

During the 1990s Islamic fundamentalism, though partially eclipsed in Pakistan, has not died out. It simmers because the social, ethnic, and economic unrest that continues to paralyze much of Pakistani public life cannot be easily or quickly ended. As crises recur, one may expect the clarion cry for a "simple" solution, one rooted in the Qur'an and in age-old precepts. Yet its appeal will be not to the masses but mainly to members of the bloated government bureaucracy. It will also have little appeal to urban, underemployed young professionals who want to distance themselves from both religious and ethnic politics. Most of its supporters will be men, though they will claim the support of women, even as they argue that their mission is to defend the honor of their own female family members.

The long-range message from Pakistan is cautionary: while no one would be foolish enough to say that religious activism or a variant of fundamentalism will not influence Pakistan's future, the lessons of the past fifty years suggest that fundamentalist ideology will continue to elicit a limited response, its declamatory excesses more evident than its programmatic achievements.

Egypt

Principal dates and rulers in the modern era:

1882	'Urabi Revolt and British Occupation
1936	Limited independence from England
1936–52	King Faruq
1952	Free Officers' Revolution
1954–70	Gamal 'Abd al-Nasser
1956	Suez Crisis
1967	June War with Israel
1970–81	Anwar Sadat
1973	October War with Israel
1979	Camp David Accords with Israel

1981	Sadat's assassination by Islamic fundamentalists
1981–	Hosni Mubarak
1992	Assassination of journalist Farag Foda by Islamic fundamentalists

Many observers think of Egypt as the heartland of the Arab and the African worlds. Located at a strategic juncture between the Mediterranean Sea and the Red Sea, in the heart of the Middle East, Egypt has spearheaded both the expansion of European commercialism and indigenous reaction to external manipulation. The anger of its intellectuals against the British occupiers was first heard in the nineteenth century and echoed in the newly founded presses of Cairo and Alexandria, which reached far beyond their borders.[11] Calling for the expulsion of foreigners, Egyptians hoped to challenge European world hegemony by counterposing to it a modernized civilization at once Arab and Islamic, with Egypt in the vanguard. Not all Egyptians were so utopian, however. Not all espoused Pan-Arabism or "greater" Egypt. Other elites, both political and commercial, accommodated to the shift in commercial and strategic options offered by the British presence. At the same time, the large majority of Egyptians experienced the colonial and post-colonial era only in an indirect sense: they remained peasants (*fellahin*), often in debt to absentee landlords, and for them survival was—and is—the overriding concern.

Two parallel but divergent groups protested against British influence in Egypt. During the early years of the twentieth century, the nationalist movement coalesced around the figure of Sa'd Zaghlul. He himself had been inspired by the leading light of Islamic reformism, Muhammad 'Abduh, and founded the opposition Wafd party on principles that reflected an elision of political independence with religious dedication to Islam. Formal independence was granted in 1922, yet British control of defense and foreign affairs persisted. Zaghlul died in 1927, still protesting. Others continued to protest till the Wafdist and the British finally signed a treaty in 1936. Yet extremists demanded total British withdrawal, a withdrawal that did not seem possible as long as King Faruq, who had succeeded to the throne in 1936, ruled.

Challenging not only the British and his royal lackey but also the Egyptian nationalists was a group called the Muslim Brothers. Formally established in 1929 under the leadership of Hasan al-

Banna, they advocated nothing less than the restoration of Islamic identity to all levels of Egyptian society, but particularly the government. They were less confident than either the reformers or early nationalists that independence from foreign rule would bring a renewed dedication to Islamic norms.

Their fears proved correct when an army coup brought the Free Officers to power in 1952, with Gamal ʿAbd al-Nasir (Nasser) assuming full control in 1954.[12] Nasser claimed to free Egypt from British tutelage, and the Suez Crisis of 1956, as well as later flirtations with the Soviet Union, seemed to confirm his nonaligned status. Yet Nasser also governed through a centralizing bureaucratic state that changed the rhetoric but little of the substance of the monarchist era. Despite the high-sounding claims made by and about Nasser, Egypt did not experience either a social or an economic revolution under his rule.

Nor did it experience a religious revolution. Nasser was not antipathetic to Islam: like other officers who cooperated in the coup of 1952, his first views had been shaped by a madrasa education. Yet religion for Nasser played essentially an instrumental role, to strengthen the bonds between Egypt and other Muslim nations, but above all to draw attention to Egypt as the hub of the Muslim world. He stopped far short of acclaiming Egypt an Islamic state. To Nasser, as to Ayub Khan in Pakistan, the *shariʿa* or Islamic law should not be used as a technical term signaling public commitment to Islamic ideals. The *shariʿa* portended a retreat from, not an advance into, the modern world. Yet for many observant Muslims, the honor of Islam was intertwined with the observance of the *shariʿa*; relaxing or denying its influence was tantamount to defaming Islam. While Nasser never officially denied the *shariʿa*, he held it at arm's length from his own ideological repertoire. In Nasser's Egypt the *shariʿa* remained, but it became an option that was voluntary rather than mandatory, its compliance private rather than public. In 1952 Nasser abolished the Mixed courts, in which British judges applied British law in Egypt, a detested legacy of colonial rule, yet two years later he launched a single state secular system that, in effect, superseded the *shariʿa* courts as well as the minority religious courts (established for Christians and Jews).

It is hardly surprising that in the same year, 1954, Nasser became the target of an assassination attempt by a member of the Muslim Brothers. Though the attempt failed, it highlighted what was already apparent to many: Nasser's socialist ideology was on a collision course with nascent Islamic fundamentalism. Fundamentalists could not gain the center of power, but they could challenge all those who used power in ways that they construed to be against the highest ideals of Islam.

Far from rejecting Islam, Nasser did not hesitate to co-opt state-appointed religious functionaries in order to issue decrees approving what he did, while at the same time denouncing the "terrorist" activities of the Muslim Brothers. As was the case in Pakistan, it was not a war between Islam and non-Islam, but between competing versions of Islam.

To his opponents, however, Nasser was merely projecting a Muslim veneer on a secular and foreign reality: he was dressing up European ideas and Western myths in Arab clothes. While Nasser may have been indulging in a game of political charades, he was also appealing to a major, crucial constituency: the Arab middle classes, who wanted to maintain the status quo of a progressive bureaucratic state. It may have been impossible for Nasser to advocate both Arab socialism, which supported class interests through government control, and economic justice for the masses. Through Nasserism, an ideology of Arab unity projected far beyond the borders of Egypt, he invoked distributive justice while pursing the interests of those who remained directly dependent on him.[13]

The year 1967 proved to be the year of destiny for Nasser. As the symbol of Arab leadership, he brought Egypt and its Arab neighbors into open confrontation with Israel. The result was a rapid and catastrophic defeat for Egypt that only confirmed in the eyes of his critics what they had said all along about Nasser: his temporizing policies could not withstand the test of time.[14]

Nasser threatened to resign, but by popular demand he remained in power. His stature was such that for a time he seemed to experience a psychological recuperation transcending his military debacle. Yet he died in 1970. The pharaonic tradition of statesmanship did not die with him. Nasser had inherited it from King Faruq, and Anwar Sadat, succeeding Nasser, adapted the same authoritarian structure of the Egyptian state to his own ends. Like Nasser, he failed to deal with the massive, underlying social inequities perpetuated by what one writer has called the "hydropolitics of the Nile."[15] Though Sadat did achieve a pyrrhic victory over

Israel in the 1973 war, the gap between the ideals of an Islamic state and the reality of a secular, pragmatic government became even more apparent in the 1970s, especially after the Camp David accords of 1978.

In October 1981 Sadat arrived at *his* moment of destiny. Was it inevitable that he would be killed by representatives of those who opposed him? Was it inevitable that his killers would be a clandestine unit of fundamentalists who had infiltrated the Egyptian army? The answer, as analysis after analysis makes clearer and clearer, is no. Khalid Islambouli and his accomplices were fixated on Sadat the image rather than Sadat the man. They blamed all the shortcomings of present-day Egypt on Sadat's refusal to enshrine the *shariʿa* as the law of the land. Instead of an Islamic state, he had tried to jumpstart the stagnant Egyptian economy through an opening (*infitah*) to the West. Instead of a reforged Arab alliance against Israel, he had made peace with Israel at Camp David. And so Islambouli and his accomplices attacked Sadat as a secular despot ignoring the ideals of both Islam and Arab unity. They wanted to kill the pharaoh. Sadat the symbol embodied the pharaonic despot whom fundamentalists, along with others, had come to revile. They killed the symbol but scarcely affected the system.

The turbulence of Egyptian politics should not obscure the issue that matters most about fundamentalism and fundamentalists: winning the battle for Islamic legitimacy. Yet fundamentalists have no monopoly on either religious rhetoric or religious praxis. Throughout the postcolonial era of Egyptian history, "Islam [has] remained the widest and most effective basis for consensus despite all efforts to promote nationalism, patriotism, secularism, and socialism."[16] But consensus for whom? Islam has come to mean divergent values and conflicting norms for different Egyptians. All attempts at constitutional legitimation in Egypt have reflected pervasive loyalty to Islam. In 1964 under Nasser and again in 1971 under Sadat, Islam was designated as the state religion of Egypt. The people's council (*majlis ash-shaʿb*), appointed by the government, has continued to receive proposals for heightening the state's public commitment to Islamic norms. Opposition political parties vie with one another as well as with the government in claiming the mantle of Islamic legitimacy.

In such an atmosphere, suffused, as it is, with the symbols and sanctity of Islam, it is imperative to identify who the fundamentalists are. It is not enough to analyze their ideological claims or to chart their public attacks. One must also see what classes of Egyptian society they represent. Those who have been identified as fundamentalist invariably come from upwardly mobile middle-class backgrounds: they are not the poor, downtrodden, and dispossessed, but rather those who have had sufficient education to perceive another reality than the one they daily confront. They are underemployed doctors or engineers, or journeymen technicians with no stable career path. They may also be marginalized merchants or disgruntled army personnel. They have enough education to frame their protest in either-or ideological categories, categories that admit of black and white but not gray. Mawdudi was a harbinger of all Islamic fundamentalists: seeing whatever was not Islam as *shirk* or unbelief, he could attack a pervasive enemy, without ever once suggesting how that enemy was to be transformed into an observant cobeliever.

The postcolonial experiences of Egypt and Pakistan provide a benchmark for some of the enduring arguments about political Islam. Separation of religion from politics became a trip wire, a shibboleth for all that was wrong with colonialism and its legacy, and all that was right about Islamic norms. Fundamentalists refuse to acknowledge the separation of church and state, waging an internal *jihad* against all who pretend to clarify and enforce such a separation. Islam, in their view, is both church and state. The Arabic words *din* (religion) and *dawla* (state) are conjoined with the meaning of Islam. In the words of an early member of the Muslim Brothers, "politics is part of religion. Caesar and what belongs to Caesar is for God Almighty alone. . . . Islam commanded a unity of life. To impose upon Islam the Christian separation of loyalties [into church and state] is to deny it its essential meaning and very existence."[17]

Islam then becomes a giant anomaly. On the one hand, it is more than a religion. It encompasses both the spiritual and the political, the private and the public domains. Attention to one sphere presumes engagement in the other. To do less is to trivialize and confound Islam. To talk about a mosque-state division in Islam is to talk about dividing Islam.

Yet at the same time, religious specialists are not in charge of making Islam into an overarching, socioeconomic, religiopolitical reality. For the Muslim Brothers and their various subgroups in Egypt, as for the Islamic Society in Pakistan, emphasis on the unity of Islam does not imply the creation of a theocracy. Sunni Muslims attach minimal importance to a class of religious specialists; the *ʿulama* are ordinary Muslims who happen to be religious functionaries. They are not endowed with the high rank or social prestige of Shiʿite clerics. Islamic fundamentalism represents the radicalizing synthesis of Muslim laymen, not clergy.

In the postcolonial era, the nation-state is the inescapable context for all public life, and the Egyptian fundamentalists who challenged the political leadership in Cairo did so by claiming that they, not the army officers turned politicians, were the true claimants to the seventh-century Medinan state inaugurated by the Prophet Muhammad. Nationalism, in their view, resurrected the kind of tribalism or *jahiliyya* that Muhammad opposed and that early Muslims temporarily overcame. In its stead, there should be a transnational patriotism that seeks the benefit of all Muslims everywhere. Sayyid Qutb, the Muslim Brother who opposed Nasser and was executed on charges of sedition in 1966, used a string of homologies to stress how Islam, if correctly defined, offered a nationalism worthy of Muslims. In true Islam, wrote Qutb, "nationalism is belief, homeland is Dar al-Islam, the ruler is God, and the constitution is the Qur'an."[18]

As secular nationalism falters in the Muslim world, one might expect religious fundamentalism, also known as Islamism, to surge forward. That would be a facile, and possibly inaccurate, expectation. Though the effective appeal of nationalism is to a limited, sophisticated urban elite, the power of the modern state allows these same elites to exercise coercive authority over a much wider segment of the population. At the same time, fundamentalists, despite the religious idiom of their discourses, are handicapped by the counterappeal of other religious authorities, and the lack of concrete goals in their stated programs. Their greatest appeal is to urban discontents with at least high-school-level education. Seldom do they appeal to the greater number of their semiliterate or uneducated countrymen. And, as in Pakistan, their rhetorical power exceeds their pragmatic accomplishments even when they provide, as some have, social, medical, and educational services that surpass those of the often corrupt, ever inefficient state bureaucracy.

If the pattern of protest that marks Islamic fundamentalism in Pakistan and Egypt is in part the legacy of British colonial rule and in part the response to regional tensions and national dilemmas arising from the post–World War II era, can the same be said for Muslim majority countries that had been under French colonial rule? To explore that question I will focus on two Arab/Muslim countries that experienced French colonial rule: Syria and Tunisia.

Syria

Principal dates and rulers:

1914–17	Ottoman conscription of Syrians during World War I led to widespread famine; Armenian massacres
1920–46	French mandate
1946	Independence
1958–63	Egyptian-Syrian alliance (United Arab Republic)
1963	Baath party comes to power
1964	First Hama riots against Baath secularism
1967	June war with Israel
1967–70	Hafiz al-Asad consolidates power in Correctionist Movement and becomes president
1973	New "secular" constitution; October war with Israel
1976	Deployment of troops to Lebanon
1982	Israeli invasion of Lebanon and subsequent de facto division of Lebanon into Syrian and Israeli spheres of influence
	Muslim Brothers' uprising in Hama crushed
1994	Death of Basil Asad, oldest son and likely successor to Hafiz al-Asad

Syria, like Egypt, remained within the Ottoman sphere of influence for nearly four centuries, from the early sixteenth to the early twentieth century. It was not till the defeat of the Turks at the end of World War I that the French established a mandate over the region. Its unpopularity led to an early uprising (1925–27), a treaty with France before World War II and finally full independence in 1946.

Independence did not bring stability, however: Syrians were merely left with a geographical entity, that piece of territory from the Mediterranean to the Euphrates that the French had ruled, together with Lebanon, since 1920. The struggle to take control of postcolonial Syria was waged along several regional, sectarian, class, and ideological lines. Over time it became a battle between a landowning, urban, mercantile elite and a rising group of rural army officers who favored modernization within a praetorian state.

It was under the banner of the Baath party that the latter group won, and since 1963 they have ruled in Syria. The current president, Hafiz al-Asad, was a rural army officer turned Baathist. He became the undisputed ruler of Syria after deposing a party rival in 1970. To maintain his power base in Damascus, he had to outwit even his own brother, the ambitious Rifaat al-Asad, whom he sent into exile in 1984.[19]

Within the context of regional politics, many observers have criticized Asad for the severity with which he has punished dissenters from his autocratic rule. The showcase for Asad's alleged brutality is his handling of the Hama rebellion in 1982. What begs for amplification, however, is the historical background to the Hama rebellion. It requires attention both to the social formation of the fundamentalist protestors who spearheaded that rebellion and to the search for religious legitimation on the part of a precarious, minoritarian regime.

The Muslim Brothers have existed in Syria almost as long as in Egypt. Appearing in the mid-1930s, they opposed the French mandate and resented the benefits it conferred on the modernizing sector of the Syrian economy. Those who supported the Brothers clustered in the region around Hama, an ancient trading center some 150 miles north of Damascus. Merchants and landlords, they numbered about one-sixth of Syria's population. In the 1960s, the Brothers sparked two organized protests against the Baathist regime. The first took the form of a series of merchant strikes in 1964 that openly challenged Baath policies as un-Islamic, secular, and therefore unacceptable. The first Hama riot forced the new government to intervene and even to shell a mosque. It was followed by another strike the next year. Once again, the government had to intervene, and once again it broke the strike with force.

When Hafiz al-Asad took control of the Baath party in 1970, the Brothers were initially silent, but by 1973 they had come to view him as an Alawite secularist. After all, Asad, like Nasser, his erstwhile hero, had sponsored a new constitution, and like Nasser's, his new constitution did not enshrine Islam as the state religion. Merchant strikes and violence spread to Hama. Asad put down the protest but at the same time declared that only a Muslim could serve as Syria's president. Yet he remained an Alawite, and many still regarded Alawites as heretics. To put to rest qualms about the Islamic status of Alawites, Asad set about projecting an Islamic image for himself and his family. He launched two architectural projects in his native village of Qardaha, situated in the heart of the Alawite mountains. For his deceased mother he built a lavish mosque, and for his oldest son Basil, who was tipped to be his successor but died in 1994, a vast funerary complex. Reminiscent of a Muslim saint's shrine, it features Qur'anic recitation and projects Basil as, above all, an observant Muslim.

From Damascus Asad increased the salaries of religious functionaries throughout Syria. Nor did he stint in his patronage of religious sites, either building new monuments or restoring historic landmarks. His pride may also be remembered as his folly: the Umayyad Mosque of Damascus now memorializes Asad through his signature on the band of one of its newly rebuilt minarets.

Throughout the 1970s the face of Syria was transformed both politically and economically. In 1973 Syria, along with Egypt, was drawn into still another war with Israel. Despite initial victories, which included the Syrian recapture of Qunaitra, both Egypt and Syria were finally defeated. Yet over twenty years later the Baathist regime continues to celebrate what is lauded on state-run television every October as "the victory of Qunaitra." Political obfuscation can succeed only because economic progress during the same period has been real, at least for some Syrians. While the highest levels of Baath leadership have remained exclusively male, some women have emerged as public figures: both the minister of education and the minister of culture are women, the latter having held her post for almost two decades. Women have also been encouraged to work, and to work at higher paying, salaried jobs where they were often trained in skills denied to previous generations of women. The Women's Union, a government-sponsored group, advocates causes such as greater female employment opportunities and increased literacy for women of all classes. The literacy rate of Syrian women and their prominence in education have become touted achievements of Baathist rule during the past three decades.

Both women and men gained from the increase of petrodollar profits in the Gulf after 1973, since some of those profits were channeled to Syria through labor and services. This meant that goods and services improved but prices also escalated. The newly rich and the newly empowered benefited at the same time that traditional mercantile classes felt slighted or even betrayed. Their frustration took on an added religious coloration when Syria intervened on behalf of the Maronite Christians and against the Palestinians, both Muslim and Christian, in the early stages of the Lebanese civil war (1976). The legacy of that intervention lingers among Muslim activists. Initially it spurred Sunni Syrians who opposed Asad to identify him as a secularist and to challenge the non-Sunni, specifically Alawi, tone of his leadership.

During this same period the Brothers expanded their influence and trained cadres in urban warfare. Mosque study circles on weekends became a recruitment nexus for their cells. When a noted Hama cleric was imprisoned and died, they also used his funeral as a rallying point for mobilizing new recruits. By 1976 they had embarked on an assassination campaign against key state officials. When Asad's brother Rifaat was attacked in February 1978, many began to suspect that there was sympathy for the Brothers even within the officer corps.

The struggle escalated in June 1979: a terrorist unit of the Brothers attacked an artillery school, killing sixty cadets and wounding many others. Asad's response was the stick and the carrot. The stick fell on the Brothers: three hundred of them were imprisoned. The carrot was extended to other members of the Sunni community, as more and more Sunnis were awarded government posts.

The Brothers continued to agitate, and a crackdown in 1980 was directed at the city of Aleppo, in the far north on the same trade route with Hama. Five thousand people were arrested, hundreds killed. In a single helicopter attack on a Brothers' outpost, two hundred of their number were killed. The local merchants of Aleppo attempted a strike, parallel to the one previously declared in Hama, but it fizzled and failed.

By spring 1980 the Baathists had introduced a special law that made membership in the Muslim Brothers an offense punishable by death. Though public membership disappeared overnight, the Brothers, operating clandestinely, tried to assassinate Asad in June 1980. They failed, but his security forces killed over five hundred Brethren who were serving time in prison.

The Brothers now became part of a united Islamic Front that opposed Asad as an unbeliever, not only because of his draconian measures against them but because of the secular constitution he introduced in 1973 at the same time that he required the president of Syria to be a Muslim. It is impossible to calculate how broad was the social basis for the Islamic Front. It seems more coherent than its counterpart in Egypt, yet it also seems more vulnerable to isolation and defeat, for behind the rhetoric of opposition to the Baathist regime there emerged a low-key success story: the constitution, combined with Syria's modernizing prosperity, allayed the fears and raised the hopes of many groups in urban areas. It also appealed to rural peasants and, of course, to loyalist elements of the army.

But the Brothers were able to strike. A bomb attack in late 1981 killed five hundred people in central Damascus. It was followed by a military plot to overthrow Asad in January 1982; over four hundred members of the army were purged.

It was against this backdrop that the rebellion in Hama occurred in February 1982. From Asad's view, it was hardly an isolated incident, but rather the latest and most portentous in a series of threatening actions by his declared enemies. His response was swift and brutal. Between ten thousand and twenty-five thousand people were killed. As whole districts were razed, many families were allegedly taken from their homes and shot en masse.

The campaign worked. Hama halted the Islamic challenge to Asad's rule. It epitomized not a religious struggle but a struggle for power in which religion was used by both sides as a mask for deeper grievances and more palpable stakes. The merchants and landlords who were the backbone of support for the Brothers and the Islamic Front numbered about one-sixth of the Syrian population. The Baath party relied on workers, peasants, minorities, and army personnel. Its constituency accounted for about one-fourth of the Syrian population. The chief issue did not concern Islam but modernization. It was not an up or down decision on Islamic statehood, but rather a process involving countless daily decisions on how the country modernizes, who benefits, and who is in charge. It was also in part regional. The merchants, landlords, and religious classes from the North resented the influence of other groups. They could appeal to some disaffected student cadres and military units but not to broader constituencies. Even though upper-middle-class professionals denounced the government as authoritarian, they were unenthusiastic about an Islamic state. Teachers and professors might sympathize with the Brothers, yet they remained in the employ of the state. Little support came from working classes or peasants. Indeed, these groups, which represented the majority of Syrians, had benefited from Baathist social policy and were also often controlled via trade unions or the Peasant Union, both of which were allied to the Baath party.[20]

If one charts political conflict on socioeconomic lines, it is possible to say of modern-day Syria that the Baath party represents a secular state with rural constituents opposing an urban mercantile class professing Sunni orthodoxy. Framed in this perspective, Islamic fundamentalism stands out in Syria for what it is everywhere: an ideology of protest that represents the interests of specific socioeconomic groups yet claims to project all of Islam under the banner of those interests. It is not often that the conflict reaches the battle proportions that it did in Hama in 1982, but when it does, the outcome is clear: the Syrian state, with its powerful economic and technological base, its professional army and security forces, can suppress any rebellion. The rebellion is labeled sedition, the rebels traitors. The state wins militarily but it also wins psychologically, for many afterward are led to applaud the rational nature of the state's response to terrorism. "The state is said to be (by its custodians, by its many, many spokesmen) the only dike against great upheaval and disorder."[21] Was it possible that many Syrians in the aftermath of Hama thought to themselves: "Better one month of Hama than fourteen years of Lebanon"?[22] If so, the chief legacy of French colonial rule in the Levant would seem to be a predisposition to accept the worst excesses of authoritarian government rather than to opt for change. Was French colonial rule therefore more destructive of indigenous resilience than its British counterpart? Not perceptibly, for comparison of Syria with its Arab neighbors does not reveal a qualitative difference. Authoritarianism and popular complicity or cooptation seem to be the rule.

Even were Hafiz al-Asad to be replaced as leader of Syria by the end of the current century, the new ruler would be, at best, an "enlightened" despot, one who invokes Islam but, like Asad, stops far short of implementing an Islamic state. After all, that state would have to straddle Shiʿi and Sunni sensibilities, since the Alawites are much closer to Iranian than Saudi notions of Islamic observance. What modern Syrian history seems to favor is the continuation of a secularist polity that genuflects toward Qom as much as Mecca, favoring Shiʿi piety around its own monument to martyrdom at Sidi Zaynab, outside Damascus, as well as commercial and political ties with Tehran.

Tunisia

Principal dates and rulers:

1881	French Protectorate
1956	Independence
1956–87	Habib Bourguiba
1987–	Zayn al-ʿAbidin Ben ʿAli
1990	An-Nahda party, also known as Le Mouvement de tendace islamique, outlawed, and its leader, Rachid al-Ghannouchi, sent into exile

Tunisia, at first glance, may seem like an unlikely candidate to include in a survey of the engagement with Muslim protest movements known as Islamic fundamentalism. It is a small North African country of seven million people, wedged between two magnets of revolutionary fervor, Algeria and Libya. If one wanted to chart the aftermath of French colonial rule and the agency of indigenous Muslim activists, one might expect to profit more from a study of Islamic fundamentalism in Algeria or even distant Morocco than Tunisia.

Tunisia, however, offers some unique characteristics that highlight the nature of Islamic fundamentalism in general. Like Syria, it was shaped by French colonial policy, above all in the educational sphere and in the development of the army. Like Syria, too, it has prospered not so much through its natural resources, which are meager, as through its ability to integrate into the commercial patterns of the larger Mediterranean world. The first of the North African French colonies to obtain independence (in 1956), it has been dominated for the past forty years by one party, the Destourian Socialist party, and shaped by one man, Habib Bourguiba, leader of the independence movement and president-for-life. At least Bourguiba was supposed to be president-for-life, but in 1987, though still alive, he was declared unfit to rule. Through a bloodless military coup he was deposed and replaced by the current president, a former securities force chief, Zayn al-ʿAbidin Ben ʿAli.

The major reason for studying Tunisia goes beyond its French connection and authoritarian politics. It has to do with the expressiveness of its ideologues: along with the fundamentalist movements in Pakistan and Egypt, the Tunisian opposition ranks as among the most articulate in the entire Muslim world.[23] It has played only a marginal role in the history of modern Tunisia, yet it has eloquently voiced both its laments and its hopes. Faced with intractable opposition, and against impossible odds, Tunisian fundamentalists throw into bold relief the dilemma of other post-colonial Muslim societies: the struggle to forge a new identity against forces identified with the colonial period and yet the desire to recuperate agency as Muslims allied with economic as well as political progress.

Tunisia resembles Syria in more than its Francophone legacy. Politically it too has the power of the central government vested in one city, the capital city. From Tunis and through Tunis all the mechanisms of the modern nation-state are channeled. Bourguiba, like Asad, defined the state in his image, though Bourguiba even more than Asad might be portrayed as a rank secularist. Bourguiba was a product of the bilingual education system that the French had introduced in order to bridge the modern and traditional cultures of Tunisia. After completing his education in France, he became a lawyer active in the nationalist movement. Immediately after World War II, he was challenged by an Islamic rival, Salah Ben Youssef. Ben Youssef based himself at the most prominent mosque, the Zaytuna, in Tunis and drew support for his cause from other Muslim countries. While Bourguiba stressed themes of progress and development, building indigenous power through trade unions and maintaining external leverage through ties with the French, Ben Youssef appealed to traditional merchant and landowner interests, accenting Arab-Islamic solidarity rather than Tunisian national identity.

Ben Youssef's challenge faded because nationalism, not Pan-Islamism, was on the ascendant in the late 1950s and 1960s. Bourguiba became president and almost immediately sponsored a Code of Personal Conduct. It was made the law of the land in August 1956. It outflanked while also delegitimating Muslim law (the *shariʿa*). Most important were its provisions in the realm of family law. Polygamy was abolished, judicial divorce granted to women, a minimum age fixed for marriage, and mutual consent of both bride and bridegroom required. Women also were given the right to vote and to hold political office. Education was made free for both men and women, at the same time that women were to be given equal pay for equal work, as well as an equal chance to be hired.[24]

The challenge of the Code of Personal Status was followed by the abolition of the *shariʿa* courts. At the same time, charitable endowments (the *habus*) were incorporated within the state bureaucracy. The Islamic educational system also became redefined as an extension of the Tunis government. Religion followed suit, as the state gave Zaytuna mosque in Tunis, together with all other mosques, maintenance allowances, at the same time that it directly subsidized preachers' salaries.

Whatever hope religious leaders may have had for intellectual or institutional independence from the Bourguiba regime was removed by still another provision: all those who sought government employment were required to be bilingual. "As a consequence of these reforms, that fraction of the political elite whose symbolic capital was based on knowledge of Arabic and Islam and on the control of Islamic institutions was dispossessed of political power and social mobility."[25]

To complete his credentials as a thoroughgoing secularist, Bourguiba proposed an unprecedented change in February 1960: he attempted to eliminate one of the defining pillars of Islamic ritual observance, the Ramadan fast. Anyone who has traveled in the Muslim world or lived in a Muslim country must be sensitive to the tenacity of the Ramadan fast. It requires all observant Muslims who have reached young adulthood to abstain from food, drink, and sexual liaison during the period from dawn to dusk for twenty-eight days.

77

How, then, could Bourguiba expect his fellow Tunisians to welcome his proposal to end the Ramadan fast? Because, he argued, such fasting impeded national development, and what was needed in Tunisia was to break the back of underdevelopment. Nothing less than a holy war or *jihad* against underdevelopment was required if Tunisia expected to enter the competitive ranks of its industrialized Mediterranean neighbors. It was not merely to get ahead but to survive that Tunisians needed to increase their productivity. And so, in the name of a higher principle, the survival of an Islamic society, Bourguiba called for the renunciation of a lower principle, the prolonged fasting of Ramadan.[26]

However flawed the logic of his appeal, Bourguiba's declaration was consistent with a pattern of ambiguity that beguiled his enemies, even as it strengthened his own support. Bourguiba never renounced Islam; he merely claimed that his own interpretation of its tenets superseded that of the traditional classes. He even sought and obtained the approval of religious functionaries for his 1956 Code of Personal Conduct. No urban revolts or assassination attempts followed its implementation. And in the 1959 constitution Bourguiba did what Asad later did: he proclaimed Islam to be the state religion and required that the president of the republic be a Muslim. At no time during his more than thirty-year rule did Bourguiba, his ministers, or his party reject the Islamic focus of Tunisian identity. They never became explicit secularists in the tradition of Kemal Mustafa Ataturk, the founder and icon of modern-day Turkey.

Even when he hit a trip wire, Bourguiba knew how to keep his balance. Unlike the Code of Personal Conduct, the banning of the Ramadan fast did not win the approval of most *ulama*. To be sure, some modernist Sheikhs did support Bourguiba, declaring, "As long as one conserves one's faith, religion can adapt."[27] Yet most religious leaders rebelled. Defying Bourguiba, they continued to urge the Ramadan fast, and in one instance, in the city of Kairouan, a mob of students attacked the governor's house. Eight deaths resulted. Other public reactions were sporadic and less violent. Even when some civil students and university students did eat in public to show their support of Bourguiba, they were ignored rather than attacked. Most Tunisians quietly persisted in keeping the fast of Ramadan, and Bourguiba turned his attention to other reforms: he restricted religious education to one hour per week in primary school, and he banned the wearing of the veil in any state-run system of education. Even without the effective ban of the Ramadan fast, he hoped that the effects of secular education would eventually produce the secular lifestyle and competitive national economy that he sought for Tunisia in the late twentieth century.

In the face of such a populist autocrat, a determined modernizer with widespread appeal, how could fundamentalists hope to effect any change? They did not pick the option of armed revolt, as in Syria, or assassination of public officials, as in Egypt and Syria. Nor did they attempt to foment large-scale civil unrest, as in Iran. The cyclical pattern of economic life in Tunisia did cause several explosive incidents in the late 1970s and early 1980s—the Black Thursday riots in Tunis in January 1978, the Gafsah revolt of January 1980, and the bread riots of January 1984—but none of these was either initiated or supported by fundamentalist groups. Unlike the Syrian case, where the socioeconomic basis for fundamentalist anger, dissent, and open revolt was evident, the leading religious activists of Tunis attempted to influence the populace at large through literary and cultural media. Several journals served to promulgate the views of an Islamic opposition to Bourguiba and his party. But the government seldom closed them down or arrested their editors. Instead, the Tunis bureaucrats selectively removed the most flagrant abuses to which the Islamists drew attention, while also stressing their own Islamic convictions and behavior. Only in December 1979 was a fundamentalist journal, *Al-Maʿrifa*, the official publication of the Mouvement de tendace islamique (MTI), banned, and then on the flimsiest of pretexts: because it dared to criticize the Saudi regime for its handling of an attack on the Meccan Grand Mosque (discussed below).

In the late 1980s, however, after the removal of Bourguiba from office, the Tunisian authorities became less tolerant of cultural protest. Bourguiba's successor, Ben ʿAli, supported a law disallowing any political group specifically affiliated with any race, creed, or religion (as had Syria and Egypt). Because the leading fundamentalist group, the MTI, headed by Rachid al-Ghannouchi, is called Le Mouvement de tendance islamique, it is now banned as a political party in Tunisia's avowedly pluralist system, and al-Ghannouchi himself has been sent into exile.

Both the ban and the exile have outraged some of the marginalized intellectual and social groups in Tunis. It may yet undermine

79

the current regime, especially if economic conditions become more desperate once Tunisia's long-protected agricultural and textile export markets are opened, as they will be in 2007, according to a free-trade agreement signed with the European Union in 1995.

Yet the social sources for fundamentalist appeal in Tunisia are as limited as they were in Syria. The major bases for recruitment are the universities. Tunisia's population is continuing to grow at a rapid rate (2.1 percent annually), with over two-thirds of its nine million citizens under twenty-five years of age. Many of those who attend university come from salaried middle classes. Not only the parents but increasingly their children are coming to face what one observer has described as "a blocked future and downward mobility,"[28] even though female literacy and life expectancy continue to soar.[29] It is fundamentalists who benefit when despair over a secular future runs high among urban professionals. Not surprisingly, over 80 percent of the membership of MTI comes from this group, as do 75 percent of its leaders. The remaining 25 percent come from white-collar and blue-collar workers, either unemployed or underemployed.

The similarity of their profile to the Islamists studied in Egypt are striking. In both instances the majority of the members are under thirty. In geographical origins both are urban or of recent rural origin. A minor difference concerns parentage: while in Egypt two-thirds of the fathers were middle-level government employees, in Tunisia almost half of the fathers were urban or rural workers. The major difference seems to reflect the social fallout from the 1956 Code of Personal Conduct: while in Egypt none of the fundamentalists came from families that had been scarred by divorce or separation, in Tunisia almost a third did come from families that had been so scarred.

Despite the adverse economic circumstances that Tunisia has faced in the 1990s, with upwardly mobile young professionals being caught in a downward cycle of frustration, it is hard to foresee how fundamentalism can enjoy more than a short-term appeal. First, there is the organizational problem: not all the fundamentalist groups coalesce under one umbrella. Their world views differ, their objectives conflict, their membership compete, each with the other. One group tries to combine socialism with Islamic radicalism: labeling its major journal *15/21*, it hopes to elide the fifteenth

Islamic century with the imminent twenty-first century of Christian, now Western preference.

More significant is the cultural antipathy of the MTI leadership to all things European. Rachid al-Ghannouchi feels himself alienated from the nationalist movement, his rights deprived since independence: he, and many of his followers, were "educated as Muslims and Arabs, while we could see the country totally molded in the French cultural identity."[30] Like the Syrian Muslim Brethren in Hama, the MTI leadership have been set adrift by the modernizing forces of their new nation-state, but unlike them, MTI has not opted for violent confrontation.

Rachid al-Ghannouchi had but slight ties to groups of the urban poor and the regionally marginalized, even before his exile to London in the early 1990s. Predictions of the late 1980s that Tunisia was on the brink of disaster, and that the government's failure to recognize MTI as a political party would bring about an alliance between Islamic and secular forces, forging links between private citizens and the military that would eventually topple the Ben ʿAli government—such predictions now seem at best premature, at worst hopelessly naive.[31]

There are at least two further reasons why Tunisia seems more stable now than it did a decade ago. One, the option of military intervention, has not been seriously broached in modern Tunisian history. Civilian political institutions are stronger in Tunis than in any neighboring North African or Middle Eastern polity, even though security forces pose an omnipresent, stifling control on social mobility and political experimentation. Another is the anomaly of women's role in Tunisian fundamentalist protests. To the surprise of some, women have actively participated in MTI. Why would young, mostly educated Tunisian women support a group that advocates an Islamic state? The women themselves seem to feel that Islamist organizations "provide well-known male acquaintances and also, by their professed code, guarantee physical respect."[32] However, a fuller explanation seems to lie in the distance between the goals of Bourguiba's secular utopia and the reality of present-day Tunis. Women have been encouraged to succeed outside traditional, domestic roles. They have tried to emulate the independent-minded women of Europe, and some, such as the teacher/activist and film maker shown in figure 4, have succeeded.

Figure 2. (right) Two
veiled women by the sea
wall in Tunis.

Figure 3. (below) A swim-
suit ad with veiled passer-
by in Tunis.

Figure 4. A light moment between the award-winning director Mouſida Tlafli (right) and Amel ben Aba, feminist, teacher, and advocate of women's rights (left).

Figure 5. A feminist perception of the new family code in Tunisia.

Yet, even after obtaining a university education, others have been denied the achievements they were taught to expect. Job discrimination and gender segregation persist, despite the longstanding Personal Status Code. Unable to work outside the home and urged by male contemporaries to remain in the home, many Tunisian women have retreated, reclaiming traditional roles while also participating in the Islamist movement.

But women's roles, like Tunisian society in general, are clearly in transition. It is important to stress that the experiment begun by Bourguiba is still young, and that it is still in limbo. Bourguiba himself gave the fundamentalists their best opening when he tried to have nine MTI members retried and hung for a crime of which they had been previously acquitted. The sympathy generated for the MTI from groups that usually did not support them alarmed other members of his party, and it was at this crucial moment, in 1987, that Ben Ali intervened to depose Bourguiba. Though Ben 'Ali's own policies have, in turn, been criticized, it is too early to say that he will not succeed in the art of ambiguity and compromise. It is, after all, a form of art that Tunisians have come to expect of their political leadership.

Above all, it is important to note that Tunisia remains "the only Arab country which has been governed by a mass-supported party, rather than by military dynastic rule, or by a group of notable families."[33] Its Personal Status Code has also been in effect for thirty-five years; by prohibiting polygamy and attempting to make men and women equal in matters of divorce and inheritance, the Tunisian code exceeds even the secular legislation of Turkey. Indeed, "the code stands out as one of the most progressive pieces of legislation ever promulgated in any Islamic country."[34] Further modified in 1993, it now provides still more explicit legal guarantees for women, especially in alimony and divorce.

The range of opportunities for Tunisian women is also reflected in their contrasting images, from traditional to modern dress: neither beach ads nor feminist cartoons are precluded from the cosmopolitan public space of modern Tunis. (See figs. 4 and 5.)

By such accomplishments, Tunisians have shown themselves to be both nimble and adaptable. Their stake in the twenty-first century, as the journal *15/21* suggests, may yet depend on adapting Islam to new global challenges, while at the same time maintaining their competitive edge in an increasingly technological and regionally unionized global economy. Civil society has continued to function even in the shell of a praetorian state, suggesting that the French colonial legacy in Tunisia may yet prove to be more positive than it has been in either Algeria or Syria.

Saudi Arabia

Principal dates and rulers:

1902–32	ʿAbd al-ʿAziz ibn Saʿud contests other Arab chiefs for control of the Arabian peninsula
1927	Treaty of Jidda, by which the British recognize ʿAbd al-ʿAziz as King of Hijaz and Najd
1932	Kingdom of Saudi Arabia consolidated
1933	First oil concession to Aramco
1953	Death of King ʿAbd al-ʿAziz
1953–64	King Saʿud
1964	King Saʿud deposed, goes into exile, replaced by King Faisal
1975	King Faisal assassinated
1979	Mecca mosque rebellion
1975–82	King Khalid
1982–	King Fahd

It is a frequent if simplistic argument that Saudi Arabia is the oldest fundamentalist state in the Muslim world. "Having established a state," argues one writer, "the House of Saud has used Islam to legitimize its dynastic rule. Saudi Arabia is unique. It was created out of a series of Islamic campaigns in modern times, and its character as a fundamentalist polity has remained unchanged since its inception in 1932. It is thus the oldest politically independent Islamic fundamentalist state in the world."[35]

Or is it? The argument for Saudi-style fundamentalism accords Islamic legitimacy to Saudi Arabia, even while ignoring evidence that the opposite conclusion is equally valid: Saudi Arabia has become a viable nation-state not by implementing Muslim norms but by using religion as a mask. In the name of Islam, the state introduces changes that would otherwise be unacceptable to a population little prepared and even less inclined to engage the modern world.

Saudi Arabia is neither old nor unique. It is a tribal theocracy of very recent origin. There was no unified political entity called Saudi Arabia until the major provinces of the Arabian peninsula had been conquered by a skilled Hijazi chieftain. That chieftain, the later King ʿAbd al-ʿAziz, believed in the puritanical Wahhabi creed. Wahhabi was a name given to the small group that ʿAbd al-ʿAziz legitimated by his bold military and diplomatic actions in the 1920s and 1930s. At first he employed religious zealots, the Ikhwan or Brothers (not to confused with the Muslim Brothers of Egypt and Syria), but by 1929 ʿAbd al-ʿAziz had outgrown his need for, and his toleration of, his erstwhile Ikhwan supporters. Aided by British weaponry, he attacked and defeated them at Sabila and later that year killed several of their leaders who, after being captured by the British, were dutifully returned to him.

Even before he entered into the treaty with Aramco in 1932, the nimble ʿAbd al-ʿAziz was using European assistance to help him dominate and outstrip his rivals on the peninsula. By the Treaty of Jiddah in 1927 he had recognized treaty borders of the sort laid down by the Great Powers after World War I. Though he claimed legitimacy for his kingdom by declaring the Qurʾan as state constitution, few among the Qurʾan's lofty verses refer to political structures. Kingship is neither affirmed nor denied in the Qurʾan, and so the only basis on which ʿAbd al-ʿAziz and his successors can claim Qurʾanic legitimacy is by alleging that the king is equal to all other believers. It is to maintain that scriptural facade, and also to perpetuate tribal custom, that ʿAbd al-ʿAziz and his successors have held open consultations where subjects can approach and ask them about any matter of public concern. That practice, however, hardly fulfills the Qurʾanic mandate (3:158) that the ruler, following the example of the Prophet Muhammad, should consult with those ruled about all matters of governance. There has never been a consultative assembly in Saudi Arabia, nor has any publicly elected body enjoyed the influence that the National Assembly did in neighboring Kuwait during the 1980s.

Saudi history pivots around two facts: (1) the holiest shrines of Islam exist in the western province of the Hijaz, and (2) one-quarter of all proven oil reserves exist underneath the sands of the eastern provinces. Every other significant dimension of Saudi life relates to one of those two "gifts." Take them away, as if by a magical, whimsical sleight of hand, and Saudi Arabia would be as important in contemporary affairs as the hapless African nation of Chad.

The king of Saudi Arabia is a twentieth-century monarch. He continues a dynasty less than sixty years old. His religious title is "Protector of the Two Holy Places." The two holy places he is committed to protect are transnational centers of Islamic ritual loyalty: the birthplace of the prophet Muhammad and his first home, Mecca; and the city where he established his first armed polity, Medina. King Fahd protects them, but not as a spiritual leader, for he can make no pronouncement that other Muslims accept as authoritative. Rather, he protects them as the head of a modern-day nation-state. His task is at once simple and impossible: to ensure the hegemony of one tribe, the al-Saʿud, over an area larger than the United States east of the Mississippi River. Not all Saudis are either Sunnis or Wahhabis; a disaffected Shiʿi populace inhabits the strategically significant eastern province of the kingdom. It is demography and economics that make King Fahd's task manageable: a minute population enjoys stupendous wealth. The total population of native Saudis is less than five million, despite published statistics to the contrary, while the vast income generated by petroleum production and export continues to provide, even with the reduced power of OPEC since the mid 1980s, the basis for large-scale modernizing strategies.

While it is easy to say that "in Saudi Arabia the ʿulama enjoy more power and prestige than in any other Sunni state" and even to claim that "they are the key element in bestowing legitimacy on the Saudi regime,"[36] their actual role is, in fact, ceremonial. No group of religious functionaries determines the dominant tone of the state, nor do they set its planning agenda. There are numerous other bureaucrats, many of them members of the royal family, most of them educated abroad, who advise the monarch on such matters.

The usefulness of the ʿulama is chiefly exemplified by the one event that will live as the true expression of Saudi Arabian fundamentalism in the twentieth century. It was not initiated by the state but against it. Its leaders did not come from the House of al-Saʿud or from then King Khalid's theological advisers but from those who had lost hope in the religious credibility of both the king and his advisers. It is known as the Mecca Mosque incident, and it inspired tremors from Wall Street to Riyadh. It is noteworthy as a showcase demonstrating how tenuous can be any nation-state's attempt to co-opt Islamic symbols and discourse.

The Muslim lunar calendar does not coincide with the common era solar calendar. The beginning of the fifteenth-century *hijri* occurred in November 1979, nearly ten months after the return of Khomeini in triumph from Paris to Tehran. The new century was inaugurated by a revolt against the Saudi monarchy that took place in the heartland of Arabia in the precinct of its holiest mosque. The leader of the movement was a disaffected National Guardsman who had become a theological autodidact. In the province adjacent to the Hijaz, Juhayman ibn Sayf al-ʿUtayba preached against the corruption of the Saudi state. He had been inspired by one of the king's theological advisers, Shaikh ʿAbd al-ʿAziz ibn Baz, and when Juhayman had first provoked the Saudi authorities in 1978 he had been arrested along with nearly one hundred of his followers. But Shaikh ibn Baz had intervened, procuring his release. Security police monitored his actions thereafter, but not with great efficiency. For Juhayman managed to evade detection as he returned to his anti-Saudi declamations. Now he not only advocated but he also planned for the overthrow of the monarchy. And he found followers. Young theological students, disillusioned and disoriented by the rapid change that took place in the kingdom during the late 1970s, joined Juhayman's movement.

Juhayman's message was simple, but his motivation was complex. He believed that King ʿAbd al-ʿAziz Ibn Saʿud had gone astray from the *shariʿa* in the 1920s: disavowing the Ikhwan, the king had become corrupted by collusion with Western forces. But Juhayman's zeal had a personal as well as a theological motivation, since his grandfather had been among the Ikhwan killed by Ibn Saʿud, with British assistance, in 1929. Preaching that the expected *mahdi*, a messianic figure for both Sunni and Shiʿi Muslims, would usher in the new century, Juhayman proclaimed his own brother-in-law as the *mahdi*. The band of modern-day Ikhwan marched on the Great Mosque at Mecca and easily gained control of its sacred precinct. Juhayman then began to preach his message of messianic imminence to the surprised congregants, fully expecting that Allah would intervene and assist his small band to overcome the expected counterattack from unbelievers, that is, from troops loyal to the Saudi regime.

Juhayman's was a bold if suicidal move. His makeshift militia, which may have numbered several hundred, overwhelmed the thin Saudi security forces. Not only did they capture the ritual center of the Islamic world, but they effectively controlled it for exactly two weeks. The authorities, embarrassed, did not try to dislodge them immediately. Instead, they first obtained a *fatwa*, or legal decree, from the ʿ*ulama*. Wards of the state, the ʿ*ulama* readily complied, providing written religious sanction to crush the revolt. The false *mahdi* and numerous others were killed in the ensuing engagement, but Juhayman was captured alive. He, along with sixty-two others deemed to be the ringleaders, were quickly tried and publicly hanged. The Saudi authorities blamed the whole incident on outside interference. International oil companies, after briefly suffering heart arrest, calmed down by the early 1980s. They were assured by their Saudi counterparts that such an eruption would never, never occur again. The Mecca incident remained just that—an untidy domestic episode. Once the main rebels had been subdued, tried, and executed, no one within Saudi Arabia attempted to address the challenge that Juhayman had briefly raised: had the House of Saʿud gone too far in its implicit accommodation to secular values?

Yet an astute observer of Saudi national life has raised just this question, though in slightly different language: "Precisely because the Sauds claim to be so Islamic," writes James Piscatori, "the decisive field of action may yet be that of ideology—not in the sense of whether Islam is compatible with the modern age, but in the sense of whether the Sauds are seen to be faithful to it."[37]

The greatest irony of the Saudi experiment in Islamic statecraft may be that the regime, from ʿAbd al-ʿAziz to Fahd, played the fundamentalist game without being fundamentalists. "How long can a society succeed when its professed symbols war with its realities?" That is a question that as yet no one is willing to answer, nor do the Saudis themselves want it to be asked, yet it may contain the distinctive, if unintended, Saudi contribution to the history of Islamic fundamentalism and its manifest contradictions.[38]

Nowhere are these contradictions more evident than in the way that the Kingdom of Saudi Arabia projects its image abroad: (1) through foreign policy initatives that have fear, mixed with hatred, of Iran at their core, and (2) through international groups that claim true Islam to be Wahhabi puritanism, with every rival version of Islamic belief and practice outlawed as heretical, Western-inspired, and blasphemous. Whether due to systemic weakness or creative marginality, Saudi efforts to influence others can produce confusing signals, as they did recently in Afghanistan. When the Taliban were resisting the government in Kabul before seizing power, as they did in mid-1996, they were described in some media reports as "Wahhabis," and yet a journal supported by Saudi sympathizers criticized this very label as itself evidence of a plot by "the Western press, Radio Kabul, Sufi Marabouts, the Voice of America and Radio Free Iran"![39]

What needs to be constantly born in mind is that the Saudi-Iranian rivalry is seldom raised to the explicit level, either in policy or in journalistic circles. It has been kept discreetly parked to one side of media attention because of United States foreign policy. Since 1979 American officialdom, with few exceptions, has remained fixated with the superseding danger of Iran to *all* American interests in the Gulf region. It is for that reason that a closer reading and more nuanced understanding of Iran occupies the next chapter of this book.

Iran

Major events and rulers since the outbreak of World War II:

1941–46	Iran occupied by Allied forces
1941–79	Muhammad Reza reigns as shah
Mar. 1951	Iranian oil nationalized; Musaddiq named prime minister
Aug. 1953	Musaddiq overthrown by CIA plot
Jan. 1963	The shah inaugurates the White revolution
June 1963	Khomeini's arrest sparks antigovernment demonstrations
Nov. 1964	Khomeini exiled, first to Turkey, then to Iraq, and finally (1978) to Paris
Jan.–Feb. 1979	The shah departs Iran; Khomeini returns
Dec. 1979	The Constitution of the Islamic Republic of Iran is ratified by popular referendum
1980–88	The Iran-Iraq war

Feb. 1989   The Salman Rushdie affair erupts when
             Khomeini issues a *fatwa* against the author
             of *The Satanic Verses*

June 1989   Khomeini dies; Khamenei is elected his succes-
             sor, with Rafsanjani becoming president of
             the Islamic Republic of Iran

May 1997   Mohammed Khatami, a moderate cleric, is
             elected to succeed Rafsanjani as president

While the above list may seem quite detailed, at least compared to the brief sidebar calendars provided for other Muslim polities, it is not. It represents what is commonly known about the Islamic Republic of Iran because Iran since Khomeini has engendered more fear, and more misunderstanding, than any modern-day Muslim government. For the same reason Iran merits closer scrutiny than any of the Arab or Asian Muslim nation-states: it is said to be the sole test case of a successful fundamentalist revolution. "Islam in Power: The Case of Iran" is how one writer depicted the last twelve years of Iranian history. Another, still more effusive, summarized the period as "Iran: Revolutionary Fundamentalism in Power."[40]

Despite such pronouncements, a longer view of the Iranian experiment is required. Not only does the Islamic Republic of Iran remain a young political experiment, but it also has not established a collective profile that takes into account all the evidence of its most recent history. There are at least two distinct approaches to understanding Iran as an Islamic fundamentalist polity. They compete with each other. They do not offer a single, coherent view of recent Iranian history.

One proposes that Iran must be evaluated as the final outcome of several experiments in Islamic radicalism/fundamentalism that have marked the postcolonial era. According to this approach, radicalism/fundamentalism is "a purely modern, or contemporary, reaction to the emergence of revolutionary nationalism and secular norms of government."[41] As the latest endeavor to rescue the political fortunes of Islam, it first rose in countries that attempted to implement a secular nationalist tradition but did not engage all sectors of their diverse societies. These would be Egypt, Syria, and Iraq. The North African countries of Algeria, Tunisia, and Libya were also radicalized in the 1960s and 1970s, but with less social disruption than Egypt, Syria, and Iraq, in part because their governments did not attempt radical agricultural reform. Still another group, consisting of Asian Muslim countries such as Indonesia, Pakistan, and Bangladesh, attempted to initiate policies of industrialization and modernization through existing patronage systems, with mixed results. In a fourth set of countries the ruling family remained as the primary nexus of the patronage network, thus precluding any wide-scale socioeconomic transformation. Saudi Arabia, Jordan, Morocco, Brunei, the United Arab Emirates, Kuwait, Oman, and Bahrain all fall into this category. Yet a fifth category ranks as the most un-Islamic group of all, since here Islam becomes "almost submerged in the interstices of national, sectarian, ethnic or religious differences within one single state."[42] This patchwork amalgam of political-social authority applies to Malaysia, Afghanistan, occupied Palestine, Lebanon, the Sudan, and Nigeria.

While the above schematization of Muslim nation-states is rife with generalities that admit of too many exceptions, it does allow its author to suggest that prerevolutionary Iran combined elements of all five. Under the shah land reform had been applied but failed: ownership patterns changed little, while agricultural production stagnated. By attempting to industrialize wholesale in the White Revolution (launched in 1963), the shah alienated bazaari merchants and artisan guilds. He also did not produce a fully modern infrastructure, except perhaps in the two extensions of the state that mattered most to him: the armed forces and security services, both of which were organized, equipped, and maintained at a high level and at great cost.

Hence by the time Khomeini raised a challenge to the shah, much of the population had become disenchanted and alienated, poised for fundamental change.

In other words, in searching for an explanation of the Iranian revolution, one must look almost entirely to internal, socioeconomic factors. But the opposite approach is also possible: to locate the revolution's source above all with reference to external factors. While conceding that rapid economic growth was disruptive and that the self-interest of traditional social groups, especially the ulama and the bazaaris, was threatened, some scholars have seen the precipitating cause for the shah's fall and Khomeini's success in

one major external development: the human rights policy of the
Carter administration during 1977. It was Carter's accent on
human rights as a major cornerstone of U.S. foreign policy, goes
the argument, that produced two unexpected developments in
Iran. First, the shah opted to curb his repressive tactics, at least
temporarily. The outburst of criticism against him was thunder-
ous. Critics, hearing other critics for the first time, were empowered to articulate their own grievances. Second, Khomeini was able
to galvanize criticism of the shah into support for his own rule.
Khomeini's insistence on drastic change was strident and uncompromising. It also was better articulated once he moved to Paris in
winter 1978, for from Paris he had ease of access to Iran, especially
through smuggled cassette tapes, that was denied him in both Iraq
and Turkey, where he had previously resided in exile. Once the
shah cracked down again on protestors, as he did in the winter and
spring of 1978, it was too late: the sources opposing him, even
though they did not know about his cancer, sensed his vulnerability, and in the figure of Khomeini as a charismatic debunker of
the shah and the West, they had a symbol around whom to rally,
a hope to propel them beyond the horror and bloodshed of mid-
1978.[43]

The problem with both the internal and external explanations
of revolutionary Iran is that neither addresses the Iranian context
except in parochial terms. The first adds up all the problems that
could be perceived in modern Muslim nation-states and then, having located them in Iran, concludes that Iran was ripe for revolution. The second lists all the possible approaches to explaining the
revolution and then determines that one or two were precipitating,
even though many others may have been contributory. What neither does is to approach head-on the problem of turning data into
evidence. To determine which data can be used as evidence, one
must construct an analytical framework that permits comparative,
cross-cultural assessments. In the case of the Islamic Republic of
Iran, no such assessment is possible unless one first devises a strategy that matches the rhetoric of Islamic Revolution with the reality
of building an Islamic nation-state in the late twentieth century.

The very first step, therefore, must be to examine major categories rather than to accept them as self-evident, at once timeless in
origin and univocal in meaning. All human language is derived, all
is socially conditioned. To understand aggregate terms like Islam

or revolution, one must specify in what ways and by what criteria they are to be invoked. Islam has already been shown to be as much a pliable symbol as a fixed system; Arab and Asian Muslim rulers use it at the same time that all contestants for power challenge their use of it. The situation is no different in Iran. What is different in Iran is the constant invocation of the term "revolution," as though this is *the* revolution, that it is also, because its supporters say it is, an *Islamic* revolution. Both claims need to be examined more carefully.

Did 1978–79 produce an *Islamic* revolution? No and yes. No, because it was more than Islamic in its genesis, it was also a Third World revolution. Yes, because Islam became the label by which it was broadcast as a legitimate transfer of power, replacing a Shiʿi-Iranian monarchy with an Iranian-Shiʿi theocracy.

Both the no and the yes require explanation.

The events of 1978–79 may be termed a Third World revolution because they exhibit several of the features characteristic of the accelerated technological era after World War I. It was a local happening, yet it was precipitated by transregional factors, not the least being Iran's economic marginalization in the 1940s and 1950s. Only oil production and its strategic location gave Iran some political leverage at the outset of the Cold War. In the 1960s and 1970s that situation changed. Increased oil prices opened up major opportunities, but mismanagement, greed, and paranoia prevented those opportunities from being realized. The White Revolution, launched in 1963 to make Iran rapidly modern and military powerful, failed. It created a crisis affecting numerous groups, not only the clerical elite. Dissatisfaction came to focus on the autocratic leader, but also on the external, colonizing forces linked to him.

A land of poets also intensifies the power of slogans: one Persian word has come to symbolize extreme dependency on foreign income, foreign military aid, foreign political adventurism, and foreign lifestyles. That word is *gharbzadegi*, "excess of the West," or, as some would have it, "Westoxification." *Gharbzadegi* was pinned on the shah as transmitter and perpetuator of the colonial past, which Iranians of nearly all classes so deeply resented. Though Iran was never directly colonized, Prime Minister Mossadegh was overthrown by CIA collusion in the early 1950s and then replaced by the shah, leaving the impression that Iran was not in control of its own destiny. And the wealth that came with oil production was suspect, benefiting only a small minority of Westernized, affluent Iranians. The dispossessed resented their lowly status, even when they had neither the means nor the hope of successful revolt.

Religion provided the vehicle of Third World protest in Iran. The years 1978–79 witnessed not only a Third World but also a religiously inspired revolt. A Shi'i Iranian monarchy became an Iranian-Shi'i theocracy. Most observers neglect to note how inextricable are the two, how thin the line between Shi'i Iranian and Iranian-Shi'i. There is no neat division of religion from national, or national from religious, in the consciousness of most Iranians. To oppose the enemy within there had to be a moral, specifically Shi'i criterion against which the enemy could be measured and found wanting. The shah was vilified not because the majority of Iranians were Shi'i rather than Sunni Muslims, nor because as Shi'i Muslims they had a deep distrust of, or outright aversion to, political power, especially when exercised by an absolute monarch. History disproves that essentialist reflex. The accommodation between shahs and their Iranian Shi'i subjects goes back to the early sixteenth century and the founding of the Safavi Empire, a vast, successful, bureaucratic, military patronage state. The crisscrossing of religious political authority and the constant need of even the most powerful monarchs to claim religious legitimacy ensure that the shah could, and did, project himself as "God's Shadow on Earth." From the Safavi period, Iranian rulers had arrogated to themselves the multivalent title "God's Shadow on Earth." Even though some have remarked that "Mohammed Reza Shah seems to have given little more than ritually dutiful attention to this aspect of his role,"[44] he never disavowed it.

Yet, in the minds of his Iranian subjects, there lingered an implicit, unescapable question: is it possible for *din* and *dunya* (the demands of religion and the lures of worldliness) to be reconciled? How does the ruler resist the latter while promoting the former? Do the Shi'i clergy, as the repositories of Islamic teaching but even more as the custodians of hope for all Iranians, deem him to be *sultan'adil* or *sultan jabir*—a just ruler or a despot? Until 1979 there was no Shi'i consensus either that monarchy was patently un-Islamic or that a cleric should rule in place of the shah. Rather, the hope for clergy and laity alike was that the shah—if not this shah, then another shah, whether from this dynasty or a successor dynasty—could be made accountable to the standards of justice, which also meant at least the appearance of rejecting, rather than promoting, colonial—which is to say, European or American—influence in Iran.

The events of 1978–79 therefore did produce a dramatic shift in the world view of Iranians. As such, they could be said to have augured a revolution, whether Third World or Iranian-Shi'i or both. Yet to Iranians, this revolution was not their *first* revolution. That distinction belongs to the Constitutional Revolution of 1905–1911, and in many ways that earlier revolution prefigured the events of 1978–79. It, too, was a revolution against the shah, though he was then a Qajar rather than a Pahlavi shah. It, too, was sparked by a protest against foreign (then British, now American) influence, involving tobacco rather than oil. It also had the support of a few influential Iranian clergy. However, the principal agenda for that revolution was strikingly different: its advocates insisted above all on the implementation of a uniquely Western democratic instrument, namely, a constitution. Hence it has been named the "Constitutional Revolution."

As firm as is collective memory of the Constitutional Revolution, dim and dreaded is the memory of another Iranian revolution, the failed "White" Revolution heralded by the late shah in January 1963. As its name suggests, it was intended to be a revolution without violence, one that would modernize Iran's economy (especially the agricultural sector) and also upgrade its military profile during the remainder of the twentieth century. The White Revolution failed, yet its deeper aspiration, to modernize Iran and make it a country benefiting from the global economic system, is one that drives the planning of many pragmatists in the current Islamic Republic of Iran.

Against this background, we must revisit the events of 1978–79. If we suppose that the ascent of Khomeini did augur an *Islamic* Revolution, to what extent was it more than a mere circulation of ruling elites under opposite ideological banners? Since most observers agree that both the Constitutional and the White Revolutions have failed, in what sense can one claim that the current, Islamic Revolution has succeeded?

It can only be said to have succeeded as a durable revolution if it embodies economic as well as political change; in other words, if it succeeds in doing what neither the Constitutional nor the White Revolution could do. It is an awesome challenge because, as indicated above, this revolution was not only Islamic but Third World, its power deriving from the marginalized disempowerment of those who protested the structures of late twentieth-century Iranian society. How could its leaders both transform their own society and alter the role of that society in the larger world community?

For many observers, it is more than an awesome challenge, it is an impossible goal. Class analysts especially are skeptical of Iranian claims. The sociologist Bryan Turner, looking at the critical transformations that have characterized Western societies, notes that in each case the presence of an autonomous, commercial middle class was required to make the transition from feudal/religious to industrial/secular culture. That class has been lacking in Middle Eastern societies, including Iran; its absence has produced the "No Revolutions" thesis that dominates much writing on the premodern and modern Middle East. Though it is an Orientalist argument, it has its Marxist counterpart, namely, that these societies, precisely because they have not undergone genuine "social" revolutions, have experienced mere political coup d'états and palace revolutions. Ernest Gellner advances a similar claim in arguing that outside Western Europe and North America no other societies could forge liberal democratic states driven by capitalist, scientifically oriented economies. Islamic Iran becomes the crucial test case proving the incompatibility of Islam and modernity, at least insofar as modernity can be defined as coeval openness to pluralist structures and technological advance.[45]

Yet the clerics who came to power in Tehran in 1978–79 are not so easily pigeonholed. Their ideology includes a platform for totally restructuring the economic, judiciary, and administrative instruments as well as the symbolic profile and political leadership of Iran. Have they succeeded? In any such evaluation two indices would seem to be crucial: the mode of political representation and the sources of income. At a formal level, neither has changed significantly since the Pahlavi period. The state has been called an Islamic Republic, yet it does not function as a democracy. There is a single party *majlis* (parliament), with courts, mosques, schools, and land law functioning under a hierarchically monitored state ideology as rigid as that which prevailed prior to 1978.

The income that allows the new government to function domestically and to prosecute its foreign policy continues to derive from the export-oriented segment of the economy. Since the fall of the shah, oil revenues as a percentage of total foreign exchange revenues have actually increased; they now constitute 80 percent of Iran's export earnings, while non-oil-related exports have continued to decline.[46]

New revolutionary institutions have been established, yet many of them shadow institutions remaining from the ancient regime, with only the personnel circulating. Particularly at the provincial level, where there is great disparity between the less and more developed provinces, almost the same procedures are followed today as were in place twelve years ago. The court system has not been reorganized. In the absence of an Islamic Retribution Bill (ratified in 1981 but not yet enacted), individual revolutionary courts and firing squads acting as neighborhood committees continue to operate. On the crucial issue of land reform, little has been done since the time of the shah.

Land reform is indeed the most evident single issue for gauging how difficult it is to implement a genuine social revolution in Iran. The 270-person *majlis* (an elected body) and the 12-member Council of Guardians (first appointed by Khomeini and now by Khamanei) have been in sharp disagreement with one another on just this point. The former has loudly advocated rapid socialization of the entire economy, including land. Social justice is its shibboleth. The latter has quietly held out for individual rights, retention of private property (with scriptural support from the Qur'an), and free trade (not restricting it to the Muslim bloc as the *majlis* has advocated). In effect, there is a continuing ideological contest between the *majlis* and the Council of Guardians. While he was alive, only the undisputed authority of the Imam (as Khomeini was affectionately and fearfully known) held together the Iranian government on these issues. But even some of his efforts at mediation failed: the 13-member council for determining the interests of the Islamic order, a body consisting of 6 members from the Council of Guardians, six from the *majlis*, and his own personal representative, which he first appointed in February 1988, still wavered on the implementation of land reform.[47]

Since Khomeini's demise, a viable policy on social change remains paralyzed by the same forces that were at work during his lifetime. Rather than focusing on ideological claims that continue to stress how the Islamic Republic is an agent for social justice acting on behalf of the dispossessed, one must look closely at the class distinctions that stymie the Islamic Revolution and its present leadership. The first, crucial point to note is the absence of the cross-class conflict contributing to the formation of a fundamentalist opposition elsewhere, especially in Syria and Egypt. Though their ideology is cross-class—indeed, universalist—in scope, the members of the ruling elite in the Islamic Republic are predominantly middle class. Nor should one think of the ideological contests within the middle class as interclass political conflicts or rivalries. It is not different classes, but different factions within the middle class, that subscribe to different types of economic policy and development strategy. And they debate as members of the same social class, arguing, in effect, about how their class relates to those beneath them, that is, the vast majority of Iranians.

There are three middle-class groups that vie with one another for the mantle of leadership in post-Khomeini revolutionary Iran. There is a conservative faction. Supported by wealthy merchants, landlords, and some high-ranking ayatollahs, they reflect the dominant merchant-clergy alliance that is often credited with having authored the events of 1978–79. They oppose planning, state ownership, and public management of the economy. They advocate free enterprise and decentralization. They oppose both the land reform bill and any increase of direct taxes. They favor free trade with Western Europe and Japan as well as with Islamic countries. They prefer agricultural exports over oil exports.

Opposed to them is a radical faction. They consist of lower- to middle-ranking clergy, many religious intelligentsia, and most revolutionary organizations. Traditional middle and lower classes in the urban centers and rural areas also support this faction. They advocate public ownership and management of large enterprises. Supporters of agriculture, they want food products consumed at home but not exported. They are against both free trade and openness to international economic forces. They stress self-reliance and confrontation with the Great Powers. They deride the conservatives as proponents of "American Islam" because the latter allow for engagement with the Great Satan. They claim that their own is "the Islam of the Prophet Muhammad" or "the Islam of the Oppressed."

Bridging the two groups is the centrist-pragmatist faction. While they are supported by the religious intelligentsia, the new middle class, and the technocrats, they also enjoy the confidence of most classes throughout Iran. They are classic fence-straddlers. They favor a market economy, but with controls. They uphold the need for socioeconomic and even further political reforms, but they equivocate on their implementation. They advocate free trade, but only within limits: they do not want Iran to be exposed to the risks of an open economy. They advocate peaceful coexistence with other Islamic nations and want to build an exemplary society rather than to export the Islamic Revolution, as the radicals propose. In 1989 they advocated a change in the constitution and succeeded in eliminating the premiership, transferring the functions of this office to a more powerful presidency.

Since the end of the Iran-Iraq War and even more since Khomeini's death, this centrist-pragmatist group has determined the future course of events in Iran. They have not yet succeeded in transforming factionalism into full-scale participatory democracy. That remains a distant goal in the Islamic Republic of Iran, but even short of that ideal, if the three factions could succeed in co-operating to the extent that they ensure enough political stability and social security to cause a sustained upturn in the economy, they may institutionalize the Islamic Revolution. However, it will be a revolution with a small r, rather than a capital R, one that allows Iran to survive as a modern-day theocracy with a mixed socioeconomic policy. The problems of ethnic and religious minorities will persist, and while Muslim Kurds and Armenian Christians may fare moderately well, Muslim Afghans and Bahai sectarians will find a cool reception even were pragmatism to reign long after Rafsanjani's departure from the presidency. [48]

What challenges and preoccupies all branches of current Iranian political culture is an ideological high-wire act: how to take account of the modern world while not disallowing or reducing the Islamic difference. On this point, the adaptability and tenacity of Islamic thinkers in Iran can be traced from the modernist Shari'ati[49] to the fundamentalist Motahhari to the pragmatist Rafsanjani. They stretch Islamic thought and its technical categories to include a range of data that is clearly engaged by the modern world, saturated even with philosophical or scientific reference, yet never loses its spiritual rootedness. While one could focus on

100

Shariʿati or Motahhari, Rafsanjani invites closer attention, if only because one seldom finds a politician with the multifaceted intellect that Rafsanjani clearly possesses. His homiletic style is revealed in Friday sermons as well as in political stump speeches. In one such sermon, he deftly defends the Islamic legal code while also implying that it can and should be adapted to changing times:

> The important point here is that the Islam which developed 1,400 years ago on the Arabian peninsula—in a settlement where the people were fundamentally nomads—was a legal code specific to that society. And even that code was promulgated slowly over a period of seven or eight years. Now the legal code, which was executed in those days for that particular nation, aspires to become the code for a world in which humanity has plunged the depths of the earth and mined resources thousands of meters below its surface, has competed in space to conquer Mars, has built formidable weapons of defense and offense from particles of atoms, and has conquered the sky, the earth and the mountains. . . . At this very moment millions of people are engaged in legal research to better human society. The Islam which was revealed some 1,400 years ago for the limited society of that time, now desires to become the fulcrum of [modern] social administration and [our] nation wants to use this fulcrum [as a weapon] to wage war on the entire imperialist world, testing its mettle by those means. Unique circumstances have arisen during the course of time. How can Islam [without adaptation] cover all these contingencies?[50]

Despite the final appeal to "wage war on the entire imperialist world," the tone of this speech is an impassioned plea for Islamic flexibility in the face of the scientific and technological advances that have shaped the modern world. It is hardly a radical or fundamentalist view of Islam, and the fact that it is made by the de facto ruler of the Islamic Republic of Iran suggests how far the first success of Islamic fundamentalism has come from the millenarian aspirations of its founding figure. If Khomeini had to swallow poison in order to accept a cease-fire with his nemesis, Saddam Hussein, he must have been jolted from his eternal sleep by the tone and the message of Rafsanjani's speech.

What the message illustrates is the extent to which the continued memory of Khomeini, which extends to the construction of a marvelous tomb complex honoring him near the Graveyard of Martyrs on the outskirts of Tehran, may cloak other realities. If one were to

Figure 6. ʿAli, the major figure in Shiʿi veneration.

Figure 7. Hussein, ʿAli's son and the major martyr of Shiʿi veneration.

observe the posters that continue to lionize Khomeini, or if one were to compare popular photos, such as those linking him iconically as well as thematically to both ʿAli and Hussein, the exemplars of Shiʿi Islam, it would be easy to assume that the Islamic Revolution persists, its ideals intact, since Khomeini's demise in 1989.

Yet the changes signaled in Rafsanjani's speech are not limited to him. They are mirrored in numerous other currents of thought in post-1989 Iran. During the past eight years, there have mushroomed within cosmopolitan circles heated debates about the future course of Iranian society. For a time the press in Iran, unlike its Arab neighbors, became so free that "newspapers, magazines, scholarly journals and books provided a forum for the dissemination of ideas that only a few years ago would have been considered dissident thinking." Intellectual populists, such as Hosain Azimi and Abdul Karim Sorush, until recently have been allowed to voice their views openly, even when they called for a reassessment of the role of religion in the Islamic Republic of Iran.[51]

Figure 8. Khomeini's official portrait.   Figure 9. Khomeini's tomb mosque.

The makers of revolutions and the builders of revolutionary nation-states may walk in the same shoes, but they do not always march to the same cadence. What was true for the Soviet Union from Lenin to Gorbachev is also now becoming true in the Islamic Republic of Iran, but within a much shorter time span. There is evidence of a broadly based rethinking of the goals of an Islamic society, one so pervasive that it has been labeled *andisheh-ye digar*, alternative thinking, which is to say, opposition to current policies framed by respected figures who accept the premise of a Shi'i state but not its current format. If a Second Republic is emerging within the chrysalis of the Islamic Republic of Iran, it will be more tolerant, of both internal dissent and external difference, than its predecessor. It will be neither an outlaw state nor a hostile civilization. Instead, it will project a development that students of late capitalism should welcome: while the world system may not be one, its parts do interconnect, and cultural distinctiveness can be maintained only if each nation-state fosters exchange with other nation-

103

states who do not share or who may in part oppose one's own motto of authenticity. Fundamentalists, whether in Iran or in Egypt or any Muslim nation-state, will always hold out hope for a radically new world order, but in the meantime they must, and they will, live within the present order.

It is necessary, however, to look at the Iranian experiment with religious nationalism at a more profound level than has been the case up till now in most public policy and journalistic quarters, especially in the United States. The great difficulty, as indicated in the previous chapter, is the overwhelming support within the American political establishment for privileging Saudi interests. That translates into permitting Saudis greater access to American institutions and also into aiding pro-Saudi Muslim groups, such as the Islamic Students of North America (ISNA) and the World Muslim Council, the group that in spring 1997 protested the statue of Muhammad in the U.S. Supreme Court building. Many of these groups have no explicit Saudi connection yet are either funded by Saudis or remain sympathetic to them; the Iranians have no counterpart to these groups and operate mostly through cultural venues that tend to differ among themselves as to what is the most appropriate stance toward religiopolitical identity generally and the regime in Tehran in particular.[52]

The global political outlook for Iran may depend on a new generation of American pragmatists assessing what the long-term loss will be for U.S. interests if implacable, uncompromising hostility by Iran to the United States is matched by equally implacable, uncompromising demonization of Iran from the U.S. Department of State. Iran, far from being an immediate threat, poses the best venue for access to inner Asia through the Caspian Basin, itself "the most promising source of new energy in the 21st century."[53]

But the greatest resource of Iran may be its mobile, entrepreneurial people, many of whom are keenly aware of advantages in the global market. Urban Iranians speak better English, and also have more acquaintance with philosophical and technical issues of the high-tech era, than do their counterparts in other Middle Eastern countries, with the partial exception of Turkey and Egypt.

Yet few observers would doubt that the major hurdle to Iranian acceptance into a larger international commity may have less to do with Washington-London-Paris-Bonn policy makers than with internal disputes about culture. The present rulers of the Islamic Republic of Iran have maintained a definite stance on women's dress codes and also women's participation in the public sphere. The accent on women remains central to a Muslim difference in projecting global norms and values.

If the difference is persistent, it is also subtle. Not only Iranian Islamists but their counterparts in other Muslim countries are slow in coming to terms with gender differences that escape the too neat binary categorization common to dogmatic pronouncements. Women—their role, their status, their future—provide a key to understanding the social dilemmas of Islamism. They also permit one to see differences internal to Muslim countries. To the extent that some Muslim men not only control women but also direct the perceptions that others have of them, the production of the Woman Question must be addressed. In part 2 I shall try to clarify what has been the impact of male ideologues, and the patriarchal order that they proclaim, on their female coreligionists. At the same time, I will attempt to chart future options that empower Muslim women in what one observer has called, referring to late-twentieth-century Iran, a "post-Islamist society."[54]

PART TWO

MUSLIM WOMEN AND ISLAMIC FUNDAMENTALISM

The Double Bind Revisited

A RECENT study of the multiple writings of Frantz Fanon made clear the importance of gender for Fanon's critique of both colonial and postcolonial Afro-Asian societies. It was Fanon's goal, never fully realized, that a new social order—at once more generous and more equal toward all its citizens—should emerge in the aftermath of colonial rule. Though far from consistent, Fanon seemed to grope toward a criterion for authentic humanism that would "take the condition of woman as a mark of the degree to which human beings in a determinate place and time have truly come into their own."[1]

By Fanon's criterion, both fundamentalists and the praetorian, neocolonialist state have failed. Both conspire to keep Muslim women in a condition of marginality. Like other Asian and African women, most Muslim women still enjoy neither the educational nor professional opportunities available to their fathers and brothers, husbands and sons. And while much more information now exists about the variety of circumstances that characterize the lives of Muslim women, the information widens rather than reduces the sense of oppression they face. Some thought that the state would in time reduce the hold of religious tradition falsely arrayed against female Muslims, but in fact, as Hisham Sharabi has shown, the modern state has itself fallen sway to neopatriarchal norms.[2] Even when literacy is dramatically improved, as in the case of Iraq, the public role of women does not change significantly.

The largest single factor handicapping women in the Muslim world is the same that inhibits men: the underdevelopment of economic opportunities for their respective nations within the current "new world order." It is not the sole factor, nor has its impact gone unchallenged, yet to begin to understand the range of options available to Muslim women, one must recognize what is not available to them: the bourgeois lifestyle that presupposes a public sphere of opportunity for both men and women with market access to resources for education and employment, communication and consumption. Such resources are not available to most Afro-Asian Muslims, either men or women, and while the frank acknowledgment of their absence may lead some to an economic determinist reading of the Muslim world, it may, and should, lead others to frame a realistic assessment of local options and future possibilities.

Since there is a limited middle class in most Muslim countries, economic inequalities still situate a few landed or mercantile rich above masses of urban and rural poor. The army remains one of the principal avenues to social and economic advancement, provided one also has the right tribal or sectarian markings to evoke trust from the ruling elite of one's country. Educational restrictions are severe. Not only are there too few universities and too many applicants, but there is also the absence of high tech institutions of quality, with the result that the few who are rich (the 8 out of 100 who can qualify for credit cards) send their children abroad. Alternatively, foreign nationals from abroad are hired to perform the functions that indigenous professionals do not know because they cannot learn them locally.

Gender asymmetry becomes reinforced by such structural limitations. While tradition may be invoked to deny women entrance into the public job market, it is in fact the prevalence of unemployed or underemployed men vying with one another for scarce jobs that ensures the continued exclusion or curtailment of Muslim women from employment in the industrial or modern sector of their respective countries.

The double bind becomes triple: being Muslim, being female, being economically marginal, would seem to exclude all but the most desparate options. Yet women's voices do register in protest against the present system. Literate women protest in writing; their illiterate sisters are spoken for by others. These are the voices to which we should be listening. Many tell a story of violence on several levels. Cognitive violence is to ignore, social violence is to reduce, the marginalized or feared group; these same women suffer a physical violence the pain of which cannot be glossed as "mere" cultural difference. Where there is resistance, challenge, and change, it needs to be highlighted, but first it must be located.

An example from Egypt illustrates the dimensions of the dilemma facing responsible scholarship on Muslim women. Few monographs have explored the ambiguous stance of veiled working women as well as Arlene MacLeod's, *Accomodating Protest: Working Women, the New Veiling, and Change in Cairo.*[3] MacLeod's Foucauldian study of middle-class women in Cairo reveals that the *muhaggabat,* or veiled women, resist through accommodation as well as protest. They do so by exhibiting that contradictory consciousness to which Gramsci drew attention: working in low-level government positions, they are responding to economic pressures that necessitate as many incomes as possible, at the same time that they are able to express Islamic loyalty through dress code. They do give religious meaning to the veil that they adopt, argues McLeod, but to the degree that their veiling remains instrumental—providing, as it does, the pretext for their being allowed by conservative relatives and friends to work—they will be alert to ways that they may oppose, rather than merely being preempted by, the increasingly Islamist tone of modern-day Cairo.

Unlike MacLeod's nuanced analysis, the public story of Muslim female fundamentalism is most often told by charting the women's groups that appear alongside men's. The very telling of the story presumes (a) that female fundamentalists share the same social and political agenda of their male counterparts and (b) that women participate in defining the public agenda for protest. Neither presumption is correct. Female fundamentalists are, by definition, concerned with private rather than public issues: the home and not the headlines motivate them. For that very reason we will rarely see the diary of a female Muslim fundamentalist; whatever she thinks and feels and hopes for is best voiced by male fundamentalists.[4] Even when women do join in public gatherings, whether to sport rifles or to shout slogans, their presence, and one imagines also their performance, is choreographed by men. The myth of the independent, voluntary female fundamentalist has no factual basis. Men create a space for representative women, and these women are representative precisely because men select and direct them to the purposes that they, the men, favor. Fundamentalists insist that women by nature are weaker than men, mentally as well as physically, and yet since women are also possessed of the ability to distract men, the Islamist mandate is to create and maintain separate public spheres. As the French political theorist Olivier Roy has observed, the true taboo for fundamentalists is coeducation (*ikhtilat*): women's track for learning must remain separate from men's.[5]

111

In what follows I will try to soften the male fixation that characterizes most studies of Islamic fundamentalism. I will look not at the manipulated women counterparts to male fundamentalists, but at the role or roles that women seek in Muslim nation-states. I will also try to assess how those roles have changed in three representative Muslim nation-states: Iran, Egypt, and Pakistan.

The choice of these three as "representative" Muslim states reflects their frequent citation in all studies that claim to grapple with Islamic values. They also touch disparate geographic regions of the vast Muslim world. Iran is both Middle Eastern and Asian, Egypt is both Middle Eastern and African, while Pakistan is South Asian, reflecting the nexus between Central Asia and the Indian subcontinent. More important, all three have had to come to terms with the commercial expansion of Western Europe and the United States, and to a considerable extent they share structural features that handicap them vis-à-vis the existing transnational order shaped by global capitalism.

In pursuing the changing circumstance of Muslim women, one could pick other countries than Iran, Egypt, and Pakistan, yet the combined geographic diversity and socioeconomic commonality they represent will at least suggest insight into patterns that may apply elsewhere in that vast domain of Asia and Africa known as the Muslim world.

Why begin with Iran? Because it is in Iran that Islamic fundamentalism began. Iran determines the standard, which is to say the male-specific, depiction of Islamic fundamentalism. It also sets the standard for women. Not only did Iran signal the return of Islamic values as a dominant element of national identity in many Muslim societies, but the women of Iran, in particular, had a history of participation in that society prior to 1979 that was so extensive, and so well documented, that examining it allows us to understand the force—some would say the fury—of Islamic fundamentalism.

The Pahlavi regime had a specific policy toward women. Embracing Euro-American norms, it tried to impose them on twentieth-century Iranian women. Its major moments include:

1935–36	Women compelled not to wear the veil in public places
7 Jan. 1937	Marked as women's day by Reza Shah
1938	First women admitted to Tehran University

1958	High Council of Women organized; later (1966) replaced by Women's Organization of Iran (WOI), with branches in all major cities
Jan. 1963	Among the six points marking the reforms known as the White Revolution, one promises women's suffrage
1967	Women accepted into the judiciary and also drafted into the police and army
1967	Family Protection Law passed, modified in 1975 to provide for mutual consent in divorce

Spanning the forty-four year period from 1935, when the veil was banned, till 1979, when the Islamic Republic of Iran came to power, these government-initiated changes produced results. Among them were the following:

· Women's Organization of Iran expanded to a network of 400 branches and 118 centers, with 51 affiliated organizations. The centers provided vocational training, literacy classes, childcare, legal and professional counseling, as well as family planning.

· The number of girls attending elementary and vocational training schools rose dramatically, increasing more than tenfold in the decade of the 1970s alone. By 1978, 33 percent of all university students were women, and many had begun to choose fields other than those marked as traditionally female occupations. For example, the number of women candidates for medical school in 1978 was higher than the number of men.

· By 1979, 2 million Iranian women (out of a total female population of 20 million) had entered the labor force. Almost 200,000 were enrolled in academic and specialized fields; another 150,000 worked as civil servants, with over 1,500 serving as managers or directors. There were over 1,800 women university professors, and women worked in the army, in the police force, as judges, pilots, engineers—in every field except religious activities. Schools of theology were the only academic institutions closed to women.

· Political space was also opened to Iranian women. Women were encouraged to run for public office. In 1978, of 1,660 candidates elected to local council, 33 were women. Twenty-two of the 270 member *majlis* were women. There was a woman cabinet member, ambassador, and governor. There were five women mayors.[6]

As heady as were these achievements for Iranian women, they depended for their continuation on government support. There were no private-sector initiatives, nor did the private sector begin to acquire an institutional autonomy that allowed it to complement or compete with government initiatives. Consequently, when government support was withdrawn with the return of Khomeini and the coming to power of the Islamic Republic of Iran, the above markings of women's public prominence were erased. They were quickly replaced by rules favoring women's absence from, or invisibility within, the public sphere:

Feb. 1979   Family Protection Law suspended

March 1979   Women no longer appointed judges or allowed
               to hold decision-making posts; public veiling
               required; childcare centers closed; women
               barred from competing in internation sports

May 1979   Coeducation banned, with women also segre-
               gated in cafeterias and on buses

Dec. 1979   The first woman to have served as a cabinet min-
               ister under the shah (a medical doctor and
               teacher who had been education minister from
               1968 to 1975) is brought to trial, condemned
               for spreading corruption on earth, and sen-
               tenced to die before a firing squad

March 1980   The First Islamic *majlis* is elected; there are 2
               women among its 270 representatives

April 1980   Universities closed indefinitely

May–July   Further steps are taken to implement compulsory
   1981   veiling, e.g., unveiled women fired from
               government jobs

July 1981   The *majlis* ratified Bill of Retribution, especially
               harsh on women offenders

Yet a skeletal reiteration of legislative or juridical measures taken against women's participation in the public sphere does not tell the full story. The Shiʿi clergy who dominate the Islamic Republic of Iran also extol those women who conform to their understanding of women's ideal roles in an ideal Islamic nation-state. Their viewpoint deserves scrutiny in its own terms, even when it rubs up against the dominant notion of who women are and what their public role ought to be.

A crucial issue is representation: representation within the clerical leadership and representation within the female population of Iran. Who speaks authoritatively for the norms established by the Islamic Republic? And to which women do those norms apply? Do they apply equally to urban and rural women, to elites and non-elites, to wealthy and poor? Such questions about female representation complicate the issue of women and fundamentalism, yet by specifying subgroups within a population too easily glossed and generalized under a single image, they allow us to nuance the future of women in an Islamic nation-state.

The authoritative spokesperson setting forth the fundamentalist view of women might be either Khomeini or Motahhari. Khomeini is the better-known figure, but Motahhari is the more consistent thinker. Khomeini's position is complicated by the seeming contradiction between some of his pronouncements, which seemed to hold out hope for women's public participation in the Islamic Republic, and his writings, which, along with the provisions of the 1979 Constitution, extolled women solely as childrearers and educators, i.e., as the denizens of domestic space.[7] Motahhari, on the other hand, has systematically delved into the question of women and women's social roles. He is no less controlling than Khomeini, but he is better grounded in his mode of argumentation. It is from his writings that we gain a unique perspective on the Iranian clerical view of women.[8]

It is a view defined by two considerations: (1) the requirements of marriage and (2) the challenge of the modern West and its social norms. So major is the West and its symbolic challenge that traditional marriage must be retained, at all costs. Motahhari is not content merely to restate what Islam does, nor how Muslims ought to behave. Instead, he frames his own views as counterarguments to the arguments of his opponents, those who advocate the heralded notions of freedom and equality. Both notions are boldly attacked in two sets of lectures, one addressing "The Rights of Women in Islam," the other, "Sexual Ethics in Islam and in the Western World." Though the second is much briefer than the first, it contains in summary form the central postulate of Motahhari's approach: women are primarily defined as sexual beings, for it is their sexuality that provides the criteria for their broader function as members of society. While disclaiming any essentialist notion of female sexuality, he dwells on what he terms "the basic need for

115

humane conditioning of natural instincts and desires."[9] This conditioning applies both to men and to women, and yet it is women who bear the burden of responsibility for allaying male concerns. The male-privileging moves that punctuate "Sexual Ethics" become starkly evident when Motahhari lists the most frequent charges that he feels permissive Westerners raise (without justification, of course) against proponents of traditional mores. They are:

1. male sense of possession of his female
2. male jealousy
3. male concern for establishing his paternity of a child
4. asceticism and monasticism based on the assumed sinfulness and wickedness of human sexual relations
5. female sense of impurity arising from her menstruating nature
6. male abstinence from sexual relations with a menstruating female
7. severe punishment at the hands of men undergone by women throughout recorded history
8. causing women to remain economically dependent on men[10]

Apart from (4), which applies to both men and women, and (5), which is a female reflex, all the other charges concern male malevolence. It is men who marginalize and subordinate women, whether due to insecurity or to a drive to power. Motahhari never refutes these charges; he seems to presume that he has removed their stigma by itemizing them serially without comment.

Despite the ad hominem form of his reasoning, Motahhari's argument does exhibit a form of logic. The logic he pursues is the logic of internal falsification, refuting the West through the West. He adduces case after case of how traditional morality works and modern laissez-faire ethics fails. Ironically, Motahhari summons as witnesses on behalf of his position prominent Western thinkers like Bertrand Russell, Will Durant, and even William James.

The major weakness of Motahhari's position lies not so much in the form of his argument as in its unspoken, and therefore unexamined, premises. He views woman first of all as a sexual being, and so defines her from the outset within a world view that excludes the social roles that many modern women have come to take for granted: freedom of mobility, equality before the law, the right to higher education (whether in university or in technical schools), and opportunities for employment in business, medicine, law, or government, with the expectation of advancement in each up to the highest level or office. Motahhari never cites these options, nor does he acknowledge them as women's rights, for none of them pertains to the foundational notion of a woman's identity, her identity as sexual being.

Motahhari's views are not his alone. They are shared by other clerical members of the Islamic Republic of Iran, by other Iranian men and women, and by non-Iranian Muslims, even by some deemed to be "progressive." One such "progressive" Muslim, a modern-day Tunisian scholar, declared that "male supremacy is fundamental in Islam."[11] If he is right, then the only true Islamic society would have to be patriarchal. But is he right? Could it be that male supremacy is not fundamental to Islam? Might it not be rather due to the construction of Islam that has developed since the time of the Prophet Muhammad, a construction that is at variance not only with the Qur'an but also with the exemplar conduct of the Prophet's own life? As early as the 1920s, a Lebanese woman activist, Nazira Zayn al-Din, made just this assertion, arguing that it was religious scholars who had occluded the gender-inclusive message of the Qur'an and relegated women to a position inferior to men.[12] And as Barbara Stowasser, in a trenchant textual analysis of women and early Islam, writes: "The fault for unjust laws and practices such as women's inequality lies not with God's revelation but with the ʿulama's interpretation of it . . . as well as with contrived or unauthentic variations of Prophetic Hadith."[13]

It is important to recognize that there is a contest about what constitutes true Islam, and that testimony from Qur'anic evidence often conflicts with later juridical decrees. It is equally important to note that women have been defined not only textually but also socially. Whether they are urban or rural matters as much as their class markings. Rural women are rarely reported, much less featured, in journalistic accounts of Muslim women. Rural women are also uneducated, often illiterate. Yet they represent the largest number of women in Iran, as also in Egypt and Pakistan.[14] Neither veiling nor polygamy characterizes their lives, and so the driving issues of both fundamentalist and feminist ideologues have little appeal since neither religious conformity nor social liberation is related to the day-to-day reality of life for these women. Arguments about women's rights vs. women's duties remain just that, arguments. They are arguments that presuppose a space for reflection denied to rural women whose social and economic value is measured by increments of survival.

Women of Deh Koh is a brilliant anthropological study of one group of rural Iranian women, a study undertaken since the establishment of the Islamic Republic of Iran. It provides several anecdotes that demonstrate how women cope. Especially gruesome is the story of a village woman's rape. This story demonstrates just how limited are a woman's options. Not only was the rapist not executed, it was the woman who was burdened by his crime; since she was no longer a virgin, her "best" hope was to have the rapist marry her. She resisted that conclusion, but fellow women villagers, in talking among themselves and with her, left no doubt that her only other option (and one that many women are driven to choose), was suicide.[15]

If women are everywhere vulnerable to men, in the countryside of Iran they are less prone to seek or support options for change than elsewhere. They live as economic dependents of their male relatives, but they also form emotional attachments to other women that preclude criticism. One of the most scathing indictments of the Islamic Republic's policy toward women also criticizes Iranian women for condoning their own lot. "The women themselves are to blame for . . . women are not conscious of their rights and either try to justify the existing laws, or raise cries for our rights without any valid backing."[16] Yet this is an urban lament, since rural women must continue to think in terms of one right: survival.

Since 1979 women, along with men, have begun to move out of the villages in greater numbers. Many recent migrants to Tehran, whose population in 1997 has swollen to 13 million, have become part of a lumpenproletariat, or lower-middle-class urban population. Changing locale has also entailed a change in the visible expressions of Islamic loyalty. In crowded, often inadequate housing, women have embraced the austere black veil or *chador* and *maghnae* (a head, shoulder, and bodice covering that leaves the face and hands free) as a passport to public space. Since all urban women must wear this uniform, they become equally conformist in the public domain but also equally free of patriarchal control restricting them to the private domain, that is, their households.

Common dress code then allows to surface the true problem of women: their place in the workforce. On this question there has been, and will continue to be, debate at all levels of Iranian society. Until Khomeini's demise, most governmental positions, except teaching and women's health, had been closed to women professionals, but for the past six years "women have been able to study whatever they want and enter all jobs." One might scoff at such a statement except that it comes from the editor of *Zanan* (Women), a bimonthly magazine focusing on women's issues that began publication in 1991 and has not shied away from such controversial topics as divorce practices, the condition of women prisoners, stereotypes of women in textbooks, the image of women in Iranian cinema, and particularly alternative readings of Qur'anic passages concerning the status of women.[17]

Zanan is a publication by and for urban women—those who have had the benefit of education, employment, and access to public space. It is they who have protested against the Islamic Republic of Iran. They have written passionately and argued effectively against patriarchal norms. Many have also projected their views through publications that have appeared in English while they were exiled to England or North America.[18]

The comparative freedom that Iranian women enjoy reflects the resilience and determination of those who have lived through both the early years of the revolution and the eight-year-long war with Iraq. It also reflects the political courage of Rafsanjani, who in a characteristic interview noted the accomplishments as well as the limits of women in the public sphere:

> After the revolution, we invited people to encourage their daughters to play a more active role in society. And we encourage them very much to send their children to higher institutes of learning and research centers. Now, about 35% of our university students are women. And about 40% of school teachers are women. We do not have many women at the level of high management, but their number is increasing in the parliament and top management. We think that the status of women has been enhanced and that their future is even better in this country.[19]

While not all clerics or parliamentarians share Rafsanjani's "liberal" view of women's role in society, there is little doubt that the situation of Iranian women is improving, partly as a result of their own efforts, but partly also with some help from engaged and supportive leaders. Iranian women are far from passive creatures confined to home and unable to participate in the public sphere; Euro-American media stereotypes die hard, but die they must if the reality of Iran is to be recognized.

EGYPT

What is true for women in Iran is also true in Egypt during the past quarter century: Islamic fundamentalism has played an increasing role in their lives.

There are at least three profiles that need to be considered. The first, and narrowest, profile focuses only on those female cadres allied with male fundamentalists. These are lower-middle- to middle-class women, often of rural background. There are few of them, and they do not speak for themselves because their self-described role does not permit their voices to be heard as individual testimonies. The second profile centers on those women who are negatively affected by fundamentalist-inspired laws, which reduce or exclude them from public space that during a prior period had seemed open to them. Also few in number, they are almost entirely second- or third-generation urban dwellers. By birth, education, and travel they have an awareness of the status of women in Europe and America, even when they criticize the excesses of "Western" feminists. The third profile is the one least often considered in discussion of fundamentalism: it is the great mass of rural women for whom the issues of fundamentalism and feminism alike are moot. As we saw in the Iranian case, it is foolish to speak of Muslim women as a single group since the social, economic, and educational profile of rural women brackets them from their urban sisters.

If we begin with urban women, it is because only in cities, and with the transformations that occur to women in Muslim cities, can the saga of Islamic fundamentalism be charted.

In the Egyptian case, as in the Iranian case, we begin with a provisional list of public events, but even as we do, we must recognize that the events of progress that they signal affect but a small number of Egyptian women, nearly all of them urban dwellers.

1923   Egyptian Feminist Union (EFU) is founded; its journal,
       L'Egyptienne, is published in French. Its upper-class
       constituents, headed by Huda Shaarawi, advocate
       social reform.

1929   First women admitted to Fuad I, later Cairo University

1930   Minimum marriage age for women raised to sixteen;
       marriage laws reformed; higher health standards
       advocated for rural women

1933   Protective legislation passed for working-class women

1936   Muslim Ladies' Association (MLA) formed as an
       alternative to, but not a competitor with, EFU

1937   EFU shifts its journal from French to Arabic language
       (becoming *al-Misriya*), but still denies even middle-
       class women educated abroad admission to its ranks

1944   National Feminine Party (NFP) founded, limited
       to Cairo

1945   League of University and Institutes' Young Women
       (LUIYW) founded. Its leader, Inji Aflatun, writes two
       major books: *80 Million Women with Us* and *We
       Egyptian Women*, arguing that women's liberation
       is compatible with Islam

1948   Daughters of the Nile Union (DNU) also founded in
       Cairo, but with branches throughout Egypt. DNU,
       along with NFP and LUIYW, advocates political
       rights, literacy, and hygiene for poor women

1970s First family planning programs inaugurated

1971   Article 40 guarantees citizens equality before the law,
       with "no discrimination made on the basis of race,
       sex, language, ideology, or belief."

1979   By law women are guaranteed thirty seats in Parliament

1979   Personal Status Law passed. Canceled in early 1985;
       most of its central provisions reinstated in a new law
       that went into effect in July 1985

1982   Arab Women's Solidarity Association founded by
       Nawal el-Saadawi. At first denied permission to
       register by the government, it was finally allowed
       to register in 1985 but then was dissolved in 1990
       along with its journal, *Nun*.

What the above list of dates and events omits is the level of inter-action between fundamentalists and feminists that moved from ini-tial cooperation to outright hostility. MLA was founded by Zaynab al-Ghazali, the leading female Islamist, as an alternative to EFU, but with the goal of furthering options for Egyptian women. However, in 1952, when Nasser and his fellow officers came to power, fundamentalists split from feminists and disavowed the latter's goal of harnessing all women to the development goals of the state. Nasser reacted by choking off fundamentalist women. He treated them less harshly than he did their male counterparts: though imprisoning Zaynab al-Ghazali in 1965, he executed her male role model, Sayyid Qutb, the following year. Sadat may be seen to have had a similarly punitive stance toward female funda-mentalists: after Zaynab al-Ghazzali's release, another female Is-lamist, Safinaz Kazim, was incarcerated on three separate occa-sions—in 1973, 1975, and 1981.

Yet attention to the names and fates of a few fundamentalist women ignores an underlying class disjuncture. Both Zaynab al-Ghazali and Safinaz Kazim were upper-middle-class Cairene women of education and privilege; while distanced from the upper-class women of the EFU, in class background they very much resembled members of the MLA or the DNU. By contrast, fundamentalist women who joined Islamic alternative groups in the 1970s and 1980s tended to be middle- or even lower-middle class.[20] This cross-class mobilization of female Islamists invites attention. It matches the growing economic disjunctures of urban Egypt during the past two decades. Women as well as men have been confronted with mammoth shortfalls between their educa-tional horizons and their occupational opportunities: each year 375,000 new people enter a workforce that already is swollen with 40 percent unemployment,[21] and so the new class lines tend to be drawn between those who are employed with any semblance of "honorable" subsistence and those who are not. Fundamentalism appeals to educated, underemployed women, as it does to their male counterparts.

Faced with such a massive, intractable economic crisis, Sadat and then Mubarak followed the policy of Nasser in manipulating both women's issues and fundamentalists toward their own Phar-aonic objectives: to maintain the state as a refuge against chaos at

122

all costs. The Constitution of 1971 is a showcase of juridical ambiguity, as Margot Badran has demonstrated in her path-breaking article on women and modern Egypt. While guaranteeing women equality before the law, it also declared: "The state guarantees a balance and accord between a woman's duties towards her family on the one hand and towards her work in society and her equality with man in the political, social and cultural spheres on the other without violating the law of the Islamic Shariʿah."[22]

In effect, the fundamentalist viewpoint that women are to be maintained in the domestic sphere and excluded from the public sphere was supported by the tone, as well as by the last clause, of the declaration above. In other ways, too, Sadat undermined women in the workforce. His famous Open Door (*infitah*) policy, inaugurated in 1974, embraced foreign investment and encouraged the private sector, but it also rescinded the state's guarantee to employ all university graduates who could not otherwise find jobs. Since women had to compete with men for the few private-sector jobs available, the Open Door became a closed door for female university graduates. With every other Egyptian facing unemployment by the mid-1980s, the state positioned itself as the constrainer of woman's public roles, the advocate of her retreat into the home.

What Sadat took away through economic policies he seemed to restore by legislative decree. Through a double move in 1979 he opened up Parliament to greater female representation and also passed the most hotly contested legislation of his entire rule, the Personal Status Laws. The Personal Status Laws gave women the right to initiate divorce, protected them in divorce actions, and also placed controls on polygyny. All this in the same year that witnessed the ratification of the Camp David Accords with Israel and the ascent to power of the Ayatollah Khomeini in Iran!

Despite the uproar that greeted the Personal Status Laws, they did not change the subsurface reality of Egyptian social culture. In the early 1980s a flood of editions of popular religious tracts appeared from Egyptian publishing houses, at the same that the charismatic preacher Muhammad Mitwalli al-Shaʿrawi rose to public prominence. Their message was the same: the happy woman is the woman in the home, an Egyptian woman who is at once obedient wife and nurturing mother. While the radical female fundamentalists like al-Ghazali and Kazim were kept at bay, the moderate fundamentalists were allowed to operate at will. They were even supported by the state under Mubarak. In 1988 Shaarawi, whose television popularity exceeds that of America's televangelists and who, unlike them, was granted free air time by the state, received a national decoration. In the same year a similar decoration was bestowed on a university professor of peasant origins, Bint al-Shati, whose prolific writings were chiefly marked by their unflagging exaltation of women's domestic roles.[23]

There was a still deeper subsurface reality of Egyptian economic life that had not changed. While statistics are notoriously inaccurate, it is still likely that the majority of Egyptian women continue to be rural rather than urban, and among rural female workers, more than two-thirds are engaged in some kind of economic productivity outside the house, whether plowing in Lower Egypt or milking cows and tending to chickens in Upper Egypt. Such women are concerned with subsistence, with managing minimal resources. Illiterate themselves, to the extent that they think of educational opportunities for their children they "harbor a suspicion that an education which at the end of university [no longer even] guarantees a poorly paying job in the government bureaucracy may not always be worth the effort."[24]

And what does occupy them beyond subsistence is family relations and, above all, marriage. When one reads accounts of the lives of such women, it is neither the platitudes of fundamentalism nor the promises of feminism but the strategies for coping with arduous circumstances and limited options that loom large. These women are far from being passive or unresourceful. Though they and their families are visited by numerous and unending afflictions, they are never left without some appropriate action to take. They are "actively and energetically involved in manipulating their and others' lives, in responding to difficulties effectively, and in discovering solutions to problems that are realistic given the limits of what is available."[25] And yet when all the opportunities for change have been mapped out, neither a religious validation of hearth and home nor a shift to education and public employment is among them. It is only a tiny fraction of urban-dwelling Egyptian women who are affected by either the fundamentalist or the feminist option— or by a newly emergent trend toward "Islamic feminism."

PAKISTAN

One reaches the same conclusions about Pakistan that one does about Egypt, though by a different historical route. The tabulation of public events prior to 1947 is difficult because it must take into account the multiple groups participating in colonial India, conjoining future Pakistanis with Muslims and Hindus who were as opposed to Partition as they were to British occupation. Indian Muslim women, for instance, were visible in the ranks of those supporting a Pan-Islamic coalition (the Khilafat movement) in 1917. They also helped to found the Muslim League, which was the prime advocacy group of an independent South Asian Muslim nation. Soon after Partition in August 1947, Muslim women became visible as Pakistani citizens. They began to organize at the national level. Among their achievements were the following:

1949   All Pakistan Women's Association (APWA) formed
        by the wife of Pakistan's first prime minister,
        Begum Liaqat Ali Khan
1956   APWA publishes a report recommending restrictions
        on *talaq* divorce and polygyny
1961   Moslem Family Laws Ordinance passed, raising the
        legal age for marriage from fourteen to sixteen for
        women, and eighteen to twenty-one for men
1973   New constitution promulgated, one of its provisions
        claiming to guarantee women's equality
1974   Married Women's Property Act and Dowry Prohibition Act passed
1979   Women's Division created at the federal level
1979   Hudood Ordinance passed, creating a special threat
        to lower-class women
1981   Women's Action Forum (WAF) formed, stressing
        feminist issues and attracting housewives, students,
        lawyers, and professional women
1982   A lay preacher, Dr. Israr Ahmad, calls for the complete seculsion of women as well as total enforcement of the veil, and a Federal Council appointed by General Zia al-Haq limits women's participation in spectator sports

1983   Law of Evidence passed, limiting women's testimony
         in court and also compensation due from murder of
         a relative

All these dates suggest again a tug-of-war between feminists and fundamentalists, with the fundamentalists in Pakistan enjoying explicit government support, at least until General Zia's death in 1988. After its founding in 1981, the Women's Action Forum (WAF) spread to all major urban centers of Pakistan, and with support of the older APWA, focused on advocating women's rights, including education, marriage choice, family planning, even abortion. WAF members were loyal citizens of the state and also devout followers of Islam, inasmuch as their members participated regularly in Qur'an classes. These feminists, like their counterparts from Egypt, Iran, and elsewhere, were seeking to find scriptural justification for Islamic norms other than those sanctioned by a neopatriarchal religious class.

The WAF strategy did appeal to some moderate Muslim males, but it did not not succeed in convincing other conservative Muslims, both male and female. The state, which was tainted by its illegal usurpation of power, nonetheless countered the WAF challenge through its own backers, female as well as male Islamists. "The women's wings of the fundamentalist *Jamaat-e Islami* and its student appendage, the *Jamiat-e Tulaba*, banded together with the newly formed *Majlis-e Khawatin* Pakistan to stymie WAF's campaign against Zia's Islamization policies."[26] At the height of this ideological battle, in 1984, the founder of the APWA, Begum Liaqat Ali Khan, challenged General Zia to a showdown. She was the leader of Pakistani women while he was the head of state. He was the instrument of religious fundamentalists, she the advocate of democratic processes and women's rights.

The drama evident in this theater of confrontation masks a deep and disturbing reality. Pakistan is less able to nurture, to educate, and to employ its women citizens than either Egypt or Iran. Pakistan is predominantly agrarian, over 75 percent of its ninety-five million population living in forty-five thousand villages in four provinces. Most women live in such abject poverty that a report by the government-sponsored Commission on the Status of Women could report that "the average rural woman of Pakistan is born in near slavery, leads a life of drudgery and dies invariably in oblivion."[27] Girls' education is even scarcer than running water or electricity. While most boys go to elementary school, some to high school, and a few even to college, most females "typically have been trapped into a traditional treadmill as maintainers of simple one- or two-room dwellings, tenders of animals, and auxiliary farm workers."[28] And, of course, they get married and produce children, an average of seven surviving children per family since only a small percentage of fertile couples practice family planning.

Yet even in the most desperate village, women continue to function, as they do in the most upper-class circles of Karachi social life, as vessels of honor. "For whatever her station in life, the Pakistani woman derives identity in the family circle as mother, wife, daughter, and sister. The stability and sanctity of family life, kinship ties and loyalties, the fabric of religious observance and custom—all these are maintained largely through women who are looked upon as preservers and upholders of social virtues."[29]

In relation to the total population of Pakistan, both feminists and fundamentalists seemed to share certain benefits. They were far more privileged than the poorer, which are also the more populous, segments of Pakistani society. In Egypt, the feminist and the fundamentalist movements also drew support from urban women of privilege: regardless of class differentiation among upper, middle, and lower classes, they all benefited from their placement in the upper third of the Cairene social scale. For Pakistani women also, markers of class location are crucial. They mirror a pattern of social hierarchy that has been historically constructed and remains deeply embedded as the "obvious" norm of social exchange, above all in urban settings. Feminism, despite its rhetorical clamor, remains socially conservative, so socially conservative that the political historian Ayesha Jalal depicts its functional stance as "the convenience of subservience." She explains:

> In Pakistan, as in other parts of the world, the class origins of those who have formed the vanguard of the "feminist" movement have been the decisive factor in the articulation of women's issues at the level of the state. Educated, urban, middle and upper class in the main, these women have toyed with notions of emancipation but carefully resisted challenging their prescribed roles in society. Such deference is merely the outward expression of a deeper and largely subjective consideration: the stability of the family unit and by implication of the social

order itself. As beneficiaries of social accommodations worked out over long periods of history, middle and upper class women everywhere have a stake in preserving the existing structures of authority, and with them the convenience of a subservience that denies them equality in the public realm but also affords privileges not available to women lower down the rungs of the social hierarchy.[30]

In the context of Pakistan, such conservatism, expressed as subservience to existing structures, means that the mere election of a woman to the highest political office does not assure that the fundamentalist cause has been stalled, the feminist advanced:

> On the face of it the election of Benazir Bhutto as prime minister . . . might well suggest that the march of history has dramatically changed course. Yet even the most visible symbol of a woman successful in the public domain has been compelled to win social approbation with measured nods to the orthodox and fundamentalist galleries. [Hence Benazir Bhutto during her time in office did not repeal either the hated Hudood Ordinance or its sequel, the Law of Evidence.][31]

While Pakistan provides a test case of how gender advocacy and class consciousness do not mesh, leaving poor urban and destitute rural women equally disempowered, the circumstances of women in Egypt and Iran are better only by degrees. The strategy for feminists has been to advocate advancement for their country, along with the improvement of opportunities for women. Hence Azar Tabari has declared that "any struggle must also fight against the overall political Islamic system that deprives women and men of the most elementary rights of choice and any kind of self-determination,"[32] while Nawal El-Saadawi has gone even further, asserting that "the complete and real liberation of women, whether in the Arab countries or the West or the Far East, can only become a fact when humanity does away with class society and exploitation for all time. . . . In other words, women can only become truly liberated under a socialist system where classes have been abolished."[33] Hers is an appealing utopian vision: it evokes a global community at once transgendered and classless. Yet it must be tempered on three counts: (1) It conceals the class-embeddedness of the speaker, a medical doctor whose writings and travel place her among the most privileged of Egypt's tiny urban elite. (2) It provides no middle ground for advocacy within the current global economic order, where classless society is not only a lofty ideal but also an unattainable option. Reallocating wealth is no easier for women than for men: how many advocates of a truly classless society would be prepared to endure the grinding poverty of El-Saadawi's rural Egyptian sisters, or their counterparts in Iran and Pakistan? (3) It downplays the historical formation of contemporary Arab/Muslim society, which has been very uneven, leaving most societies with impoverished masses (Egypt and Algeria) or expatriate workers who amount to indentured servants (Saudi Arabia and the Gulf States). Not only capitalism but industrialization and corporatization have reinforced divisions among humankind within as well as between different societies. Socialism in the mid-1990s represents a spent force.

Pakistani women are, and will continue to be, deprived of the opportunity to work. Their irreversible deprivation underscores the global, international specter that daunts feminists and fundamentalists alike: "In the final analysis, the integration of women in the wage-labor force hangs on a solution to the Arab [read: Egyptian, Iranian, Pakistani] economic crisis. This in turn depends on the political will to achieve *real* national independence and regional self-reliance. If the past is anything to go by, little will be achieved in the foreseeable future."[34]

Because feminists have neither the internal mechanisms nor the external supports to further their agenda, it will remain possible for others, especially fundamentalist others, female as well as male, to propound their solution to the no-win economic dilemma. As new generations crowd out the old, more and more young people will continue to migrate to cities. They will seek education and employment, only to meet with dissatisfaction and poverty. The most visible group to blame will be "the modernizers," those who seem to have succeeded by defending the current order. A major group standing against the modernizers will be the Islamists or fundamentalists, those who articulate an indigenous set of codes, grounded in one reading of the Islamic past. The fundamentalists will claim to provide a safety-net against the disruptions and disappointments of emerging economic order. Since no such safety-net exists, the fraud of fundamentalism will become evident, at least to some. Yet the fundamentalist protest will persist. Even when its proponents do not succeed in gaining direct political power, they will have succeeded to the extent that they have made conformity to religious norms the litmus test of cultural authenticity. Even though a theocratic experiment is unlikely for either Egypt or Pakistan, elites in both countries will experience the impulse, from the government as well as from the opposition, to seek an Islamic solution to nagging problems. Women will be drawn into the fray from both sides, and their voices will merit close attention, etching sharply the contradictions that face Muslim society as a whole.

The Shah Bano Case

NOWHERE have the contradictions posed by an Islamist solution become more evident than in the case of a South Asian Muslim divorcee who sought support from her husband through the court system. To examine the case of Shah Bano is to call attention to the pivotal yet problematic role of one mode of governance, the judiciary, as it functions in the three major Muslim states of South Asia: India, Pakistan, and Bangladesh. I will argue two points that emerge when one looks at women as an independent category and the judiciary as a crucial dimension of governance. The first is that women are made to represent the cultural norms shared by men and women alike throughout Muslim South Asia. The second is that court cases involving women's legal rights not only reflect boundary markings between Muslim and other communities, they also heighten tensions about their maintenance, even as they complicate notions of what it is to be both Asian and Muslim in the late twentieth century of the common era.

Shah Bano was the daughter of a police constable.[1] At an early age she had been married to her first cousin, Muhammad Ahmad Khan. During more than forty years of marriage she had borne him five children. Then one day in 1975, according to her account, he evicted her from their home. At first he paid her a maintenance sum, as was required by Islamic law, but he ceased payment after some two and a half years. When she applied to the district court for redress, he divorced her. Uttering the formula disapproved by the Prophet but authorized by the Hanafi school of law, he declared: "I divorce you, I divorce you, I divorce you."[2]

At that point they were fully divorced, but, complying with a further provision of Islamic law, Muhammad Ahmad Khan repaid Shah Bano the dower of about three hundred dollars that he had set aside at the time of their marriage. Legally he had fulfilled all his responsibilities to her.

Shah Bano, however, was left impoverished. She had no means to support herself, having worked only as a housewife for over

131

forty years in the domicile from which she was now debarred. She sued her former husband by going to the magistrate of a provincial court. The magistrate ruled that Muhammad Ahmad Khan, having violated the intent of Muslim Personal Law, was obliged to continue paying Shah Bano her maintenance. The court awarded her the sum of roughly two dollars a month. She appealed the amount of that award, and two years later, in 1980, the High Court of her state (Madhya Pradesh) awarded Shah Bano approximately twenty-three dollars a month.

It was at that point that Muhammad Ahmad Khan appealed the High Court's decision. A lawyer himself, he took the case to the Indian Supreme Court, arguing that he had fulfilled all the provisions of Muslim Personal Law and hence had no more financial obligations toward his former spouse.

The Shah Bano case dragged on for another five years. Without the financial support of "fairly well-off male family members (in this case, Shah Bano's sons),"[3] she could not have pursued her appeal. Finally, in 1985, seven years after she had begun litigation in the lower courts, Shah Bano was vindicated: the Indian Supreme Court upheld the Madhya Pradesh High Court judgment, and her former husband had to comply with its verdict. The Supreme Court justices, in dismissing Muhammad Ahmad Khan's appeal, cited the Criminal Procedure Code of 1973, one section of which referred to "the maintenance of wives, children and parents."[4]

None of the above narrative makes Shah Bano exceptional. Neither her plight nor the length of her legal battles lacks precedents. Numerous are the studies of South Asian women that underscore the discrimination they continue to experience even after the attention drawn to Third World women during the International Women's Decade (1975–1985).[5] It is no small irony that Shah Bano's legal vindication came just as the International Women's Decade was ending, but the favorable outcome of her case had more to do with a legislative act than with public advocacy of women's rights: it was a change in the Code of Criminal Procedure (often abbreviated Cr.P.C.) enacted in 1973 that made possible the reconsideration of provisions for divorced Muslim women. Under this code, two Muslim women had been awarded maintenance—in 1979 and again in 1980—and it was their cases, though reviewed and modified in the Shah Bano judgment, that provided the precedent with reference to which the Supreme Court opted to rule in favor of Shah Bano.

The legal drama, and its political consequence, are dense. Often the case seems to remain only a watershed for identity politics in the continuing struggle for inclusive norms within postcolonial India. What needs to be stressed alternatively is the nature of the legal system that made all three cases possible. All three women resided neither in Bangladesh nor in Pakistan, the two majoritarian Muslim nations of the subcontinent, but in the Republic of India. As Indian citizens, they lived under an ad hoc system evolved since British colonial rule. It was a system that tended to separate criminal law from Muslim personal law. Throughout the nineteenth and the early twentieth centuries there was no uniform manner of applying Muslim family law within the lower courts. On the one hand, the number of rules applied to questions of marriage and inheritance were restricted, while on the other hand, they were enforced through a strict hierarchical structure where appeals moved haltingly from a subordinate district judge to a state high court to the London Privy Council, replaced after 1947 by the Indian Supreme Court.[6]

Due to the omissions and excesses of this system, it is not surprising that customary law, unfavorable to women, was often applied instead of the more favorable terms of Islamic law. Muslim women in the western and northern regions of India were especially vulnerable to facing the denial of property inheritance and dowry settlements, both provided to them under the *shari'a* or Islamic law. Finally, in 1937, under pressure from Muslim elites, the Shariat Law was passed. It required all Indian Muslims to be governed solely by Islamic juridical norms in family matters, namely, in marriage, divorce, maintenance, adoption, succession, and inheritance. But at independence ten years later, Parliament passed an All India Criminal Procedure Code that applied, as its title suggests, to all Indian citizens, whatever their religious affiliations; one of its provisions stipulated "the maintenance of wife, children and parents." It was that provision which the Supreme Court justices cited in the 1979 and 1980 cases and again in 1985 when they ruled in favor of Shah Bano and against Muhammad Ahmad Khan.[7]

Personal law, in effect, acquired a double tracking, one pertaining to the Muslim community, the other to common Indian citizenship. While that double tracking created tension between secular and religious authorities after Independence, such tension was nonetheless successfully negotiated prior to 1985. Were the issue itself a sufficient provocation, then both the 1979 and the 1980 cases should have set off a nationwide row. In fact, they did not.

The case of Shah Bano became decisive for one reason: its timing. It did not occur in the mid-1970s, when Mrs. Gandhi's declaration of a state of emergency had muzzled the court system, nor will it occur again in the mid-1990s, for reasons that will be made clear below. It was the changed climate of religious identity in the mid-1980s that set the stage for the Shah Bano debacle. There were several necessary conditions, but the one sufficient condition was timing: it was in the mid-1980s, and only in the mid-1980s, that there surfaced an issue that signaled how permeable and volatile were the boundaries of Muslim identity. That issue was Muslim Personal Law, that is, law that applied to the personal status of each Muslim within the family domain. Personal law became the litmus test of Indian Muslim collective identity, its fragility underscored by the creation in 1972 of an All India Muslim Personal Law Board to maintain and defend its application.[8]

Even so, personal law by itself would not have created the Shah Bano debacle. The case came to public attention in the aftermath of Indira Gandhi's assassination at the hands of Sikh extremists. Riots in Delhi and elsewhere had shredded the myth of communal harmony in the Republic of India. Everyone had become more aware and more worried about his or her markings as a Hindu or a Muslim or a Sikh or a tribal. While Sikhs, not Muslims, had been the primary targets of the Delhi riots, Muslims still felt vulnerable.

It was in this charged atmosphere that demagogues sought pretexts to "prove" that the ruling party was but a front for furthering Hindu hegemony, at the expense of all minorities but especially the largest, which was the Muslim, minority. The Shah Bano case provided Muslim ideologues, supported and abetted by the All India Muslim Personal Law Board, with "clear" evidence that there was a juridical slide toward uniform civil codes, codes that would enforce majoritarian Hindu values on all Indians. Rajiv Gandhi's Congress-I was then the ruling party. When Congress-I supported the Supreme Court decision, an incensed Muslim politician ran against the Congress-I candidate (who also happened to be a Muslim). The demagogue won, lambasting the anti-Muslim impact of the Shah Bano judgment. How could Muslims preserve their separate identity, he argued, if even their personal laws were subject to arbitration in the higher, "secular" courts of India? The Muslim Personal Law Board, having won a victory at the regional level, ratcheted its claims to the next level. Its members pressed on the national front, appealing to legislators, ministers, and, of course, journalists. They were abetted by Muhammad Ahmad Khan, a barrister arguing his own case! Together the aggrieved former spouse and representatives of the Muslim Personal Law Board carried the banner of Muslim juridical autonomy to several members of Parliament, their every move broadcast by the press.

The role of the press in dramatizing the Shah Bano case has been considerable. In volume of print and decibels of emotion it exceeds all other tragedy-laced spectacles, even the storming of the Sikh golden temple in Amritsar, even the assassination of Mrs. Gandhi and later her son, Rajiv. It exceeds even the Rushdie affair, with which it has sometimes been linked, notably by Gayatri Spivak.[9] The Shah Bano case exceeds all these because it concerns a process that has tapped into communal fears, and drawn out appeals to communal loyalty, not witnessed since independence. Its only competitor for sustained media attention is the Ayodhya mandir/Babri masjid dispute. That dispute erupted in 1986 as a politically motivated effort to reclaim all of India as "Hindu" by pinpointing, with scant historical evidence,[10] one pilgrimage site as the birthplace of the god Ram and then alleging that sixteenth-century Mughal invaders built a mosque on this same site in order to affirm their superiority over Hinduism.

Important though the Ayodhya dispute is, in a real sense it occupies adjacent space on the same spectrum of communally marked confrontation as Shah Bano. Ayodhya becomes the sequel to Shah Bano since it was the latter that pushed Muslim-Hindu antagonism to new levels. Unlike the local protagonists of previous communal riots, the India-wide Hindu protagonists of Ayodhya's sacral purity used the media to stage a grievance identical to that of the Shah Bano case, namely, that Muslim and Hindu world views were finally incommensurate and that the Republic of India could not grant both equal representation.

In such a charged atmosphere the value of religious identity is heightened, and appeals to creedal shibboleths abound. The ideological weapon wielded on both sides quickly became identified as fundamentalism. It was fundamentalism Indian-style, but it was still the bugbear of fundamentalism. The challenge was thrown down by the demagogue who used Shah Bano as the rallying cry for his own election to Parliament in 1985. Syed Shahabuddin decried the Supreme Court decision as "clear" evidence of Hindu contempt for Muslim law. He opposed it not only for himself and for his Muslim constituents but also for all believing Muslims who, like himself, were fundamentalists. Fundamentalists? Yes, fundamentalists, because to be a true Muslim, in his view, was to bind oneself to the literal revelation of the Qur'an. "Historically," declared Syed Shahabaddin, "the Qur'an was revealed to the Prophet 1400 years ago but it is the final message of God to mankind. Not one syllable is subject to change. . . . It is in this sense that the Muslim is by definition a fundamentalist."[11]

There are, of course, enormous contradictions in this assertion, since the Qur'an itself is subject to variant interpretations *within* the believing community of Muslims. Despite the consensus shared by all Muslims that the Qur'an is the final message of God's final messenger, its rare legal passages engender multiple interpretations, arising as they do in a myriad of human circumstances. When Syed Shahabuddin and his followers appeal to Qur'anic finality, they are really staking out a claim for themselves as the sole valid interpreters of what they take to be the simple, singular meaning mandated by Qur'anic verses. Yet other, equally devout Muslims can challenge those claims and offer in their stead equally valid alternative readings of both the Holy Qur'an and Islamic history.

In a time of crisis, to those who perceive themselves at risk, a dispassionate view of the Qur'an may be less plausible than the unequivocal reading claimed by Syed Shahabuddin and other "fundamentalists." The mid-1980s were such a time of crisis for many Indians. India's Muslim "fundamentalists" challenged the Shah Bano ruling at a moment when the center seemed to be unraveling. Their appeal to Parliament to reverse the Shah Bano decree seemed implausible, and the uproar about Shah Bano would have quickly subsided had their appeal failed. But for a variety of political considerations both the Congress-I and Prime Minister Rajiv Gandhi perceived themselves as vulnerable to "the Muslim vote." Out of expediency the Indian Parliament in 1986 passed a bill often referred to as the Muslim Women's Bill.[12] That bill withdrew the right of Muslim women to appeal for maintenance under the Criminal Procedure Code. In other words, after 1986 Shah Bano could have no successors, for the Muslim Women (Protection of Rights on Divorce) Bill, in fact, discriminated against Muslim women: it removed the right of any Muslim woman to juridical appeal for redress of the award made to her under Muslim Personal Law.

Damaging though that outcome may be to the invisible seam of multiculturalism without which Indian democracy cannot function, its most dire consequences may yet be muted by the logic of its initial success. Rather than closing debate on the Shah Bano case, the legislative reversal of the Supreme Court ruling raised new questions about who has the right to speak on behalf of the Muslim community. The Supreme Court judge who read the majority decision made his own claim to best understand Muslim interests when in concluding his argument for the court's ruling he justified it as "more in keeping with the Quran than the traditional interpretation by Muslims of the Shariat."[13] His move to separate the purity of Qur'anic principles from the obfuscation of Muslim jurists was followed by others, including a score of journalists. In an exchange that enlivened the *Illustrated Weekly of India* during early March 1986, a Hindu journalist, Arun Shouri, argued that "while there was much oppression of women under Islamic law, the Quran, rightly interpreted, would make possible the removal of the injustices they suffered." But, according to his respondent, the Islamic scholar Rafiq Zakaria, Shouri only seemed to be concerned about true Islam; his stated concern actually masked a contempt for Muslims and a not so subtle attempt to undermine Muslim religious identity. Nor did the debate disappear once the Muslim Women Bill became law: women's groups opposed the government's stand in favor of the bill, with the result that leading Muslims spoke out on *both* sides of the issue.[14] Seldom before had religious identity and gender parity been so publicly framed in antithetical, competing terms. No wonder that Shah Bano subsequently rejected the court verdict in her favor and occasioned still another round of debate about the meaning of her subjectivity as a Muslim woman.[15]

What is too easily ignored in the heat of the debate is the further limiting effect it has on the claims of Islamic fundamentalists. Islamic fundamentalism spurs competitors, also religious ideo-

logues, also "fundamentalists."[16] The Islamist move is countered
by the effort of Sikh and Hindu others to mark *their* community
boundaries with shibboleths. Each shibboleth is said to echo an
element of scriptural, linguistic, or ethnic purity. Collectively such
shibboleths are upheld as fundamental dicta, that all insiders must
defend, but which outsiders also must respect.

While the outcome of ideological warfare, with its frequent
eruption into physical violence, is not clear, one thing has now
become clear. Though seldom stressed, the status of women in
fundamentalist discourse is crucial. Laws governing women have
provided the touchstone for Islamist identity in the maelstrom of
Indian politics. While much more could be said about how several
groups have manipulated the Shah Bano case to their own perceived advantage,[17] that narrative obscures rather than illumines
the significance of Shah Bano's gender. It is only when Shah Bano
has been highlighted as a Muslim *woman* litigant in modern-day
India that one can begin to assess how other Muslim women fare
in the judicial systems of Bangladesh and Pakistan.

FEMALE LITIGANTS IN PAKISTAN AND BANGLADESH

There are no Shah Banos in the Pakistan of the 1950s and 1960s,
nor in the Pakistan and Bangladesh of the 1970s, 1980s, and
1990s. Despite the attention directed to the implications of the
Shah Bano case within India, no one has yet examined its implication for India's Muslim neighbors.[18] To ask why Shah Bano is a
distinctly Indian test case is to make a comparative move across
territorial borders by presuming that Islam as a variable can be
tested in each postcolonial state. It is also a move that reveals the
major divergences between the advocacy groups claiming allegiance to Islamic fundamentals as they strive to dominate the social
and political life of the subcontinent in the 1990s.

One would like to believe, for instance, that there are no test
cases of female appellants in Pakistani or Bangladeshi courts because as majoritarian Muslim nations, Pakistan and Bangladesh
treat their women citizens fairly, providing them with the entitle-
ments specified in the Qur'an and in Muslim law. Such is not the
case. If one could measure, one would probably find as many infractions of Muslim fundamentals in the cases of divorcees or

widows in Pakistan and Bangladesh as in India, and one would also probably find most of these infractions committed by devout Muslims who ignore the "clear" reading of the Qur'an, not so much because it is expedient to do so but because they feel themselves to be legally "protected" from its application to them. They are "protected" because Muslim law is continually being reinterpreted and adjudicated, making it impossible to chart a single, direct line of interpretation from seventh-century scripture to twentieth-century juridical norms. There is no "clear" reading of the Qur'an as law, just as there is not of the Bible or the Torah, or the Adi Granth or the Vedas. Scriptures are themselves symbol systems that allow for multiple, often conflicting, extrapolations of their legal mandates.

Yet there is more than juridical ambiguity that accounts for the absence of publicized cases involving women and personal law in both Pakistan and Bangladesh. One must also look to structural features that have determined, and so delimited, each country's mode of governance. One must confront, in particular, the colonial legacy of Pakistan and Bangladesh. At the most general level their colonial legacy is the same as that of India. It can be traced to the calculated imposition of British administrative norms. The new norms were designed to meet the needs of competing interest groups, but they also impelled these same groups to continue to compete with one another. The final demarcations of territory in 1947 further ensured that groups defined and controlled as rivals would find no intrinsic basis for national cohesion after Independence.[19] Even if one demurs from the wag who quipped that "British rule in India began on 14 August 1947,"[20] one must acknowledge that the structures defining governance in Pakistan and India *after* 1947 diverged more and more from one another. Both nations, and later Bangladesh, had inherited the threefold division of governance into executive, legislative, and judicial branches. But the three branches did not function with equal authority in each polity. It is in examining differences between them that one can begin to understand the ideology of control that has been obsessed with women's status since the mid-1980s, that is, since the advent of competing religious fundamentalisms.

The space created for Shah Bano to protest came out of the mixed legal system inherited from the Raj. On paper Bangladesh and Pakistan have a judicial system similar to India's, one where

139

criminal law parallels but also diverges from Muslim Personal Law. Yet only in India does one find an independent judiciary functioning as a third branch of government, at once separate from and unbridled by its legislative and executive branches. The Indian court system, despite many challenges, has maintained its autonomous role since 1947. It continues to be

> a single, integrated, hierarchical system, consisting of the Supreme Court of India at the top, high courts in the states, and lower courts in the district and local areas. *The idea of the independence of the judiciary, introduced by the British, has struck deep roots in India.* The Constitution guarantees security of tenure for judges . . . and outlines an exhaustive procedure for dismissal on charges of incompetence or misconduct. . . . Given India's diverse and contentious social groups, the judiciary overall has played an indispensable role in mediating social conflict. Not only the educated elites concentrated in the cities but also the poorer rural and urban sectors of the population have made frequent use of the courts, and Indians in general have gained the reputation of being a highly litigious people.[21]

While opponents of the Shah Bano case have contested the Supreme Court's ruling, they have had to go to great lengths to mitigate its effect. Despite the political debacle produced by the subsequent Muslim Women Bill, the very process that produced the Shah Bano case demands attention if we are to understand why no Shah Banos have litigated their grievances in either Pakistan or Bangladesh.

It is executive supremacy, rather than judicial autonomy, that characterizes the postindependence polities of Pakistan and, since 1971, Pakistan and Bangladesh. From its inception in 1947 Pakistan functioned as a Punjabi-based militocracy, where the influence of British-trained senior army officers determined the political culture of first Karachi and then Islamabad. Although Bengalis resisted West Pakistani disdain for their culture and waged a successful war of independence, with Indian assistance and at great cost, the asymmetry of governance that prevailed in Islamabad was transferred to bhaka. During the past two decades the military has dominated all levels of governance in Bangladesh. Sheikh Mujib, through the Awami party, guided his countrymen to independence and was twice elected to office with massive pluralities. Yet, because of his close ties with India, he lost the confidence of the army,

140

for despite the fact that India had assisted Bangladesh to gain independence, the officer corps had inherited from their Pakistani counterparts a deep anti-Indian bias. In 1975 a group of young army officers invaded Mujib's Dhaka residence and another residence where some of his family lived, assassinating Mujib and nine of his closest relatives. They justified their mass murder in part because of Mujib's alleged subservience to India.[22] In 1981 Mujib's successor, Zia ar-Rahman, who had tried to form his own political party and to bring new groups into Dhakan public life, was also assassinated by the army. Zia's successor was an army general, Husain Ershad, who imposed martial law on Bangladesh and suppressed all rival political parties. When at last Ershad was forced to hold elections in 1988, the entire opposition boycotted the polls, producing a voter turnout of less than 3 percent! In such circumstances it was nonsensical to talk of a democratic polity: Bangladesh, even more than Pakistan, functioned as a one-party militocracy till the early 1990s. Though the Constitution of 1972, later modified in 1977 and 1988, provided for independent legislative, executive, and judicial branches of government, the legislature consisted of Ershad appointees, as did the court system at all levels, even after Begum Khaleda Zia, the widow of the general assassinated in 1981, became prime minister of Bangladesh in 1990.

While Begum Khaleda Zia is seen as an ineffective executive, her successor, Hasina Wazed, is not. Elected prime minister in June 1996, Hasina Wazed is one of the two surviving members of Sheikh Mujib's family. She promises to usher Bangladesh into a new era of internal justice and external respect. Yet the path beyond military domination remains perilous; it has been difficult even for Hasina Wazed to bring the still living murderers of her own family to trial. In late April 1997 she did succeed in beginning a process of litigation that, when it culminates in 1998, will perhaps demonstrate that at last, more than twenty-five years after its separation from Pakistan, Bangladesh is "finally becoming a nation under law."[23]

Despite the repressive, single-party regime that prevailed in Bangladesh till recently, women still enjoy some benefits. There is a tradition going back to Zia ar-Rahman of Bengali participation in the cause of Women in Development (WID). This program channels international aid to women's cooperatives in the poor rural areas that constitute most of Bangladesh. Since both Zia and

Ershad found it expedient to mobilize at least some women into government-sponsored activities, it is not surprising that two women, though rivals of each other, have made it to the highest executive office, with first Begum Khaleda Zia and now Hasina Wazed serving as prime minister of their nation.

Personal law, however, has fared less well. Not till 1985 were family courts even set up. Though they were said to have been given "exclusive jurisdiction to deal with cases relating to parental and conjugal rights, thereby expediting their resolution,"[24] one may wonder how efficient these courts were. Changes at the executive level may accelerate the snail pace of litigation and appeal, but the legacy of martial law lingers, and as recently as 1987 "there were 29 Supreme Court judges dealing with 21,600 cases."[25]

Throughout the 1980s the cases selected as well as the decisions rendered by the Bangladeshi judiciary were also subject to review by the executive. Since Ershad attempted to make Islam the defining badge of national identity, he did not tolerate a case that questioned personal law, even if the litigant based her plea on Qur'anic precedent. Women, most of them rural, poor, and illiterate, remain subordinate to norms that are un-Islamic because the state-sponsored version of Islam reflects surface expediency rather than scriptural zeal. What few rights Bangladeshi women have gained come from left-wing parties or grass-roots organizations; the anaemic judiciary has left them no other avenue of redress.

The legal situation of women in Pakistan reflects a postcolonial asymmetry that more nearly mirrors the condition of Bangladesh than India. Pakistan, like Bangladesh, is plagued by a history of military interventionism. What seems on paper to be a tripartite government of executive, legislative, and judiciary powers turns out to be a long executive arm enveloping and so curtailing both the legislature and the courts. The high profile of Pakistan in international politics has deflected attention from its structural deficiencies. Unlike Delhi, Islamabad did not develop a legislature that could be regularly elected from different regions and so represent plural constituencies at the center, nor did it sponsor a judiciary that could be freed of political pressure from the head of state. Again, the role of the army provides the principal narrative tracing political power in Pakistan's fifty year history. The first ten years of a lackluster experiment with parliamentary democracy ended in 1958 when a military coup by General Mohammad Ayub Khan took control of Islamabad. Ten years later Ayub Khan was, in turn, removed from power on charges of corruption and inefficiency, to be replaced by General Mohammad Yahya Khan. Yahya suffered both a military defeat by India and the territorial loss of East Pakistan in 1971. He was replaced by a popularly elected prime minister, Zulfikar Ali Bhutto, whose brand of Islamic socialism produced a 1973 Constitution for Pakistan. His insecurities, however, led him to rig elections in 1977, or at least that was the claim made by his adversaries. The uproar that followed the "disclosure" of rigging provided the cover for an ambitious general to invoke martial law and eventually declare himself president of Pakistan. Zia al-Haqq not only replaced Bhutto, he engineered the latter's execution through a mock trial on trumped up charges. The Lahore High Court as well as the Supreme Court were divided in their decisions to support the government's case against Bhutto, but in the end they both capitulated, and Bhutto was hanged in 1979. Zia proceeded to rule through a small junta consisting of senior generals close to him. His disdain for other branches of government was made evident by his cynical manipulation of elections to the National Assembly but even more by his assault on the courts.

Zia's opposition to the judiciary took two parallel and complementary forms. One was to subordinate the judiciary to the chief executive. This he did through the Provisional Constitutional Order of 1981. When the chief justice and four other justices of the Supreme Court, along with several high court judges, refused to accept this 1981 Order, Zia fired them and replaced them with his own appointees.[26] Still more subversive of judicial independence was Zia's move to impose military courts and Shari'at courts on the traditional court system. The former was to provide security, the latter to introduce Islamic orthodoxy into the fabric of Pakistani society. Both turned out to be extensions of Zia's power-sated personality, and the status of women, in particular, was problematized by the agency of the Shari'at courts.

The benchmark of Pakistan's effort to provide legal rights for all its citizens was the Family Law Ordinance of 1961. Introduced by Ayub Khan when he was attempting to extend the bases for his own limited claim to legitimacy, its provisions were hardly radical, yet they did curtail polygyny and also enhanced women's rights in the event of divorce. The bill also raised the legal age of marriage for both females (from fourteen to sixteen) and males (from eighteen to twenty-one).

For religious zealots and political conservatives, the Family Law Ordinance was wrong because it interfered in the private domain, which only Muslim law courts could regulate. Bureaucratic and ideological impediments limited enforcement of the ordinance, and it has functioned more as a symbolic point of attack by fundamentalists than as an instrument of large-scale social change. Its bearing on women's status since 1979 has been almost entirely overshadowed by the moves that Zia made to define criminal justice for women. Three ordinances shaped the tone of Zia's allegedly Islamic reforms: the Hudood Ordinance, the Qisas and Diyat Ordinance, and the proposed Law of Evidence. Each downgraded women to a juridical value roughly equivalent to half the value accorded men. It also exalted patriarchal norms to such a definitional cloud zone that adultery and rape became indistinguishable.[27] Not only were there no Shah Banos in Zia's Pakistani courts, but the equivalent case of a woman whose litigation drew nationwide attention was the victim of a double rape who was herself convicted of adultery and punished for her "crime." Under Zia's Hudood ordinance there was both *zina* (adultery) and *zina bil-jabr* (adultery by force, i.e., rape). But the latter crime had to be established by the same procedure as the former, that is, it required the testimony of four pious adult male witnesses. In the case of adultery, such testimony is hard to come by, but in the case of rape, it boggles the mind to think of four pious Muslim males witnessing the act without intervening on behalf of the intended victim!

These obvious contradictions in the Hudood ordinance did not concern the single-minded Zia, and their crowning mockery became evident in the Safia Bibi case. Safia, the daughter of a poor peasant, had been employed in the local landlord's house as a domestic servant. Virtually blind, she could only do minimal chores. She was eighteen years old. According to the statement she made to the police, she was raped first by the landlord's son and then by the landlord himself. As a result she became pregnant and gave birth to an illegitimate child who later died. It was after the death of the child that her father registered a case of rape. The sessions judge in a lower provincial court acquitted both the son and the father of the crime, claiming insufficient evidence to prove rape under the Hudood Ordinance. Had he stopped his judgment here, the case would scarcely have merited mention in the press, but he then went on to note that Safia Bibi's self-confessed pregnancy was evidence supporting a charge of adultery against her. Having ruled that she did in fact commit adultery, he then gave her what he later claimed to be a light sentence: on account of her young age and near blindness, he sentenced her only to public lashing (fifteen lashes), three years imprisonment, and a fine of Rs. 1,000. When his ruling became public in July 1983, there was an outburst of indignation from several quarters. Especially effective was the advocacy of Safia Bibi's case by the Women's Action Forum, calling attention to the illogic of a judge sentencing a rape victim for adultery on the basis of her own testimony![28]

So embarrassing was the Safia Bibi case to Zia's credibility that the Federal Shariʿat Court intervened the following month (August 1983) and requested that the case be transferred to it for review.[29] Chief Justice Aftab Hussein overruled the session judge and, clearly distinguishing between rape and adultery, dismissed the case of Safia Bibi. He also added a note of sympathy for the victim.

The Safia Bibi case underscores what is evident about justice in Pakistan during the past two and a half decades. It depends on the shaky autonomy of an appointed court, the Federal Shariʿat Court, to overrule misguided convictions in the lower courts, at the same time that other instruments of Pakistan's militocracy, notably the Islamic Ideology Council and the Qazi Courts, are indifferent to changes in women's status. Their indifference mirrors the indifference of most Pakistani women to their judicial status. There is renewed hope for some women litigants in the reemergence of the Supreme Court in Pakistan as a vigorous, independent voice during the late 1990s. Yet the litigations that take place continue to have a distinct class coloration. The majority of feminists argue within the urban, upper-middle-class professional ranks of the Punjab and Sind. They do not represent women from other provinces, nor do they represent the vast numbers of rural, illiterate women who account for the majority of Pakistan's female population.[30]

It is dangerous to make too much of the class bias in the feminist movement:[31] most sociopolitical protest movements in the Islamic world are limited to urban settings and to the multiple groups that are at once spawned and alienated by urban conditions. Yet its limited class basis should not obscure the fact that Pakistan, in Nikki Keddie's view, "has the most effective and militant women's movement of any Muslim country."[32] During the 1980s urban groups of professional women, joined by sympathetic male counterparts, did succeed in protesting against a system that masks authoritarian control through the creation of feeble alternatives to executive power.

The excesses of Zia thrived in the cracks: he attempted to reduce or to manipulate the other two branches of government, exploiting their intrinsic weakness to his own ends. Instead of vesting an independent judiciary with the right to pursue guidelines for Islamic justice, Zia sidestepped the existing courts. He supplanted them with courts that reflected his own one-person interpretation of what constituted Islamic orthodoxy. Ironically, the Federal Shari'at Court that was designed to project and enact Zia's views became independent of him in certain instances,[33] at the same time that the Supreme Court of Pakistan appealed to the constitution as the basis for its own noninterference in the process of Islamization, leaving that task to the executive branch.[34]

The shallowness of Zia's moves are further demonstrated by the inability of Islamic groups to win votes in nationwide elections: the people who do care about Islam are not convinced that state-sponsored fundamentalism represents the true intent of Islamic communitarian norms. Not only feminists and moderate professionals but also respected lawyers and judges are intent to remove the judicial process from the arbitrary dictates of a nonjurist ruler, whether Zia or one of his successors.

One must ask the tough structural question: can Pakistan (or Bangladesh) forge a representative, effective polity when one of its three branches of governance functions undaunted, and unchallenged, by the existence of the other two? Not likely. Yet Zia's legacy continues ten years after his death. It continues because a militocracy does not quickly or easily reform itself. Moreover, his successors have been handicapped. The first premiership of Benazir Bhutto was so marred by programmatic contradictions and political opposition that her mere survival became more important than any moves to establish a fairer, more durable polity. Her successor Nawaz Sharif concerned himself with pleasing conservative supporters and military interest groups; he never ventured to intervene in the judicial process. While the Shariʿah Ordinance of 1988 was never enacted,[35] the Federal Shariʿat Court introduced by Zia continues to function under his successors, including Benazir Bhutto, during her second term in office as prime minister, and now Nawaz Sharif in his second term. One must note the evident good will of some of justices sitting in the Federal Shariʿat Court, but the court as a whole still stops short of functioning as an independent judiciary. In its present form it makes democracy in Pakistan a distant rather than an imminent prospect.

The focus on women's status through the Shah Bano case goes to the heart of many issues raised in the age of Islamic fundamentalism. It is often said—and with considerable truth—that the early Islamic movement effected a revolution in the status of Arab women.[36] Muslim norms provided new rights for women, within limits. The Qurʾan makes explicit that male and female believers alike inherit Paradise. In all matters of faith women are, as Stowasser aptly notes, "the spiritual and sexual equals of men."[37] Stipulations concerning divorce and inheritance law also mark an advance over prior practices, and even the oft-cited permission for Muslim men to take up to four wives is hedged with restrictions (Q.4:3: "If you fear that you will not do justice, then marry only one."). Throughout most periods of history Muslim wives have been accorded provisions of justice, even while dependent on their husbands to interpret of what is meant by justice. For Islam, like all premodern societies, remained patriarchal in its norms and values. The Qurʾan, like the Torah, the Bible, and the Vedas, mirrors those patriarchal standards. Men count twice as much as women in giving legal testimony, and it is incumbent on men to maintain women, with proportionately greater responsibilities in public matters (Q.4:34).

Reading the Qurʾan in tandem with early Islamic history remains, for Muslims, both an act of piety and an interpretive challenge. How does one respond in successive eras to divine revelation? Is submission to the will of God best accomplished by conforming to the patterns of earlier epochs? Or does one have to search anew for the spirit of God's directive and Muhammad's example and try to apply their guidance to today's challenges? In South Asia, as elsewhere, such questions have been raised with insistent urgency in the modern period. Nineteenth- and early-twentieth-century reformers like Sayyid Ahmad Khan and Amir

147

Ali argued that the spirit of Qur'an and *hadith* alike required the Muslim community to participate in an ongoing effort to improve the social status of women. Contemporary Muslim writers, such as the late Fazlur Rahman, have followed in the same tradition.[38] Despite the controversy of such efforts, no one can escape the question posed by the foremost twentieth-century intellectual from Muslim South Asia. For the poet-philosopher Muhammad Iqbal that question was: can Islamic law, including its provisions for women, develop and change or not? His own answer was an unflinching "Yes." "I have no doubt," he wrote in his most famous theological essay, "that a deeper study of the enormous legal literature of Islam is sure to rid the modern critic of the superficial opinion that the Law of Islam is stationary and incapable of development."[39] And the principle of development rested, above all, on the practice of *ijtihad* as a vehicle for returning to authoritative sources and reexamining them in the light of present-day conditions. Iqbal's was an unabashed reformist voice.

Yet those who oppose Iqbal and all other reformist voices argue that there is no going back, except by way of emulating, without change, the example of earlier generations. For such Muslims, adherence to Islamic tradition, understood as a network of practices ordained by prior custom, becomes the benchmark of Islamic identity, over and against the military, economic, and intellectual power of non-Muslim communities. In South Asia, as elsewhere, Muslims who perceive themselves above all to be engaged in intercommunal struggles dismiss the reformist argument as an alien import: reflecting Western influence, it dilutes true Islam and debilitates its present profile. They consider loyalty to the Muslim community as primary, its core defined, above all, by willingness to subject one's personal and family life—fully and without question—to traditional legal norms. The advocacy of such norms in a charged public forum for explicit group interests is not, however, part of Islamic tradition, and so the nontraditional advocacy of traditional norms is most often called fundamentalism or, less accurately, "neo-traditionalism."

At present, the reformist voices have become muted, or attenuated, in public debates where Islam is invoked. It is the neo-traditionalist or fundamentalist approach to Islam that dominates the intercommunal disputes of South Asia. Politicians understand the negative as well as positive force of a fundamentalist agenda and so often become its most ardent supporters. As long as re-formist voices are denied equal access to both media and policy forums, they will have difficulty reshaping institutions that apply to the range of Muslim social life, including those affecting the status of women.

As a consequence, there are no Shah Banos in Pakistan. There have been none in Bangladesh. A cross-national comparison of South Asia's major states confers on the Republic of India a pivotal distinctiveness: despite its struggles with an independent judiciary, India has maintained a claim to impartial review that extends to female as well as male litigants. In Pakistan women continue to suffer from an ad hoc judicial review system that affects too few rural women, at the same time that it is subject to manipulation, rather than consultation, from the center. In Bangladesh one is confronted not only with the neglect of women's rights but also with the absence of all but a few women from any public scrutiny. In part the anonymity of Bangladeshi women is a legacy of that country's belated and brutal entry into the comity of nations, yet postcolonial independence, first from England, then from Paki-stan, has not allowed an independent judiciary to emerge in Dhaka. Justice through litigation has become the expectation for a mere handful of Bangladeshis, while the continuing co-optation of the federal courts by the executive branch signals just how difficult it has become, and will remain, for Bangladeshi women to counter fundamentalist or other state-directed ideologies.

THE FUTURE OF ISLAMIC FUNDAMENTALISM

In recent decades the emphasis of scholars, journalists, and policy makers alike has been almost exclusively on Islamic fundamental-ism. The result has been a deficit in understanding the actual na-ture of Muslim social and cultural values in the modern period. For there is no concerted, uniform movement called Islamic funda-mentalism. It varies due to many factors, and after situating it within a broader historical context, we must still examine specific local contexts. The beginning of each of its several manifestations must be ratcheted to specific regions, its ideologues traced to spe-cific countries and then sorted out into specific classes, and specific groups of men and women. At the same time, one must examine the limits of fundamentalism, to gauge why its appeal is not greater and for what reasons the largest number of pious, observant Muslims remain nonfundamentalist in their outlook as also in their behavior.

It is too easy to follow the opposite course. One can read numerous statements from leading Muslim thinkers and from Euro-American analysts attesting both to the unity of the Islamic world and to its exceptionalism. All Muslims think alike, we are told, and no one else thinks as they do. While Muslims, from the time of the Prophet Muhammad, have been enjoined to function as one community, the foundational ideal has not become a sustainable reality: Muslims have failed to cohere as a single, cohesive group, either politically or ideologically. Their failure is no worse than that of Jews, divided into three major and other minor sects for more than a hundred years, and Christians, likewise divided and subdivided into numerous competing sects since the Reformation. Why, then, should we be surprised that Muslims have failed to obtain either a structural coherence or a creedal/ritual/juridical uniformity? In premodern times there were already Muslim sects, not merely the familiar Sunni-Shi'i faultline but myriad internal divisions within both Sunni and Shi'i communities. More importantly, in modern times sectarian divisions have been surpassed by national ideologies of Islamic identity. Some have tried to suggest that since World War II the major difference is between Islamic states and Muslim states, the latter resting on demographic indices, the former on dedication to a uniform religious culture. But this distinction is moot, for it belies an underlying common function of both Islamic and Muslim states: both states define Islam for their citizens rather than acknowledging an independent or polyphonous source of religious authority. The major characteristic of all modern-day Muslim societies is the centralized authority exercised by the state on behalf of whichever form of Islam best suits its rulers. As one scholar has noted about the profile of statist Islam:

> This rise of "officialized," government-supported forms of Islam and Islamic ideologies is . . . one of the most important developments of Islam in Muslim countries since the mid-century. The government itself benefits from this "officialized" version of Islam because it gives a religious legitimation to the state and its politics, however hard they may

be on the population. But this "officialized" Islam inevitably evokes responses among the population, including political and religious opponents of the established regime, and these will also be expressed in terms of Islam. As soon as the centralization of state power leads to particular state supported definitions of Islam, its opponents will develop alternative definitions such as one finds in Islamist circles all over the present-day Muslim world.[40]

This point can be expanded. Not only does the state define Islam, but its definition competes with the definition of other Muslim nation-states. Hence the irony that all Muslims, while clinging to ideals of collective solidarity, live within Muslim nation-states that compete with one another. Most were created since World War II, often by colonial administration and imperial diplomacy. As *independent* nation-states they must compete with one another, for, though free from direct foreign rule, they remain separated from the political and social loyalties that characterize their Muslim neighbors. No new state has disappeared (despite the further partition of Pakistan in 1971 with the creation of Bangladesh, and despite the 1990 Iraqi invasion that placed Kuwait's future at risk). Nor have any two states combined, though several attempts were made both by Nasser of Egypt and later by Qaddafi of Libya. Why, we might ask, should Muslim nation-states combine? Could anyone imagine Canada, the United States, and Mexico becoming federated as the Union of American States? As preposterous as that scheme sounds, even more preposterous would be the suggestion that such a federation is mandated on religious grounds, since the majority population of all three is Christian! Yet a parallel suggestion is regularly put forth by those who look at the Muslim world. "Aha!" they exclaim: "The hold of their religion on them is stronger than ours on us. They can unite against us, and we must fear their collective hostility."

This fear would be dismissable if made only by Serbian nationalists trying to cow their Muslim neighbors, as it was in the early 1990s, or by Jewish settlers seeking to curtail a Palestinian presence in West Bank and Gaza. But it is also made by many respectable American academic and foreign policy pundits. It is given credibility because some Muslim leaders, such as Muammar Qaddafi and Saddam Hussein, deliberately play on such fears. Yet the discerning observer must remember time and again to separate the rhetoric from the reality, the ideals proclaiming unity from the institutions, especially the nation-state, mandating competition. Islam is no different from Judaism or Christianity. Living in a world of compromise, it cannot meet either the goals of founding figures or the ideals of present-day spokesmen.

A related and equally important rule of thumb is to ask: Whose Islam? Whose Islamic revivalism? Or whose Islamic fundamentalism? Is it Arabs or Persians, Africans or Asians who are drawing attention to Islam? Is it those in power or those seeking power? Is it men or women or teenagers? The greatest problem for the best informed non-Muslims, even when they are sincere and well-intentioned, is the absence of acquaintance with real-life Muslims. The only Muslims who are known to most Europeans are Muslims from abroad living either as expatriates or as temporary laborers in their midst. Such Muslims are refugees from the economic, and often also the political, climate in their country of origin. Though concerned about their distant coreligionists, these refugees do not inevitably mirror the outlook or aspirations of those back home. By contrast, in the United States there exist both émigré and indigenous, or African American, Muslims. Despite their small numbers (less than two million[41]), they are no less heterogeneous than Protestant or Catholic or Jewish Americans. They consist of immigrants from Middle Eastern, African, and Asian Muslim nations as well as indigenous converts.

Neither Americans nor Europeans have cause to fear the growth of self-confident Muslim communities in their midst. The great difficulty is to separate the Muslims represented—and too often misrepresented—in the media from the Muslims resident next door. To acknowledge diversity is the first step toward placing Islamic fundamentalism in its proper perspective, and replacing a negative image of Islam with a proper vision of its norms and values. Europeans, like Americans, should learn more about real-life Muslims. Few of them resemble the feared Muslim fanatic or his gun-toting accomplices or his veiled female companions.[42] And indeed, one sees in the voices of Muslim modernists the continuity of an Islamic alternative to both fundamentalism and praetorian neo-colonialism.

I have explored above the answers of a Muhammad Iqbal and also an ʿAli Shariʿati. But how does one frame their contribution, along with that of Izetbegovic and other Muslim modernists? To do so with any hope of interpretive, cross-cultural affirmation, one must introduce a category that does not limit God to the mosque, the school, the court, or the seat of government. One must find a new word that demotes religion and politics alike from their current prestige ranking. In English the most suitable word might be "mentality" or "world view." It eschews a kind of linguistic reductionism by admitting the role of imagination and historical change. It also collates the givenness of key ideas and values with the equally important property of adopting "models of behavior inherited from different traditions."[43]

Muslim thinkers in the context of the late twentieth century who have exhibited the ability to be both traditional and modern can and do embrace elements from the Islamic past while also espousing "models of behavior" from other sources. They are not less Muslim for being adaptive. They exposit a world view or mentality that may over time generate powerful changes, even though they are largely ignored in the current debate. Among their number, in addition to Izetbegovic, Shariati, and Iqbal, one needs to add the names of Egyptian jurist ʿAli ʿAbd ar-Raziq, Algerian semiotician Mohammed Arkoun,[44] and Sudanese exegete Mahmoud Taha.[45]

Though ʿAli ʿAbd ar-Raziq achieved fame—or rather, notoriety—in the early part of the century, the issues he raised continue to inform alternate views of Islam that inform internal debates about the profile of a distinctive Muslim world view, at least in Sunni Muslim circles. For the furor that surrounded ʿAli ʿAbd ar-Raziq concerned the debate about the Caliphate. The Caliphate stood at the apogee of Sunni Muslim symbolic structures, just as the Imamate occupied that rung for Shiʿi Muslims. And it was at the height of Ataturk's challenge to the Caliphate that many Muslims in adjacent countriues, including India, rallied to the support of the Caliphate.[46] At the height of this debate over the Caliphate, ʿAli ʿAbd ar-Raziq, himself a Shaykh at al-Azhar, posed to other Egyptian scholars a challenge to the very notion of political-religious symbiosis as crucial to Islamic life. His book, *al-Islam wa usul al-hukm* (Islam and the bases of governance), caused an uproar that led eventually to his trial and also his dismissal from the post he held at al-Azhar. As Leonard Binder has deftly shown in his extended analysis of ʿAli ʿAbd ar-Raziq's trial,[47] it was not easy for him to maintain his initial position, and he may have been browbeaten into reversing himself, but the notoriety of his case suggests that he went to the heart of a major issue and provided an alternative that could not be dismissed out of hand, namely, that there is a religious core to Islamic identity that may take multiple political forms, and by the same token, that there is no single political structure announced by the Prophet, perpetuated by the first three Caliphs, or sanctioned by practice in subsequent Muslim dynasties. It is the opposite of current thinking in Islamic fundamentalist circles but also in much of popular perception about the Muslim difference in religio-political norms.

Arkoun is alive and well because he forged his boldly revisionist view of Islam from Paris, not from Algiers. His is a powerful appeal to the transformative power of the Qur'an and its applicability to a range of modern issues, including equality for women and human rights for religious as well as ethnic minorities. He also privileges myth over history, suggesting that there is a narrative kernel in the Qur'an that supersedes all other markers of its revelatory impulse. The task of scholars and activists alike, in Arkoun's view, is to separate mythic from both mythological and ideological invocations of the Qur'anic fact.[48]

One of the ironies of Arkoun's approach is its relocation in English via translations, or references to his works in English-language theoretical works such as Binder's *Islamic Liberalism*. It is ironic because Arkoun's methodology presupposes an acquaintance with, and acceptance of, French discursive subtleties that often elude or just plain annoy English readers and Anglo-American scholars. Binder, who devotes a long section to Arkoun in his own assessment of Islamic liberalism, still has to take him to task for not accepting "either the historicity or the validity of what happened in Iran."[49] Yet Binder misses, or chooses to avoid, the linchpin of Arkoun's argument: that the Qur'anic myth can never be fully or adequately reappropriated at any moment in history. Every reading is also a misreading. Every truth is also a lie, and so on. Arkoun does privilege post-Enlightenment, poststructuralist methods in his assessment of the Islamic world view, but his approach merits sustained attention, despite its obtuseness for American pragmatists or their British counterparts.

Taha, on the other hand, wrote in Arabic but, like Arkoun, has achieved notoriety in his land of origin as well as in some American academic circles. A Sufi exemplar with distinctive exegetical perspectives, he evolved a way of reading the Qur'an that directly assaulted the traditional approach of most Sunni Muslim scholars. His provocation was more virulent than Arkoun's and more lethal than 'Ali 'Abd ar-Raziq's because he remained in his native Sudan. Tolerated for a time, he was subjected to a mock trial, conviction, and execution, all engineered by the then ruler of Sudan, General Numeiri, in the late 1980s. Numeiri has ceased to rule Sudan, but Taha's radical view of the Qur'an still inspires debate. Like both 'Ali 'Abd ar-Raziq and Mohammed Arkoun, he would be deemed heretical by many Muslims, and yet his legacy is to provoke a continuing debate about what comprises an authentic Muslim world view and attendant practice of Muslim norms.

By examining these and other Muslim provocateurs, one begins to see how Islam as world view does more than locate Islam beyond the ideological fray of religion and politics. It also posits Islam as a symbolic resource that has not been exhausted by its relation to Europe and to the triple process of colonialism, postcolonialism, and neocolonialism. But it also requires seeing Islam as less than a sufficient explanation for the ills or the hopes of all Muslims. Islam is but one of several variables determining the social fabric of Muslim communities in Asia, Africa, and America. It does not itself determine the dominant culture, nor does it provide the sole, or even the most adequate, ideology for protesting the disruptive qualities of the high-tech era. In such circumstances Muslims may protest with violence, but they protest as aggrieved parties on the margins of a world system that they did not create and cannot control but in which they participate and refuse not to be counted.

One would like to linger on the hope embedded in the work and vision of Izetbegovic and company. However, they represent but one stratum of modern-day Islam, and their Muslim opponents are numerous. There are also non-Muslims who continue to fear what some Muslims proclaim as the cornerstone of faith, namely, *jihad*. Is not *jihad* holy war, and is it not always to be waged against the infidel? These are frequent questions, and they need to be addressed, all the more so because new ideological challenges face the increasingly visible Muslim community of Southeast Asia. Unlike their West Asian coreligionists, Southeast Asian Muslims see their battle as economic. Recently that battle has been captioned as

155

"Islam and Corporate Culture." And so at the end of a book exploring Islamic diversity and underscoring the potential for accommodation in the Muslim world, it is salutary to explore both *jihad* and corporate culture. *Jihad* and corporate culture exist together in the minds of many Malay Muslims, but till now they have not been highlighted in an overview of sociocultural tensions and opportunities that face contemporary Muslims, Malay and non-Malay. The time has come to make that step.

Convergent Signposts: *Jihad* and Corporate Culture

TWO TECHNICAL terms that circulate in the contemporary Muslim world are "jihad" and "corporate culture." One is Arabic and has a long, contested history, mostly applied to the older Muslim regions of Africa and Asia. The other is English and has a lifetime of perhaps a decade, mostly in Southeast Asia, above all in Malaysia. It would seem incongruous to compare the two terms except that together they address the central question of this book: how do Muslim countries in the postcolonial—and now post–Cold War—era move from confrontation to accommodation?

The very word jihad connotes violence. It is most often translated into English as "holy war," war waged against non-Muslims, a kind of Crusade in reverse. Jihad could be, and was, invoked in Muslim protests against European colonial rule, for it embodies ideology; it translates thought into action; it mobilizes the committed for a cause perceived as both just and necessary. But jihad also has a history in Islamic religion prior to the anticolonial and then nationalist movements. All proponents of jihad, whether intellectuals or politicians, are ideologues, but more importantly they are *religious* ideologues. For Muslims, as for others, religion and ideology merge, and during the modern or high-tech era, their merger is crucial for understanding the ambiguities of violence in an Islamic context.[1]

The same prologue informs the brief history of corporate culture as a Muslim idiom. It has no Arabic equivalent. It arises as a technical term describing the framework for competitive business in the high-tech era. The countries most renowned for their attention to corporate culture are non-Muslim industrial powers: Japan and the United States.

Yet Muslim proponents of corporate culture are now in evidence, nowhere more so than in 1990s' Malaysia. And, like proponents of jihad, they are motivated by both religion and ideology since they are intent on applying religious guidelines to the special conditions of late capitalist society in Southeast Asia.

If post–Cold War events have offered any single lesson, it is that historical antecedents do not determine the present or dictate the future: neither Muslim nation-states nor urban sectors of wage-earning Muslims are bound by the premodern legacy or symbolic capital of centrist Islam. There are discrete local and global factors informing Malay expansion into what the sociologist Clive Kessler has called cultural modernity. One is corporate culture, portending the accommodation of Islamic norms and values in the once alien terrain of late capitalist economics. The other is Chinese pluralism, the networking of a specifically Chinese world view under the rubric of Confucianism, Taoism, and/or Buddhism. Like corporate culture, Chinese pluralism too has been a domain where Islam until recently has been either a minor player or a reluctant outsider.

The challenge of Chinese pluralism needs to be assessed, but only after corporate culture. For, despite its recent origins and geographic restriction, corporate culture has as much right to be considered in a Muslim context as does jihad. Muslims, like Christians and Jews, like Hindus and Buddhists and Sikhs, must be modern to survive. They are inescapably moderns because they live at a point in time best labeled the high-tech era. They experience modernity even when they do not fully embrace modernism. And one of the most radical consequences of modernity is to transform every theology or philosophy into a species of ideology that matches the requirements of the present age.

The transformation of jihad into a modern ideology has been uneven. Its accommodation to practical exigencies, while seldom admitted among Sunni theorists, is showcased among their Shiʿi counterparts. Wherever one looks, whether to a "secular" Iranian ideologue such as ʿAli Shariʿati or a clerical theoretician such as Ayatollah Motahhari,[2] one finds Iranian Shiʿis consciously reflecting on the needs of the present age, and the shifts that it requires.

Equally important, however, is the reduced attention to jihad in some quarters. While jihad may retain its rhetorical appeal in a North African, Middle Eastern, or even South Asian context, for Southeast Asians, and especially for Malay Muslims, jihad (understood as an appeal to armed struggle) has already been bypassed by the need to situate Islam in the context of international economics.[3] As the second epigraph for this volume suggests, jihad has come to mean the advocacy of social justice in a widening circle that also includes economic participation and prosperity for Muslims.

The dominant Malay accent on corporate culture seeks to locate an Islamic dimension parallel to the commercial culture of the most economically advanced countries while not reflexively imitative of them. It seeks to operate not against the G-7, the core group of high-tech, industrialized countries, but within that alternative group of nation-states clustered as the G-15, that is, South-to-South countries that have experienced rapid growth in recent years and are now pledged to support one another in trade, commerce, and industry, even while recognizing their individual and common subordination to the G-7.[4]

The example of Malaysia helps to highlight a pattern of change that may begin to appear in other Muslim nation-states in the next phase of the post–Cold War era. While some may continue to link national interests to narrowly ethnic goals (Malays against Chinese), many others are attempting to move beyond ethno-nationalism to higher collective opportunities (Malaysians among regional economic powers).

The constant theme of Malaysian public life is mobilization in economic terms for the future. While it can be directed abroad, as it is in the G-15 meetings, it may also motivate a domestic audience, specifically Malays, who have yet to attain economic prominence equivalent to their Chinese countrymen and women. The prime minister is a weathervane of new dispositions. Mahathir could not be a successful Malay politician unless he advocated a set of policies that would advance his own basic constituency within UNMO, the political party that brought him to power and remains his primary base of support. Does Mahathir always live up to his professed goals? Of course not; neither does any public figure. The larger question is whether he can maneuver the G-15 or any South-to-South alternative group to avert the Greater China identity that many see as *the* future for the entire region.

The question seems to have already been answered by a new and aggressive breed of image purveyors. Among their venues is the Asian Marketing column regularly featured in *The Asian Wall Street Journal*. For marketing people, ever alert to the power of advertising slogans, there is but one caption that fits the entire Asia-Pacific region: "Greater China." All the region consists of growth triangles knit together under the umbrella of Greater China. Marketers take account of variant cultural traditions, such as the "globalization of the world through multinational brands, music, film, and television," but they always defer to Greater China as the telos for the region as a whole.[5]

Malaysia, like most of Southeast Asia, lives in the shadow of Greater China. Mahathir has charted the kind of values needed if Malaysia is to achieve regional recognition. It was in his 1991 address labeled "Vision 2020" that Mahathir first launched his program for making Malaysia a fully developed country, able to strut with those countries already regarded as "developed." Mahathir acknowledges that Malaysia has not yet reached the next level of economic recognition. The liminal status of his country partially explains why membership in the G-15 is so important to him: paralleling the G-7, it reminds those other top-rank countries that the second-rank countries cannot be ignored. It also reminds the Muslim world that no Muslim country has made it to the top: only Malaysia, along with Algeria, Egypt, Indonesia, Senegal, and Nigeria—who happen also to be members of the G-15—are possible contenders. And for there to be an Islamic difference in the Greater China Co-Prosperity Sphere, one must forge a broad-scale economic strategy that takes account of cultural difference while accenting Islamic norms.

In other words, it is the symbolism as much as the reality of Malaysia's economic achievements that are framed in Vision 2020. One much respected Malaysian academic told me: "It does not matter where Malaysia is in actual economic standings; it does matter how it projects its economic weight in geopolitical terms. A major economic heavyweight like Japan often appears to be either quiescent or subservient on global matters, while another economic giant, South Korea, has scarcely any independent foreign policy."[6]

No wonder, then, that there are few places in Malaysia today where Vision 2020 is not discussed, and when discussed, it is invariably in terms of the relatedness of values, that is, Islamic values, to economic growth. The lexical linchpin behind this bid to become globally competitive is corporate culture.

To the extent that every vision needs an ideological engine, the engine in Malaysia is IKIM, a think tank established at government initiative to project Islamic values. It is IKIM that engages Corporate Culture as both Islamic and Malay. IKIM is the acronym for the Institute of Islamic Understanding Malaysia: it parallels but turns to practical ends the work of another recently founded institution, the International Islamic University, or IIU. In trying to promote Islamic understanding, IKIM publishes a wide variety of books on specialized topics. One major new IKIM publication consists of an edited volume titled *Quality and Productivity: Creating a Difference in Modern Industry and Corporations*. Though the initial essays stress Islamic precedents for corporate culture, gleaned from the Qur'an, the life of the Prophet, and early Muslim history, it is a thin Islamic veneer, since no contributor claims that corporate culture emanates from either Islamic scripture or the Muslim past. Instead, the sole cross-cultural essay stands back from Malay self-absorption and lays out two variant models for economic growth. One, deriving from the United States and favoring productivity over quality, prevailed through World War II. The second, linked to Japan and opting for quality, has achieved spectacular results from the early 1950s to the present.[7]

While the narrative about corporate culture is honed to contemporary history and global economics, the narrative about jihad is the opposite. Its symbolic force is evoked from the past, especially the colonial past, with the implication that Muslims should not change in their implacable posture of enmity to the West—creedal and ideological, at the least, and, if need be, political and military as well. Economics seems to be absent, unimportant for jihad advocates.

Yet jihad does entail change. It is not the same yesterday, today, and tomorrow. And it is not the same for all Muslims. Those who contest its applicability have equal claim to being devout Muslims, whether Sunni or Shi'i, legist or Sufi in their affiliations, and they do take stock of economic as well as historical markers.

Complicating the use of jihad is the series of historical asymmetries it infers between Muslim and Christian mentalities. Concealed within these asymmetries is a series of power relations. They obscure understanding and falsify judgment unless they are brought into the open. Before leaping to the analysis of a freighted

161

term such as jihad, we must first take account of these asymmetries and their impact on cross-cultural judgments.

One asymmetry looms over all others and has to be placed in the foreground. It is a material difference that has become the hallmark of arrogance vs. weakness. Most beneficiaries of the technical age are also citizens of the G-7. Whether European or American, we speak from a moment in world history during which Christian, or at least residually Christian, polities dominate the discourse about global hegemony. From a *Muslim* perspective, American and European world views are naturally, necessarily conjoined, since neither the United States nor its European allies project an agenda that depends upon, or considers, Muslim interests.

Two international crises underscore the subordination of Muslim interests and sensibilities to a homogeneous globalism. First was the publication and then hyped-up promotion of Salman Rushdie's *The Satanic Verses* in the late 1980s. It was not an equal contest between competing world views. Rather, it confirmed what has been evident since World War II: Muslim sensibilities seldom register, except negatively, among Euro-American opinion setters. As one wag put it, we love to hate the Ayatollah and all his fanatic followers.

The recent Balkan conflict provided further confirmation that if Muslims count, it is only in a negative sense. In late 1995 the United States government joined NATO forces trying to broker a peace in the former Yugoslavia. Yet it was global politics, not consideration for Bosnian Muslims, that prompted the change in U.S. foreign policy, just as it is the potential for a "Muslim backlash," not the concern for Muslim sensibilities, that prompts U.S. interest in most African or Asian countries with large Muslim populations.

Yet there will never be a "Muslim backlash," for there is no concerted strategy among any two Muslim polities. Muslim polities are not now, nor have they ever been, a political bloc. Lame and ludicrous is the effort of polemicists like Frances Fukuyama and Samuel Huntington to portray Muslim governments as both unified and adamant in opposing the West and "Western interests." The historian Roy Mottahedeh rightly observed that "the actual agreed-upon content of Islamic government remains very limited and, more often than not, severely disputed."[8]

Unfortunately, advocates of Western exceptionalism outnumber historians of transnational cultural movements. West-is-Best advocates proliferate; they are not limited to politicians and policy mavens. Even American observers who seem to be culturally sensitive hit a tripwire when it comes to Islam, revealing how very "present-minded"[9] most Americans are prone to be.

In the case of Malaysia an egregious offender is James Fallows, Washington editor for *The Atlantic Monthly* and frequent commentator on National Public Radio. In a recent book, Fallows describes the new East Asian ascendancy in economics and increasingly in politics. He devotes a major section to Malaysia. He praises Malay commercial adventurism, yet he also contrasts Malaysia with Thailand, accenting the cultural deficit that Malaysia brings to global harmony. "Thailand is libertine," he observes, but "most of Malaysia's population is Muslim."[10] In other words, libertine is the opposite of Muslim, and everything about Islam inhibits or limits. It especially limits Western influence, since "in its political tone Malaysian life has become more and more aggressively anti-Western . . . in part . . . due to the worldwide rise of fundamentalist Islam."[11]

These words would be less jarring had Fallows never visited Malaysia, but in fact he spent two years in Kuala Lumpur during the 1980s. He saw what he expected to see, filtering all his impressions of Malaysia through an international media fixation with Islamic fundamentalism. So narrow is this fixation that it made all representations of Islamic loyalty seem like but another turn away from the West and toward religiously inspired acrimony or worse.

Reference to fundamentalism allows Fallows to keep Malay cultural pride at bay: as Muslims, Malays remain not only foreign but other.

Nor is Fallows' implicit judgment his alone. It is shared by numerous highbrow global commentators. Despite other differences, the elites of Euro-America are presumed to have a common destiny: it is we who share—and also *preserve*—the legacy of globally diffuse, multinational capitalism. No longer Russians but Afro-Asian Muslims, elites and nonelites alike, become the other to us; they are also the lesser, because now the weaker, other.

A second asymmetry underscores, and enhances, the first asymmetry between "Christian" Euro-America and "Muslim" Afro-Asia. It is too often ignored because it addresses power as constructive rather than destructive. It interprets power as part of the potential good rather than the necessary evil that marks human existence. It is a major Muslim-Christian difference, since power, far from being alien to the first Muslims, was integral to their self-identity. From the outset, the Prophet Muhammad and his companions had to confront power—political and military, economic and social, cultural and religious. The Qur'an, as the foundational text inscribing Muslim self-identity, projected the benefits as well as the limits of power. Qur'anic revelations addressed circumstances of social transformation, portending a better life in this world as well as the next. Both the order and content of the Qur'an became fixed as a single, unchanging scripture almost at once, even before the earliest period of Muslim expansionism. Yet Christians deferred entering the brutish world of politics, and Christian rulers only harnessed scriptural authority to the exigencies of political life after Christianity itself became a state religion. The time lag between Jesus's death and Christian rule was nearly three hundred years, with the result that ethical norms construed by the first, urban Christians did not engage Roman institutions of statecraft and warfare except oppositionally. While the Emperor Constantine did augur the constructive use of power by Christians, the interlude between Jesus's death and his conversion produced other influences—gnostic and stoic, Greek and Roman—that implicitly shaped Christian efforts to appropriate power. These same influences also complicated the subsequent strategy of Christian rulers and theorists in justifying war. Even today, in a post-Christian world tone-deaf to the ultimacy of religious values, Christian wariness of power continues to infuse public discourse in Europe and in America. It makes still more difficult a clear perception of the Muslim difference that often places jihad in the foreground.

Western Christian versus Asian Muslim—each label suggests uneasy accommodations to perceptual differences as well as historical asymmetries. What is true for jihad is also true for corporate culture. If Christians are ill at ease with power, Muslims recoil at profit. It is Europeans and, by extension, Americans who have the chief claim on developing capitalism as a world-encompassing mercantile and commercial world view. The Japanese have adopted, and now exceeded, Euro-American models of capitalist productivity and profit. Yet the word "profit" retains a negative connotation in Islamic parlance, at least to the extent that it connotes "excessive, personal gain." When corporate culture is discussed by Muslim members of the Pacific prosperity club, such as Malaysia and Indonesia, the term "profit" is frequently downplayed or else paired with "social responsibility."[12]

How, then, can one bridge the historical distance from developing to developed world? The G-15 can work for Malaysia only if it connects Malaysian interests to those of other economic powerhouses in Asia, like Indonesia and India.[13] So far the recognition by political leaders, business leaders, and trendsetting opinion makers that Malaysia belongs to the front tier and not the back tier or middle tier of nations has been slow to emerge, despite the hype in some quarters.[14]

At the same time, the risk of going too far forward too fast stalks all Malay modernizers. Profitability without social responsibility might lead Malays in Malaysia by the year 2020, if not sooner, to be crazed with material concerns and become neglectful of their rich Islamic heritage. To avert that possibility, Mahathir has seemed to pick an untainted successor, an embodiment of cultural purity and religious high-mindedness. At least many observers feel that it was for this reason that he selected, then groomed, Anwar Ibrahim, the former leader of the Islamic Students' movement, to be his deputy prime minister.[15]

But the larger lesson of the Malaysian dalliance with corporate culture may be to reinforce the autonomy of religion on the spiritual plane: religion as religion can converge with neither economics nor culture. Ideology often obscures the automony of religion since a parochial cultural view can project itself as a universal ethical norm. The stress on individual human rights within the United Nations, for instance, is not universally applied since economic rights, often translated as basic survival rights, have often been denied to marginalized countries. Consider the examples of post-1991 Iraq and Burma/Myanmar.

The opposite danger also looms large: a universal view may become projected into a parochial one, especially when the high-tech era encourages a selective reading of premodern history. Here the major victim is Islamic civilization itself. Luxuriant in the premodern period, it is now in danger of being squandered by too many nation-state orthodoxies, competing with each other, and often canceling each other out, all in the name of Allah's will and for the common good of the Muslim community.

Finally, there is the danger of appropriating a single global economic pattern or a particular political order as if it were a universal good, as if it had been sacralized by God and hence was incumbent on all believers to uphold and pursue. With reference to Islam, as to other universal religions, it needs to be said again and again: neither Islam nor Buddhism nor Christianity is a culture; the major social function of each is to criticize, and so to purify, cultures that already exist.[16]

Because religion cannot be fully harnessed to any social or economic system, believers are often faced with a painful, if inchoate, dilemma: they can talk about the existing order only in its own terms, not in a specifically religious idiom. In the case of Islam and corporate culture in Malaysia, that means abandoning the usual effort to relate a new approach to Qur'anic antecedents when the objective is not advocacy of Islamic economics but Muslim participation in global economics. Othman Alhabshi, the deputy director general of IKIM, faced just this dilemma when he wanted to address all Malaysians, and not just Malay Muslims, in his essay "Corporate Ethics in the Management of Organisations." He omitted the words Muslim and Islam and any reference to Qur'an, *hadith*, or *shari'a*, yet at the crucial point in his argument, after noting how corporations today differ from their predecessors (they are fewer in number, more transnational, at once more efficient and more aggressive, but also less accountable), he tried to define corporate ethics vs. corporate culture:

> Corporate culture is the way the corporation conducts itself. It encompasses the mission, objectives, strategies, plans, values and beliefs of a corporation. What determines corporate culture is really the mission and the set of values and beliefs that the corporation is committed to. The mission can be quite independently decided, but the objectives, strategies and plans will have to be influenced both by the mission and the values. In this fashion, one can say that corporate culture is the corporation's special way of conducting itself, whilst corporate ethics is the very thing that determines the formulation of mission, objectives, strategies, plans, programmes, etc. which is actually the corporate culture. It is in this sense that corporate ethics forms the basis for corporate culture or the principal determinant of corporate culture.[17]

166

So which is it—mission subsumed under culture, or culture, meaning values and ethics, determining mission? Alhabshi, though he never cites market forces or the global economy, seems to say that value-driven perspectives can shape corporate culture no matter what the mission. Such abstract, often convoluted reasoning would be unnecessary if Alhabshi were addressing a Muslim audience, but he is trying to appeal to non-Muslims as well as to Muslims. A year earlier in the same journal he had pronounced that Islam *is* the way, the only way, to achieve Vision 2020.[18] He is closer to realeconomik when he detheologizes his ethical message, since the overall pattern of change in East Asia and globally suggests that the dynamics of corporate culture will continue to restrict the counterforce of value-directed ethics, however plausibly framed, however earnestly advocated.

Still another limitation emerges from Malay-Chinese relations. It is the second of two simultaneous fronts for the expansion of Islamic norms in East Asia, as Malay and Chinese come to symbolize Islam and East Asia in the near-term future. The challenge involves more than sorting out Malaysia's multiracial society on quota lines, a practice that began with the preindependence accords of 1957. Political dominance was decreed to Malays, with safeguards for Chinese, Indians, and others. But since Malays were underrepresented in professions and business, the federal constitution stipulated that they receive preferential treatment in the award of both university scholarships and business contracts.

Political maturity has been deferred in Malaysia because Malays continue to be represented in just one political party, UNMO, with PAS as the Islamic spoiler, and Chinese and Indians each having separate political parties but little effective power. For instance, in 1991 the Chinese political party, known as the Malaysian Chinese Association, proposed spending M$5 million on a Chinese cultural center. But UNMO objected to this public testimony to Chinese culture within Malaysia, and MCA had to withdraw its proposal.[19]

Mahathir has survived as prime minister of Malaysia for over fifteen years in part because he continues to recognize the potential political damage of having competing ethnic consitutencies, each ratcheting up the claims of its group against other Malays perceived as both other and rival. In mid-1995 he made still another plea for "Bangsa Malaysia," namely, for people to "identify themselves with the country, speak Bahasa Malaysia, and accept the Constitution" and ultimately remove the special bumiputra privileges that apply mainly to Muslim Malays. [20]

Yet, however Mahathir engineers the move to genuine Malayness, executive decisions alone will not resolve the crucial dilemma for Malay identity. Pluralism has to be grounded in civil society, as it functions parallel to, but not always in tandem with, the state and political society. Crucial questions remain: how can Chinese and Malay actually integrate? Beyond the orbit of Kuala Lumpur politics, how do other Malaysians approach the vast chasm between two world views and their civilizational antecedents? And what is to be the role of Malay women?

The tentative answer appears in two conferences with identical titles, but different subtitles, that were convened in Malaysia in 1995. Most of the papers wallowed in vague generalities, offering ad hominem testimonials on behalf of Islamic universalism without exploring how that universalism accommodates the equally persistent universalism of Chinese, most of whom are not now and never will be Muslim. With the exception of one paper (discussed below) that talked about pre-Muslim cultural values and the need for Muslims to affirm them, the presenters, all of them Muslim, relied on ex cathedra pronouncements about history or doctrine and broke no new ground. Moreover, the shift in format from the first to the second conference suggested an increasing intellectual isolationism on the part of most Muslim participants. The general tenor of the first conference, despite the sterility of most of the papers, was to promote a civilizational dialogue, but by the convening of the second conference, a bare six months later, the recurrent accent had shifted to the universality of Islam. It was as if to underscore the universality of Islam that nearly all the papers highlighted a Chinese Muslim diaspora from the People's Republic of China to several parts of Asia. Ignored in the rush to combine Muslim and Chinese everywhere was the content of what might constitute a common Chinese-Muslim world view and set of practices. Grand appeals to the function of a Confucian rhetoric in Muslim guise, or an Islamic interpretation of the *Analects of Confucius*, only reinforced an incipient inclusivism.

If the above conferences do move beyond form to substance, and if the first rather than the second portends future developments, a long-term reflowering of Malayness as a composite pluralist culture is possible, and not only corporate culture but also transnational tolerance may be the outcome.

The role of women, however, is less clear. While Sisters in Islam has been functioning for over a decade from Kuala Lumpur and includes some pioneering women intellectuals in its ranks, their primary impact has come through the monograph on Qur'anic interpretation authored by an African American scholar teaching in Malaysia. Amina Wadud-Muhsin's *Qur'an and Woman* gives generous and deserved credit to the Malay activist Dr. Chandra Muzaffar at the same time that it provides fresh insight into the Islamic/Qur'anic view of women's roles.[21] Within Malaysia itself, however, the impact of the book seems negligible, and when a government-sponsored think tank like IKIM does write about religion as a social force, it is without women participants; rather, it is male authors who discuss not only politics, law, and economics, but also education and the family.[22]

Despite the underutilization of women in charting Vision 2020, it does not follow that the dominant future for Malays, as for other Muslims, will be to pursue the urge to cultural isolationism, confrontation, and war, as has been argued by theorists like Huntington and Fukuyama and journalists like Fallows and the anonymous contributors to *The Economist*.

Attention to the very construct jihad shows how subtle, yet determinative, can be the Muslim difference from Southeast Asia. It reflects an intra-Muslim struggle as much as a Muslim struggle with non-Muslim others. Consider Mahathir's reflection on the dilemma of his country vis-à-vis the Gulf War and the Balkan conflict. In both cases, Malaysia was forced to comply with the actions of the dominant Western powers. In a unipolar world, "might alone makes right," as Shaykh Fadlallah noted in his theorizations on jihad (discussed below). But Mahathir also had to voice his frustration after Iraq's defeat. On the one hand, he denounced Iraq for its greed, but on the other, he denounced "those who hold back the Muslim people and nations by drawing their attention to the next world to the neglect of duties and potentials in this world." He was, in effect, reprimanding his own constituents, Malays who remained backward not only compared with the industrial world but also with their Chinese copatriots. To them, his message was

169

progress not procrastination. "The truth is that if Muslims cannot go after progress in this world and succeed like the non-Muslims, then there is the likelihood that they will become frustrated and eventually lose their faith in Islam. Poverty and weakness will lead to apostasy, so there shall be no hereafter for them."

Vision 2020 becomes more than a vague slogan; it holds out the sole alternative to a backward, weak Malaysia, lumped together with a backward, weak Muslim world.

Is Mahathir's vision so different from traditional jihad? His plea is for an all-out effort not with weapons and war but with brains and technology. Malaysia in 2020 should be nothing less than "an advanced nation capable of self-upliftment through the mastery of knowledge and skills," and at the same time a nation "professing high moral values and able to complete with other advanced nations in all fields."[23]

While the day for parity on a global scale has not yet arrived for Malaysia, it is possible to see how a Muslim perspective revalues both the Gulf War and the Balkan conflict. Yet it is difficult to hear either Mahathir's dissent from the Western public policy view of justice or his concomitant appeal for a Muslim perspective on global events. At the close of the twentieth century, it is the Fukuyamas and Huntingtons, together with the Fallowses and yellow press internationalists, who continue to dominate most media representation of issues that shape Islam and Muslims.

While Muslims themselves must bear some responsibility for being an absent or negative voice in the major geopolitical issues of the day, it is still necessary to note that they are victimized, along with most of the South, by the structure of international news. Not only English-language media but English-language media reflecting specifically North European-North American viewpoints dominates: 90 percent of international news comes from the standard wire-services of Europe and America. Even the Saudi purchase of United Press International will not change the nature of news, especially since the Saudis themselves are masters at the double standard of professing one set of ideals and pursuing with blinkers another, opposite value standard.[24]

More importantly, the level of debate about international issues is already remote from, and may even be seen to cover up, ground-level realities. Few newspapers or periodicals, and no news programs on televison or radio, attend to structural disparities between the G-7 countries and the rest of the world. Instead, the Fukuyama/Huntington thesis,[25] as Chandra Muzaffar pointedly observed, has sparked a pseudo-debate. It serves as a smokescreen camouflaging the real post-1989 global crisis: the monopoly of resources, and so policy options for change, by the major advanced industrial nations, the G-7.[26]

In other words, a Muslim world power, despite the hype that such a power is to be feared by the West, is remote if not impossible, and instead countries like Malaysia must aim for limited economic progress while also holding out for "profitability with social responsibility."[27] The twin challenge facing Malaysia and the Muslim world, in Mahathir's words, is twofold: "to re-create a living civilization of Islam that was once dynamic and thriving, and to make a positive contribution to the predicament facing mankind."[28] Not more Muslims but better Muslims, not a regression to fundamentalism "which tends to be preoccupied with forms and symbols, rituals and practices,"[29] but a progress to corporate culture both within and beyond the *umma*.

The obstacles, of course, are evident. Two loom largest: (1) Malaysia itself is politically unified but not culturally uniform. The values espoused by upwardly mobile middle-class Malays may not be shared by their coreligionists who are not urban or their countrymen who are not Muslims, namely, the significant Chinese minority and the prominent, if less numerous, Indian minority. One writer has even gone so far as to suggest that the ethic Mahathir labels as "Islamic," implying its resonance with the universal norms of Islam, is in fact class-based, driven by Mahathir's own authoritarian, petit bourgeois upbringing that stressed values which sound strangely Confucian or Calvinist rather than intrinsically Islamic: "diligence, thrift, striving, perseverance, self-improvement, self-reliance, and attainment."[30] (2) The move to inscribe corporate culture as an Islamic ethos for the New Malay may be conflictual. It may represent not a step forward for Islam but a regression from Muslim norms of family loyalty and social responsibility. After all, the cornerstone of corporate culture is greed, not need. Can even skilled politicians like Mahathir or his likely successor, Anwar Ibrahim, engineer a social revolution in Malay economic thinking while also putting "fear of God" into those who engage in bribery or corruption? Bribery persists, as does corruption, though their scale and significance remain open to debate.[31]

171

The other side of Mahathir's and Malaysia's struggle to find an Islamic ethic that works in a pluralist, modernizing society is the rearguard engagement with jihad. Jihad has not disappeared, either from the historical memory or from the symbolic repertoire of Muslim societies. How can one keep in check the tendency to see the Islamic engagement with jihad as either (a) a systemic flaw of Islam as a universal religion or (b) a uniform characteristic of all Muslims in all circumstances? The only safety valve is constant vigilance, looking at Islamic norms as specific cultural constructs and the modern world as a further set of sociocultural constructs.

To the extent that jihad and corporate culture can be summarized as competing Muslim world views, they go beyond the contrasting visions of late-twentieth-century Islamic leaders, such as Ayatollah Khomeini and Mohammed Mahathir, and one needs to reevaluate jihad before claiming that it is the enemy of all progress, either in economics or in civil society.

Jihad is best approached as a multivalent category of reference within the Islamic symbol system. It is not limited to "holy war," nor is it decisive to the Qur'an if one considers all the themes and counterthemes of that book of revelation on its own terms. It is especially important to see how jihad has itself been subject to change, from the earliest period of Muslim history to the Sunni-Shi'i appropriation of religious authority to modern-day revisionist packagings of Muslim norms and values.

It is necessary to begin with the Qur'an. A crucial principle, internal to the Qur'an, is that of abrogation (*naskh*). The Qur'an provides the basis for its own continuously revised interpretation (2:106, 13:37, 16:101, 22:52). God's transcendence above human knowing, His sovereignty beyond human attempts to appropriate, and so limit, His power extends even to His final self-disclosure in prophecy, the Qur'an. The Qur'an ended prophecy but not divine intervention in human affairs. While Muhammad lived, the book remained open; it could always be updated. With his death (in 632 C.E.), the question of leadership for his community also raised the related question: what would be the nature, and the limits, of ongoing divine intervention? Sunnis and Shi'is have responded to these twin problems in opposite ways. The Sunnis have closed the book, applying its 'clear' directives to juridical legislation. They have also closed ranks around a discrete set of leaders who defend the book and the will of the majority. They are caliphs, their shibboleth is order, their fear is sedition/discord/disbelief.[32] Shi'is accepted the book but often located decisive meanings within the ambiguous or allegorical verses (3:7), at the same time that they posited a continuing source of oral revelation in a set of leaders who are related to the Prophet Muhammad both by kinship and by piety. They are imams, their shibboleth is justice, their fear is tyranny/oppression/disbelief.

While belief in the Qur'an and rejection of disbelief are traits common to both Sunni and Shi'i Muslims, that commonality does not allow the construction of a theory of either just war or revolution that would lump them together under one umbrella rubric labeled "The Muslim View of Jihad." Rather, acknowledging difference as basic to any sociology of Islam, we must pursue an alternate strategy. We must nuance discussion of jihad, first by recognizing it as a leitmotif of Islamic ideology, and second by exploring its variant expressions among Sunni and Shi'i theorists as well as Sunni and Shi'i activists.

Especially marked is the Shi'ite difference. For Imami or 12er Shi'is, who comprise the majority of the Shi'ite community, jihad is not indefinitely deferred, nor is it held in abeyance till the return of the hidden Imam. Jihad is constantly extolled. And it can be waged not only by the hidden Imam but by one who has been chosen by the Imam, an individual whose scholarship and piety ensures that he has been commissioned by the Imam, that is, a Shi'i cleric. And also, the enemy against whom jihad must be waged is not merely the outsider "infidel" or non-Muslim. It is also those Muslims who have not accepted true Islam. Since true Islam can only be Imami Shi'i Islam, there are many enemies who are other "Muslims." As one student of the classical Imami juridical sources has noted, the classification of enemy encompasses "the entire hateful Sunni world, a world held responsible for all the harassment and persecution to which the Shi'is were subjected throughout the ages."[33]

While the legal position of Imami jurists has seldom translated into day-to-day action, it is foolhardy, as well as wrong, to deny that there is a Shi'i difference on the issue of "holy war" in Islam. The Shi'i difference is not only real, it is also pervasive. To highlight that difference and bring it into discussion at the level that it merits, we will explore the best known, and least understood, Sunni and Shi'i cases.

The textbook Sunni case for jihad comes from the dissident group in Egypt (also named al-Jihad), which not only plotted against the pharaoh but killed him. President Sadat fell to assassin bullets in October 1981. Those who killed him invoked jihad as their cause; an ideologue who supported the same cause wrote a short tract titled *al-Farida al-Gha'iba* (The missing precept), which pointedly referred to jihad. Both the group and its ideology have been the subject of intensive scrutiny from many quarters. They have also spawned look-alike groups in other dissident circles of the current skewed political system called the Middle East.[34] Yet none of the vast, and still growing, literature about them challenges the above conclusions: Jihad does not succeed in mobilizing an ideology that could replace the modern nation-state with an alternate polity. Those who advocate jihad have been reduced to the role of terrorists even when, as in the case of the Palestinian Jihad group and also Hamas, they are counterrevolutionaries struggling to reclaim a national homeland.

The anachronism of jihad-type groups may be seen from the fate of those who have attempted to fulfill the vision inspiring Sadat's assassins. Those who invoke jihad have neither mass support nor the military firepower to challenge the omnipresent, and nearly omnipotent, Egyptian security forces. And why does jihad no longer generate popular appeal nor pose a threat to nation-state polities in the Sunni Muslim world? Fouad Ajami, himself a scholar turned news analyst, has provided an answer at once simple and grim. Jihad advocates function as terrorists, with all the hope and fear that the enterprise of terrorism evokes. Yet "when terrorism becomes commonplace . . . it can be accepted. What begins as a challenge to the state ends up confirming its rationality. . . . The state is said to be (by its custodians, by its many, many spokespersons) the only dike against great upheaval and disorder [read: *fitna*]. This is a game that all states play; this also happens to be a game at which the Egyptian state is particularly skilled."[35] And it is a game that they continue to play relentlessly in the mid-1990s. When Egyptian terrorists, stifled at home, bombed the Egyptian embassy in Islamabad, the bodies of "martyrs" were brought home to a state-sponsored funeral that featured loud outcries against the tyranny of terrorists. In other words, the state continues to make clear to doubtful outsiders, and also protesting insiders, that "it is the only dike against *fitna*."

While further eruptions of jihad-coded violence will take place in the Sunni Muslim world, they will be minor irritations rather than large-scale threats to the authoritarian regimes who continue to control all the instruments of state power, not only military and political, not only social and economic, but also religious and ideological. "There is substantial evidence," notes the historian Emmanuel Sivan, "of a long-standing and conscious effort on the part of territorial states to create a network of symbol-laden, stylized and repetitive social activities to define a meaningful focus of group loyalty, i.e., the national entity." As a result, Sunni fundamentalists "seem quite pessimistic as to their own chances. Most of their work takes place in the private sphere (e.g., in mosques that are privately-owned and not state-controlled, or in voluntary and welfare associations). They see the public sphere dominated by the state and its 'secular religion.' "[36]

At the same time, there has been an attempt at broad-scale revisionism on the meaning of jihad among the proponents of a modern Sunni world view. Chief among them is Muhammad Shahrur, a Syrian engineer turned Qur'anic exegete. In his most recent book of essays, *Dirasat Islamiyat Mu'asirat (fi dawlah wal-mujtama')* (Contemporary Islamic studies of the state and society), Shahrur argues that the first meaning of jihad is to defend freedom of belief and to oppose compulsion in religion. It then becomes extended to include protection of a community by those who uphold freedom of belief, along with other rights, and it is always directed against tyranny (*'unf*). While Shahrur's views are not shared by all Syrian scholars, especially those who view with contempt any nonspecialist advocating a new approach to Qur'anic interpretation, his is a weather vane of critical inquiry, and it opens up possibilities worthy of future exploration.[37]

Among Shi'i Muslims, however, there has already emerged a different canon for measuring state power and also for projecting the ideological role of jihad. The Shi'i difference might be summarized with reference to a major contemporary Iranian theorist on jihad, coupled with a unique ethnographic account of jihad from a regional, rural Iranian perspective. Both help to inform not only the Shi'i-Sunni distinction on "holy war" but also the new invocation of jihad as struggle by Mahathir in Southeast Asia.

The theoretician whose writings seem most apt is Ayatollah Mortaza Motahhari, discussed in an earlier chapter for his approach to the roles of Muslim women. Motahhari was among the foremost Iranian clerics, a man whom Khomeini once described as "the fruit of my life" and "a part of my flesh." Although he was killed in 1979 at the outset of the Iranian Revolution, his numerous speeches, articles, and pamphlets are still widely quoted, and several, including a small pamphlet titled *Jihad: The Holy War of Islam and Its Legitimacy in the Quran*, have been translated into English. The pamphlet itself sorts out into a series of four lectures, all of which were delivered in the early 1960s, long before the Iranian Revolution and probably as part of a monthly debating colloquium (*guftar-i mah*), attended by secularists as well as clerics. We are less concerned to look at the Qur'anic justifications for jihad that Motahhari adduces than to delineate what stands out as an approach at once distinctively Shi'ite in method and characteristically modern in tone. Distinctively Shi'ite is the subtlety of exegetical techniques, so subtle that an entire lecture (#4) is dedicated to the question of abrogated verses. In Motahhari's view, abrogation requires always interpreting the unconditional as the conditional, so that a general injunction about jihad (e.g., 9:73 "O Prophet! Fight the *kuffar* [disbelievers] and hypocrites and be stern against them) must be qualified by the following, more complete *aya* (2:190): "And fight in the path of God with those who are fighting with you and do not transgress, God loves not those who transgress." While Sunni *fuqaha* or jurists use a variety of *hadiths* or Prophetic traditions to justify what would be called *jus in bello*, Motahhari is able to set forth specific guidelines solely with reference to an inferential reading of Surah 2:190. In his view, the only enemy to be opposed are soldiers on the battlefield, and even then only after they have been declared transgressors.[38]

Jihad, for Motahhari, is always defensive. Aggression is an absolute, unmitigated evil. He excoriates aggression yet quickly adds "all war, on all sides, is not always aggression. War can be aggression but it can also be a reply to aggression, for sometimes the reply to aggression must be given by force."[39] Since only defensive war is justified, one is obliged to delineate what it is that must be defended. On this point, again using the exegetical principle of interpreting the unconditional through the conditional, Motahhari reasons that all oppressed Muslims can be defended, including and especially the Palestinians. "We may be in a situation," he suggests,

176

whereby a party has not transgressed against us but has committed some type of injustice against a group from another people, who may be Muslims, or who may be non-Muslims. If they are Muslims—like today's plight of the Palestinians who have been exiled from their homes, whose wealth has been seized, who have been subjected to all kinds of transgression—while, for the moment, the transgressor has no intentions against us, is it permissible for us in such circumstances to hurry to the help of those oppressed Muslims and deliver them or is this not permissible? Certainly [it is]."[40]

If defensive war can be justified on behalf of the Palestinians, it can also be cast in a still larger frame of reference. It is one thing to fight against transgression that afflicts one's rights as an individual or a tribe or a nation. While such assertion of self-defense is justified, there is a still higher form of defense. According to Motahhari,

There exists something superior to the rights of the individual or nation. Something more holy, more sacred, the defense of which in accordance to the human conscience is higher than the defense of individual rights. And that something is the rights of humanity. [He goes on to detail what is meant by such rights, and then concludes]. I do not think that anyone has any doubts that the holiest form of jihad and the holiest form of war is that which is fought in defense of humanity and of humanity's rights.

Such a paean to idealism demands a practical illustration of its feasibility, and Motahhari goes on to provide it:

During the period in which the Algerians were at war with the French colonialists, a group of Europeans helped them in their war and the jihad of such people was holier than the jihad of the Algerians, because the Algerians were defending the cause of their own rights, while the cause of the others was more ethical and more sacred than that of the Algerians.[41]

In short, any group of people who are fighting for freedom of belief or freedom of thought deserves support from outsiders, and those who offer such support, even if they be non-Muslims supporting other non-Muslims, are waging the greatest jihad, a jihad on behalf of the universal rights of humanity.

Few contemporary Muslim ideologues rival Motahhari in expanding and redefining jihad. Within a Shi'i frame of reference, one might be the renowned spokesperson for the Shi'i community of southern Lebanon, Shaykh Muhammad Husain Fadlallah. Shaykh Fadlallah underscores the feasibility of jihad as a kind of da'wa. Unlike classical jurists, he argues that da'wa or calling the world to Islam cannot be implemented apart from jihad. For Shaykh Fadlallah, jihad is always dynamic, always interactive; it is not, in the absence of the Hidden Imam, restricted to reactive or defensive strategies. In Foucauldian terms, Shaykh Fadlallah asserts that power (quwwa) is the generic, foundational quality of human life. The major question becomes how to relate the universal urge to secure power in a distinctly Islamic framework. His response is to affirm jihad as a subcategory of quwwa that is also inseparable from da'wa. Jihad is both required and legalized by the Islamic need for power.[42] Unlike Motahhari, however, Shaykh Fadlallah does not project the scope of jihad beyond the boundaries of the Muslim community (Dar al-Islam), nor does he suggest that non-Muslims can wage jihad, including the best of all jihads, which is the jihad waged on behalf of humankind.

If Motahhari remains the foremost Shi'i theorist on jihad, the imaginative thrust of his rhetoric has thus far not translated into ground-level tactical successes for the Islamic Republic of Iran. Instead, there has emerged a practical reexamination of jihad precisely because of its widespread invocation to justify not just waging the war against Iraq but using very young, untrained combatants to face a professional army furnished with modern weapons, both legal and illegal. Iranian reactions to the jihad against Iraq provide us with a unique case instance about Muslim resort to "holy war." The official justification for conducting a war that in the end claimed more than a million lives, most of them Iranian youth, was the necessary struggle between Islam and blasphemy. Ayatollah Khomeini was masterful in shaping the discourse of debate in terms of category differences that seemed airtight and inflexible. In speech after speech throughout the 1980s, he forced his internal adversaries to oppose not only the war but also God, Islam, and the Prophet Muhammad as well as the glorious revolution and its fruit, the Islamic Republic of Iran. "The war between Iran and the Iraqi Baathis," he onced declared, " is the war between Islam and infidelity, between the Qur'an and atheism."[43]

If opposition to the Iran-Iraq War was deemed both blasphemous and traitorous, it nonetheless managed to surface. It surfaced especially in families whose children became martyrs to God's cause. Some of these voices of dissent have been narrated by an Austrian anthropologist, Reinhold Loeffler. In an extraordinary book, *Islam in Practice: Religious Beliefs in a Persian Village*, Loeffler provides numerous interviews he conducted in a village of southern Iran. There he distilled poignant voices of outrage against the dominant ideology of the Islamic Republic of Iran. Some of his informants criticized the regime largely in secular terms, such as the following:

> Now, young men with no proper training go to the front and are senselessly killed. I don't believe they are martyrs going to paradise. Who knows how many young men have been killed. If there had been a strong army, as there was under the Shah, this would not have happened. Also, when this reverend sir came to power, he immediately started to attack the whole world, made everybody his enemy. He should first have set the affairs of the country right, and then, like the Prophet, worked to gradually establish Islam and to create an example of true Islamic life. Then the world would have said, "Look, how truly human that society is," and come toward Islam all by itself.[44]

But others faulted Khomeini for identifying too closely with the Last Imam:

> He also claims to be the representative of the Last Imam, that is, that he came to prepare the way for the coming of the Last Imam. I know this cannot be true because the Last Imam himself does not know when God will order him to come. [The speaker goes on to enumerate what he perceives to be Khomeini's principal shortcomings, e.g., his flamboyance, haughtiness and vengefulness. But what most distances Khomeini from "the great ones," in his view, is lack of compassion.] Finally, the prophets and Imams were kind and compassionate. Before his final battle the Imam Husayn exempted his followers from the obligation of jihad so that they might save their lives. Khomeini, however, pitilessly incites people to go to their deaths. All these things showed and show that his claims are unjustified. He is not what he pretends to be.[45]

Hardest for many Iranians were those moments when family members quarreled among themselves about whether or not the Iran-Iraq War was a holy war. A father-son dispute went like this:

My son now is telling me about the true Islam; they have to fight a holy war (he says) and of necessity get killed. I tell him *there is no holy war in the absence of the Last Imam*. He shouts at me saying I do not understand a thing. These young ones are like unfledged birds. When they try to fly, they fall from the tree and a cat eats them. They cannot discern the right road. I tell him to stay out of everything, to mind his own business, and do his studies; it's not the right time. But he won't listen. He will get hurt.[46]

The bitterest lament of all conjoins despair about the war dead with betrayal of the deepest ideals of Shi'ism, to strive for justice, which is to say, freedom and humanity:

Some of the clergy wore their garb to gather people around themselves and make them devoted to themselves. But they did not pursue the essence of religion, that is, freedom and humanity. The Imam Husayn whom they are flaunting so much now—again only outwardly, not in truth—fought for that freedom and humanity and in this struggle sacrificed himself and his family. The Muharram celebration should be a remembrance of this and a reminder for us to follow his order to do the same, that is, not to submit to oppression but to fight it. But the mullahs never taught us that. . . . They were right when they called for a revolution against the Shah because he was an oppressor. *But I don't think that this was a real revolution*. The clergy do not allow it that those basic principles, freedom and humanity, become established. In the past it was repression by the Shah, now it is repression by the clergy.

They refuse to stop this war in which our young men are being killed for no reason. They simply tell them that if they get killed, they will go to paradise. This is a very cheap thing to say. Is there a proof of it? Of course we believe in the after-world. But in a matter of such gravity, when thousands and thousands of young men are sent to their deaths in this belief, one should have especially strong evidence. We are seeing what is going on and we know they are telling lies, but we cannot say it. If we open up our mouths, they shut them by force. Like our former landlords, they have gathered a bunch of illiterate youngsters around themselves by giving them much more money than they could otherwise earn and telling them to suppress us.[47]

These are admittedly random voices, taken from but one village by a single anthropologist. They do not include women's voices, nor do they record the same voice over a span of years, except in rare instances. Yet the sample is reflective of a range of popular sentiments about the Islamic Republic of Iran and its rulers. It demonstrates that despite an elaborate mobilization campaign by the government, as well as efforts both material and symbolic either to accommodate bereaved families or to force compliance with the war effort, many Iranians doubted the "divine-demonic" nature of the Iran-Iraq War; they resisted its classification as a "holy war."

Perhaps even more significant for the future of the Islamic Republic of Iran is the way in which the very concept of jihad has been expanded to include a social, and also an economic, rather than a purely military or political dimension. While complaints are rife about how badly some members of the clerical leadership have handled their political responsibilities since 1979, one also reads about the extensive efforts to bring social justice to Iranian villages. *Jihad Sazendegi* was created in 1979 as a grass-roots movement to bring rural Iran into the modern age. Despite the promise of the White Revolution under the shah, rural Iran remained a symbol of bureaucratic incompetence, compounded by royal neglect. The task of *Jihad Sazendegi* was to construct rural roads, electric lines, portable water systems, sewerage systems, schools, mosques, and health clinics. The pace of improvements was slowed down by the eight year Iran-Iraq War, but by 1990, according to official sources, 50,000 kilometers of rural roads had been built, more than 10,000 villages provided clean water, and almost 5,000 new village schools built.[48] One could quickly add that the urban poor, the so-called *mostazafin*, did not fare as well under the Islamic Republic of Iran, yet the government has tried to cope with the worst urban areas, at the same time that it has maintained its level of rural development. In both urban and rural arenas the notion of jihad is central to mobilizing public interest, and grass-roots involvement. Economic jihad, admittedly less glamorous and less dangerous than military jihad, remains a high priority for post-1989 Iran.

· · · · ·

From the above examples of jihad "holy war," it becomes clear that the rhetoric of "holy war" changes its relevance in the actual circumstances of Muslim polities past and present. Above all, one cannot trace just war theory in an Islamic context without first delineating differences between Sunni and Shiʿi norms. For Sunni

Muslims, the invocation of jihad is framed by the hegemonic strictures of the modern nation-state. No rival group within the boundaries of a majoritarian Muslim country has the power to wage war on a transregional, much less international, scale. Jihad has become little more than a pejorative codeword for random protest against excesses committed by the regime in power.

For Shiʿi Muslims, the situation seems to be more favorable, at least initially. One nation-state has adopted an explicit religious ideology and under the guise of jihad has waged war over a protracted period of time, with great cost of life and pain to the families of both martyrs and survivors. That nation, of course, is the Islamic Republic of Iran. The war it waged for eight years was against the avowedly secular, Baʿathist regime of Iraq. Yet the jihad invoked in the name of Islam by Ayatollah Khomeini failed to attain its goals. The atheist opponent was not defeated, nor was the hated enemy deposed. Even had Iranian forces been militarily successful, there would have been many devout Shiʿis who would have continued to question the appropriateness of such a war: can there be any invocation of jihad in the absence of the Hidden Imam? Can anyone, even a learned, pious cleric, convince others that he has been designated as the Hidden Imam's vicar? For many, especially illiterate or semiliterate Iranian peasants, the answer to that question was and remains "No"!

While jihad retains its symbolic valence as more than a battle cry for both Sunni and Shiʿi Muslims, the major mobilizing cry for Shiʿis remains the call to justice, symbolized by the injustice perpetrated against Husayn on the plain of Karbala, Iraq, in the late seventh century. One may reasonably doubt that the pragmatic limits to political/military jihad will curtail or deplete the spiritual élan that motivates those for whom history has still to disclose the will of a just God.[49]

If there is to be a sequel to jingoistic jihad, it may well be the alternative force of corporate culture. In the case of Malaysia, corporate culture proposes to forsake military zeal for another, more difficult battle: parity on the playing fields of free-market capitalism. In casting Mahathir as a negative voice for the future of cooperative internationalism, Fallows emphasizes two themes, both of which he ascribes unflinchingly to Mahathir: anti-Westernism and opposition to individual rights.[50] In fact, the outlook of Mahathir is more complex. It is not to reject democracy or individual rights but rather to accent the impossibility of any shift in Malaysia's status unless and until the country as a whole attains economic prowess at the global level. Whatever his shortcomings, he has tried to lead through his own example, warding off the inevitable suspicion that he would be prone to the kind of nepotism widely recognized as inextricable with Suharto and his key cohorts in neighboring Indonesia. Personal integrity, sacrifice, hard work— all are part of the image that Mahathir nurtures and projects. But he is well aware that Malays will be leery of his intentions to the extent that they have progressed less than the Chinese during the accelerated economic growth of the early 1990s. Relative to their own past Malays have already made substantial gains. Many of the younger professional class may dare to hope that under a slogan of "corporate culture with Islamic values," they will be carried to a new level of prosperity unknown to Malays of the past.

Perhaps urban Malays, who are fond of talking about Malaysia as a model for other Muslim countries, can in this one area at least devise a product worth exporting: economic jihad, the advocacy of a modern Islamic profile that combines commerce with compassion. The alternatives are grim: either a failed experiment in modernization in one of the Asian Muslim countries best poised to succeed in the Pacific century, or else an economic success story that has a Muslim patina but no Islamic core, one scarred by personal greed and self-interest rather than ennobled by a collective will committed to decency and decorum at home, justice and persistence abroad.

What seems to be more important in terms of Malaysia and Southeast Asian Islam generally is to see the multivalence of jihad as a concept that can apply to the East as well as to the West. The overwhelming rhetoric remains Islam vs. the West. But what is equally necessary is a jihad in the East, one that asserts the Islamic dimension to East Asian prosperity, not by showing how Islam is almost the same as Confucianism but rather how an Islamic difference can provide pluralism with a moral edge that includes the welfare of all and not merely the advocacy of Muslim superiority. That task has barely begun, but it is most evident in the report of a Singaporan Muslim on the cultural benefits of non-Muslims in the Greater China sphere.

Unlike others, who talk only in vague generalities about what it means to be Muslim and Malay, Riduan Wu Chia Chung Ibn Ab-

183

dullah argues that the cultural values, the family structure, and the lifestyles, including dress and eating habits, of Chinese Malaysians are not inferior to those of their Muslim Malay neighbors and political rulers. He even goes so far as to list what are acceptable Muslim approaches to Chinese ritual celebrations: Chinese New Year—yes; Qing Ming (visitation of ancestral graves)—qualified yes (don't worship them); Festival of the Hungry Ghosts—no (implies a consumer society in Hell, which is outside the bounds of acceptable Muslim belief); Funeral rites—yes; Tea Ceremony—yes. In short, he advocates an elastic practice of Islam, especially by Chinese converts to Islam, and encourages "Muslims (whether Chinese or otherwise) to attend traditional ceremonies as a mark of respect for the living and the dead while also avoiding participation in the rituals of ancestor worship that compromise Allah's Unity and Uniqueness."[51]

Even if one does not accept all the directives of Riduan Wu Chia, he has identified in graphic terms the ways that Muslim and non-Muslim values can elide in South-east Asia.

What has not yet been done is to probe the notion of jihad to the East in terms that anticipate the future of Islam as a global community embedded in an Asian as well as a non-Asian context. Jihad to the East needs to be embraced as a project where Southeast Asian Muslims can and should play a distinctive role in the future, even before 2020.

And it will have its most pivotal expression not in Malay or Chinese but in English. Why? Because whatever the outcome of Vision 2020, it is, like many dreams in Malaysia, couched in English. Mahathir was criticized in early 1994 for announcing that in university-level curricula scientific and technical subjects could be taught in English. English is a residue of the colonial experience, but it is also Malaysia's bridge to the competitive world of free-market capitalism where its leaders have pledged to make every effort to succeed. Those who protested the move to make English a science language felt that Malay would be threatened, but Prabhasa Malay has now taken deep roots in both the Chinese and Malay communities. Mahathir's was a shrewd move to keep Malaysia's cherished educational system competitive with its regional, and also global, rivals.

Mahathir also garners additional attention because of his own proclivity to speak in English. It is sometimes joked about Mahathir that he knows, and uses, English better than he does Prabhasa Malay. Throughout Southeast Asia those from countries where British colonial rule prevailed have tended to make sure that English became the language of international preference, at least for ruling elites. Their preference has prevailed during the post-colonial period. Yet, of the three ASEAN leaders who speak English—Mahathir in Malaysia, Lee in Singapore, and Ramos in the Philippines—Mahathir is the only one who is a Muslim, a Muslim representing a secular state in which Islam is the official religion.

Not only for Malays but also for other Muslims, the future may yet belong to those who learn to wage economic jihad in English. There will still be competition and confrontation; some things do not change. Yet the terms of engagement will have shifted: accommodation more than violence will be the preferred outcome for Muslims as for non-Muslims.

Notes

INTRODUCTION
ISLAM ACROSS TIME AND CULTURES

1. A paraphrase from Dr. Tawfik Abdullah, dinner conversation in Jakarta, Indonesia, 12 May 1983.

2. I am alluding to a 1990s version of the scare book genre. It comes from "an internationally recognized scholar in the field of comparative religions, the cults and the occult." Robert Morey has written more than twenty popular books. His favorite targets begin with M: Mormons, Masons, and now Muslims. In *The Islamic Invasion: Confronting the World's Fastest Growing Religion* (Eugene, Ore.: Harvest House, 1992), Morey ridicules both Islam and Muslims. His chief premise is at once simplistic and antagonistic: Islam is but "a form of cultural imperialism in which the religion and culture of seventh-century Arabia have been raised to the status of divine law" (19). Distortions, half-truths, and innuendos abound, yet the book continues to be adopted as a required text in some college-level religion courses.

3. Elaine Sciolino, "Seeing Green etc." *The New York Times Week in Review*, 21 January 1996. The bait-and-switch tone of this essay only reinforces the popular fixation on "political Islam" as the major issue, displacing concerns with other dimensions of Islamic culture and contemporary history.

4. Again the book by Morey is representative of a spate of books that reduce Islam in America to "the Black Muslim Movement," and the history of that movement since 1975, when Elijah Muhammad died, to the provocations of Louis Farrakhan (172–173). No mention is made of Elijah Muhammad's son and principal successor, Warith D. Muhammad, who happens to be both a "moderate" Muslim and a Republican!

5. For the larger picture of Bosnia, we now at last have a competent, nonpartisan history that calls into question most journalistic assessments and foreign policy initiatives. See Noel Malcolm, *Bosnia: A Short History* (New York: New York University Press, 1994), esp. 218–22 on Alija Izetbgovic. The best journalistic account remains Roy Gutmann, *Witness to Genocide* (New York: Macmillan, 1993), while a masterful documentary overview, calling into sharp question the Balkan peace process, has been provided by Rabia Ali and Lawrence Lifschultz. *Why Bosnia? Writings on the Balkan War* (Stoney Creek: The Pamphleteer's Press, 1993).

6. Frances Fukuyama, *The End of History and the Last Man* (New York: Free Press, 1992), and Samuel P. Huntington, "The Clash of Civili-

zations?" *Foreign Affairs* 72.3 (Summer 1993): 22–49. Both authors presume that the Cold War ended a major phase in modern history, and both also project Euro-American triumphalism as the logical outcome of post-1989 global capitalism. Huntington's essay, in particular, has drawn a lot of criticism, and among the most trenchant is Roy P. Mottahedeh, "The Clash of Civilizations: an Islamicist's Critique," *Harvard Middle Eastern and Islamic Review* 2.2 (1996): 1–26. Mottahedeh, rather than simply deriding his Harvard colleague for rampant essentialism and pseudo-argumentation, calls attention to the need for broader discussion of what shapes, and also limits, "large transnational cultural entities"(24).

7. Anonymous, "The Shape of the World: The Nation-State is Dead, Long Live the Nation-State," *The Economist* 23 (Dec. 95–5 Jan. 96): 17–18.

8. See Bruce Kapferer, "Nationalist Ideology and a Comparative Anthropology," *Ethnos* 54. 3–4 (1991): 161–99.

9. I have exposed the limits to this kind of thinking elsewhere, in *Defenders of God: The Fundamentalist Revolt against the Modern Age* (San Francisco: Harper & Row, 1989), 91–95.

10. Sadik al-Azm, "Islamic Fundamentalism Reconsidered," *South Asia Bulletin* 13.1 & 2 (1993): 95.

11. Robert Segal, "Joachim Wach and the History of Religions," *Religious Studies Review* 20.3 (July 1994): 200.

12. Gayatri Spivak, "Postcoloniality and Its Implications for Cultural Studies," plenary speech delivered at the 1988 convention of the Modern Language Association in San Francisco.

13. Jose Casanova. *Public Religions in the Modern World* (Chicago: University of Chicago Press, 1994): 166.

14. I take the term "perspectivist" from Steven Lukes, "Relativism in its Place," in Martin Hollis and Steven Lukes, eds., *Rationality and Relativism* (Cambridge: MIT Press, 1982), 298–305, though I disagree with Lukes that perspectivism can have only a weak form (deferring to actors' perspectives) or a strong form (acknowledging the interpreter's perspective). Lukes follows too closely Said's dictum, quoted at the end of his essay: "the student must feel he or she is answerable to and in uncoercive contact with the culture or people being studied" (305). This is a false criterion of authentic scholarship, since students will always decide what represents the culture being studied (elite or popular, textual or nontextual sources) and also which people (certainly not all the people) studied they will hold themselves accountable to. My perspectivism announces that freedom and tolerance, understood as cultural pluralism and religious multicreedalism, are decisive. One may say either that they finally do matter (weak form) or that they, and they alone, count as universal desiderata (strong form).

15. Daniel Pick, *War Machine: The Rationalisation of Slaughter in the Modern Age* (New Haven: Yale University Press, 1993), 158.

16. On the overlapping relationship of missions and missionaries with the larger colonial project of reorienting colonized subjects, see especially the evocative case study by Johannes Fabian, *Language and Colonial Power: The Appropriation of Swahili in the Former Belgian Congo 1880–1938* (New York: Cambridge University Press, 1986).

17. Izetbegovic, *Islam between East and West* (Indianapolis: American Trust Publications, 1984), 175.

18. Izetbegovic here identifies religion with "weak religion," or purely spiritual religion as identified by some Western, specifically Christian, authors. His project is to retain the applicability of the ideal while modifying the practice of Islam as a religion of harmony or balance between the spiritual and secular domains.

19. Ibid., 180–81.

20. Benedict Anderson, *Imagined Communities: Reflections on the Origin and Spread of Nationalism* (London: Verso, 1983), 116–40.

21. Lawrence, *Defenders of God*, 83–87.

22. It is on this point that both Benedict Anderson and Mark Juergensmeyer need to be corrected. The former speaks only about religion as a weakened social variable, a once dominant purveyor of values now in decline at the moment that nationalism enters its most virulent phase, i.e., late nineteenth century Western Europe (Anderson, *Imagined Communities*, 12f). Anderson never considers religion as a social force that did not weaken for all citizens of the major European nations (and the United States), nor does he recognize religion as a residual symbol world still important to so-called secular elites. Juergensmeyer, on the other hand, is overly concerned to see how religious actors and secular nationalist leaders can merge their common concerns in a future step-down from Armageddon. His is a prescriptive rather than descriptive task. The continuing incommensurability of religion and nationalism is for him an obstacle to be overcome rather than a scenario to be monitored, yet his work has the singular value of charting the numerous instances of that oxymoronic phenomenon called religious nationalism, pleading against current evidence for its peaceful advance into the next century; see Mark Juergensmeyer, *The New Cold War? Religious Nationalism Confronts the Secular State* (Berkeley and Los Angeles: University of California Press, 1993), esp. 193–202.

23. It is a mark of how thoroughly secular the debate about civil society has become that religion enters not as an independent variable but rather as a substratum of trust, justice, benevolence. From Kant to Strauss to Habermas, one can trace the effort to invoke a transcendent morality without positing the need for a Transcendent Being, and the chief debate

becomes why nationalism produced one kind of civil society in Western Europe and a very different kind in Eastern Europe. While there is much of value to pursuing this debate in its own terms, it ignores the larger shift from metaphysical to instrumental notions of truth; see Adam B. Seligman, *The Idea of a Civil Society* (Princeton: Princeton University Press, 1992), esp. 156–66.

24. Harold Bloom, *The American Religion: The Emergence of a Post-Christian Nation* (New York: Simon & Schuster, 1992), 16–17.

25. Abdallah Laroui, *The Crisis of the Arab Intellectual: Traditionalism or Historicism?* (Berkeley and Los Angeles: University of California Press, 1976), 174.

26. Liah Greenfeld, *Nationalism: Five Roads to Modernity* (Cambridge: Harvard University Press, 1993).

27. Among several exponents of this view, three stand out: Ernest Gellner, *Nations and Nationalism* (Ithaca: Cornell University Press, 1983) and *Conditions of Liberty: Civil Society and Its Rivals* (New York: Allen Lane/The Penguin Press, 1994); Eric Hobsbawm, *Nations and Nationalism since* 1870 (London: Canto Press, 1991); and Frances Fukuyama, *The End of History and the Last Man* (New York: Free Press, 1992).

28. Richard Falk, *The Endangered Planet* (New York: Vintage/Random House, 1971), 227.

29. See, e.g., Basil Davidson, *The Black Man's Burden: Africa and the Curse of the Nation-State* (New York: Times Books/Random House, 1992), for a particularly strong critique of the postcolonial legacy in sub-Saharan Africa.

30. Ranajit Guha, *Subaltern Studies* (Delhi: Oxford University Press, 1985), 4:vii.

31. All the volumes of *Subaltern Studies* articulate this viewpoint, as do Gayatri Spivak, *In Other Worlds: Essays in Cultural Politics* (New York: Methuen, 1987), and Robert Young, *White Mythologies: Writing History and the West* (London and New York: Routledge, 1990).

32. The political theorist Kenneth Waltz, for instance, treats the four P's as but four flashpoints in an argument for the danger posed by interdependence in a convergent world system; see Kenneth N. Waltz, *Theory of International Politics* (New York: McGraw-Hill, 1979), 139.

33. See Juergensmeyer, *The New Cold War?* 193–202.

34. Ibid., 50.

35. For the clearest exposition of this theory, see Bryan Turner, *Marx and the End of Orientalism* (London: George Allen Unwin, 1983), 67f. But equally damning of the absence of social change among Muslim nation-states, using the Universal Declaration of Human Rights as a yardstick, or rather a bully club, is Martin Kramer, "Islam versus Democ-

racy," *Commentary* 95.1 (Jan. 1993): 35–42. Overlooking the differentiation within and between Muslim societies is not only short-sighted, it also reinforces the cultural stereotypes invoked by such glibly ahistorical commentators as Fukuyama and Huntington in order to stoke the prospect of a "New Cold War."

36. Jalal Al-i Ahmad, *Occidentosis: A Plague from the West* (Berkeley: Mizan Press, 1984), 33–34.

37. With these few words I am sidestepping moves to privilege insider above outsider use of referents to the transcendent. One such move is to isolate God as the real object of reflection for prophets, saints, and lesser believers, while marking God as merely the *theoretical* object of consideration for theologians and other academics. A parallel move, common even before Max Weber but dominant in much academic writing about religion since his time, is to separate interpretation from explanation, claiming for one discipline (the history of religions) the sole ability to *explain* religious phenomena while allowing the social sciences the related but less exalted task of *interpreting* these same phenomena. Robert Segal has exposed how this move has played out in the dominant branch of history of religion; especially in *Religious Studies Review* 20.3 (July 1994): 197–201. Another move, which has gained prominence among neo-Tillichians in mainline Protestant circles, is to distinguish between first-order and second-order discourse, as does George Lindbeck, *The Nature of Doctrine: Religion and Theology in a Postliberal Age* (Philadelphia: Westminster, 1984).

The problem with all these moves, whether polemical or apologetic or both, is their implicit ranking of those who engage in God-talk while ignoring the major issue: is there or is there not a nonmaterial force influencing, perhaps even directing, human activity? The realm of the imagination has not hesitated to say YES, and even though the voices do not accord the Other the same name, it is necessary to accent the common ground that they occupy vis-à-vis rank materialists, closet atheists, or scientizing triumphalists, all of whom deny the very existence of the Other, except, of course, as "a figment of the imagination."

38. Muhammad Qutb, *Islam: The Misunderstood Religion* (Damascus: The Holy Koran Publishing House, 1977), 52.

39. Sayyid Qutb, *Maʿalim fi't-Tariq* (Milestones on the Path) (Cairo: Dar ash-Shuruq, 1964), 146. One of Sayyid Qutb's most popular tracts, it has often been translated into English, and the above quotation can be found also in Sayyid Qutb, *Milestones* (Cedar Rapids, Iowa: Unity Publishing, n.d.), 126. On the rhetoric of *hakimiyya*, there now exists the unprecedented and invaluable two-part study of Islamic fundamentalism in a comparative context by Sadik al-Azm; see "Islamic Fundamentalism Reconsidered."

40. Ahmad Moussalli, *Radical Islamic Fundamentalism: The Ideological and Political Discourse of Sayyid Qutb* (Beirut: American University of Beirut, 1992), 241.

41. Raimundo Panikkar, "Religion or Politics: The Western Dilemma" in Ninian Smart and Peter Merkl, eds., *Religion and Politics in the Modern World* (New York: New York University Press, 1983), 46.

42. Jacob Landau, *The Politics of Pan-Islam: Ideology and Organization* (Oxford: Oxford University Press, 1990), 311.

43. James Piscatori, *Islam in a World of Nation-States* (Cambridge: Cambridge University Press, 1986), 77. Not only on this point but in his general approach, Piscatori highlights the need for constant vigilance in separating rhetoric from outcome, polemics from pragmatic action. His book confirms a hopeful, long-range view of Muslim polities that is at variance with most media assessments even as it is consonant with the arguments here advanced. For a useful update of his approach, see the analysis forged with Dale Eickelman in *Muslim Politics* (Princeton: Princeton University Press, 1996).

44. Albert Hourani, *Islam in European Thought* (Cambridge: Cambridge University Press, 1991), 73.

45. Bassam Tibi, *Arab Nationalism: A Critical Enquiry* (New York: St. Martin's Press, [1981] 1990), 87.

46. Leonard Binder, *Islamic Liberalism* (Chicago: University of Chicago Press, 1988), 280.

47. Marilyn Waldman, "The Islamic World," *Encyclopaedia Britannica Macropaedia* (Chicago: Britannica Publishing, 1987), 130.

48. The most egregrious examples of this approach are James Bill and Carl Leiden, *Politics in the Middle East* (Boston: Little, Brown, 1979), and Edward Mortimer, *Faith and Power: The Politics of Islam* (New York: Random House, 1982). More nuanced, balancing Islam as world view with attention to numerous, often competing Muslim ideologies, especially in the introduction and conclusion, is James Piscatori, ed. *Islam in the Political Process* (Cambridge: Cambridge University Press, 1983).

49. The most subtle example of this approach is Clifford Geertz, *Islam Observed: Religious Development in Morocco and Indonesia* (Chicago: University of Chicago Press, 1968), though one must quickly add in defense of Geertz's approach that he tries to retrieve a cultural boundedness for *all* social existence that earlier analysts of Muslim history largely ignored. Other scholars, less sensitive than Geertz to the colonial optic, include Christopher Harrison, *France and Islam in West Africa, 1860–1960* (New York: Cambridge University Press, 1988), and Ian Talbot, *The Punjab and the Raj, 1849–1947* (Riverdale: Riverdale Company, 1988).

50. David Laitin, *Hegemony and Culture: Politics and Religious Change among the Yoruba* (Chicago: University of Chicago Press, 1986), 164–69, has detailed the similarities and differences in a West African context.

51. Richard Fox, "East of Said," in Richard Fox, ed. *Nationalist Ideologies and the Production of National Cultures* (Washington, D.C.: American Anthropological Association, 1990).

52. For a broad global view of this protracted rivalry, see Geoffrey Barraclough, ed., *The Times Atlas of World History* (Maplewood, N.J.: Hammond, 1982), 207–95. For a region-specific view that takes account of all of Asia, see Rhoads Murphey, *A History of Asia* (New York: HarperCollins, 1992).

53. Huri Islamoglu-Inan, ed., *The Ottoman Empire and the World-Economy* (Cambridge: Cambridge University Press, 1987), and Resat Kasaba, *The Ottoman Empire and the World Economy: The Nineteenth Century* (Albany: State University of New York Press, 1988).

54. Turner, *Marx and the End of Orientalism*, highlights this argument, especially in chaper 4.

55. Delacroix's thesis is restated in Lisa Anderson, "Obligation and Accountability: Islamic Politics in North Africa," *Daedalus* 120.3 (1991): 93–121.

56. Georges Corm, *Fragmentation of the Middle East: The Last Thirty Years* (London: Hutchinson, 1988), 137.

57. For a thorough, often critical review of these trends, one can do no better than Hooshang Amirahmadi, *Revolution and Economic Transition: The Iranian Experience* (Albany: State University of New York Press, 1990).

58. Marshall Hodgson, *The Venture of Islam: Conscience and History in a World Civilization* (Chicago: University of Chicago Press, 1979), 3:176–222.

59. Michael Gilsenan, *Recognizing Islam: Religion and Society in the Modern Arab World* (New York: Pantheon, 1982), 215.

60. Charles Barone, *Marxist Thought on Imperialism: Survey and Critique* (Armonk, N.Y.: M. E. Sharpe, 1985), 115f, provides a keen exposition and broad-scale critique of Marxist theory on this point.

61. The degree of influence can be overstated, however, as is the case with the unidirectional and triumphalist thesis of Theodore Van Laue in *The World Revolution of Westernization* (New York: Oxford University Press, 1987).

62. For the Iranian case, there is much evidence of global patterns impinging on local contexts, often with unanticipated consequences. See especially Paul Vieille and Farhad Khosrokhavar, *Le Discours populaire*

de la revolution iranienne, 2 vols. (Paris: Contemporaneite, 1990), and also Erika Friedl, *Women of Deh Koh: Women's Lives in an Iranian Village* (Washington, D.C.: Smithsonian, 1989), the companion study to Reinhold Loeffler, *Islam and Practice: Religious Lives in a Persian Village* (Albany: State University of New York Press, 1988).

63. I agree with James Piscatori that we cannot absolutize successive stages of Muslim protest, implying that the rhythm of history explains *all* social change and potential development; see his critique of Hamid Enayat in *Islam in a World of Nation-States*, (1986) 36. Yet it still seems valuable to differentiate the sequence of public responses to British, French, and Dutch colonial empires. The unexpected has happened and will continue to happen, but sketching patterns of possibility can help understand a long-term process, even when the next turn in the road remains invisible, and the road itself very bumpy.

CHAPTER 1
THE THREE PHASES OF MODERN-DAY ISLAM

1. Osman Bakar, "Towards a Positive World-view of Islam," in Abdul Monir Yaacob and Ahmad Faiz Abdul Rahman, *Towards a Positive Islamic World-View: Malaysian and American Perspectives* (Kuala Lumpur: Institute of Islamic Understanding 1994), 38.

2. See, e.g., Immanuel Wallerstein, *The Capitalist World-System* (Cambridge: Cambridge University Press, 1979), though the best summary of his work and its impact remains Charles Ragin and Daniel Chirot, "The World System of Immanuel Wallerstein: Sociology and Politics as History," in Theda Skocpol, ed., *Vision and Method in Historical Sociology* (New York: Cambridge University Press, 1984), 276–312.

3. Eric Hoffer, "Islam and Modernization," *The Spectator* (Spring 1980): 1.

4. Corm, *Fragmentation of the Middle East*, 133. I am indebted to Corm's insightful book for many of the revisionist, often radical interpretations of Middle Eastern society reflected in these pages.

5. Ibid., 90.

6. The boldest articulation of the either-or thesis concerning Islam and modernization comes from the political scientist Bassam Tibi, *The Crisis of Modern Islam: A Preindustrial Culture in the Scientific-Technological Age* (Salt Lake City: University of Utah Press, 1989), and *Islam and the Cultural Accommodation of Social Change* (Boulder: Westview Press, 1990).

7. For a broad delineation of the postcolonial dilemmas faced by many Middle Eastern and North African societies, see Philip S. Khoury and Joseph Kostiner, eds. *Tribes and State Formation in the Middle East*

(Berkeley: University of California Press, 1990). The most persuasive review of democracy as an element of Muslim political discourse, despite occasional lapses into economic determinist arguments, is provided in Ghassan Salame, ed., *Democracy without Democrats? The Renewal of Politics in the Muslim World* (London: I.B. Tauris, 1994).

CHAPTER 2
ISLAMIC REVIVALISM

1. On the specific problems of nomenclature for Islamic fundamentalism, see my chapter "Muslim Fundamentalist Movements: Reflections toward a New Approach," in Barbara F. Stowasser, ed., *The Islamic Impulse* (London: Croom Helm, 1987), 15–36; and also chapter 4 in *Defenders of God*. Similar points have been made by Sadik al-Azm in his two-part essay noted above.

2. Ihab Hassan, "The Culture of Postmodernism," in Monique Chefdor et al., *Modernism: Challenges and Perspectives* (Urbana: University of Illinois Press, 1986), 307.

3. Norma Salem, "Tunisia," in Shireen T. Hunter, ed., *The Politics of Islamic Revivalism* (Bloomington: University of Indiana Press, 1988), 167, n. 7. Elsewhere I deal with a similar set of issues about terminology, arguing that to choose and defend specific cross-cultural constructs is the only way that comparative studies can finally produce some explanatory yield (see *Defenders of God*, 90–96). Sadik al-Azm is even more emphatic about the need for cross-cultural categories when he declares: "I would like to argue broadly for the epistemological legitimacy, scientific integrity and critical applicability of such supposedly modern Western and Christian-derived concepts as 'Fundamentalism' and 'Revivalism' in the study of the contemporary Islamist phenomenon." "Islamic Fundamentalism Reconsidered," 95.

4. A recapitulation of both the Arabian Wahhabis and the Indian revivalists sometimes confused with them, the Barelwis and Faraidis, is set forth in Ira M. Lapidus, *A History of Islamic Societies* (Cambridge: Cambridge University Press, 1988), 673–75, 720–22.

5. Much scholarship still routinely considers the Padris, like the Barelwis, Faraidis, and, of course, Wahhabis, as prototypical fundamentalists. The Padris were said to represent "the intensification of Islamic fundamentalism evident elsewhere in the [Southeast Asian] region" during the early nineteenth century. See A. C. Milner, "Islam and the Muslim State" in M. B. Hooker, ed., *Islam in South-east Asia* (Leiden: E. J. Brill, 1983), 47. It is just such an uncritical reading of all Islamically motivated protest as fundamentalist that mandates a reconsideration of recent Muslim history.

CHAPTER 3
ISLAMIC REFORM

1. This level of critique against reformers has been especially associated with the leading advocate of cultural or Althusserian Marxism in Morocco, Abdallah Laroui, whose views are etched in *The Crisis of the Arab Intellectual*, esp. 153–77.

2. Youssef M. Choueiri, *Islamic Fundamentalism* (Boston: Twayne, 1990), 35. I am indebted to Choueiri for his clear exposition of Islamic fundamentalism, demarcating it from both revivalism and reformism in a diachronic sequence that mirrors my own approach. I do, however, disagree with Choueiri on the label denoting the last phase. He prefers "radicalism," glossing the term fundamentalism as applicable to *all* three phases of recent Islamic protest. The term "radical," unlike revivalism and reformism, has no positive referent. It presupposes some other norm. That norm, in an Islamic context, is a strict religious code or sense of inalterable, all-encompassing fundamentals; hence I use "fundamentalism" in preference to "radicalism" to denote the last and most significant phase of Islamic protest in recent history.

3. Jean Leca, "Democratization in the Arab World," in Salame, ed. *Democracy without Democrats?*, 61. I use the phrase in a more general sense than does Leca, who confines it to the nonmonarchical states of the Arab world, even though the practice of citizen surveillance among the monarchies differs little from that of their "republican" counterparts.

4. Gellner, *Nations and Nationalism*, 138. Put even more starkly in subsequent essays is Gellner's view that what characterizes the modern Middle East and, by extension, the whole Muslim world is "a kind of tribalism in a new milieu and idiom . . . strong religion, strong state, weak civil society, and the fragile ideological power (*'asabiyya*) of quasi-kin, quasi-territorial patronage—that seems to be the heritage (of Islam in the modern world)." Ernest Gellner, "Tribalism and State in the Middle East" in Khoury/Kostiner, *Tribes and State Formation*, 125–26. The problem with this view is its parochialism: it prejudges the future of all Muslims by one, limited reading of the Islamic past. There are other options possible, if the current economic order does not inscribe the same or greater inequities on Africa and South/Southeast Asia as it has in the immediate past.

5. Kenneth Cragg, *The House of Islam* (Belmont, Calif.: Dickenson, 1982), 96.

6. Richard W. Bulliet, *Islam: The View from the Edge* (New York: Columbia University Press, 1994), 205, though Bulliet is principally concerned with the coercive redirection of education and curbing of the

power base of the ulama, intentionally or unintentionally, through "Europeanization."

7. Even when allowance is made for Fanon's emotive appeal to undifferentiated masses, whom he lauded as the sole harbingers of cultural authenticity, it is his posthumous classic, *Les Damnes de la terre*, translated as *The Wretched of the Earth* (New York: Grove, 1961/1963), that augured the grim irony of postcolonial dependence more clearly than any other writing of the nationalist resistance period, just as his *Sociologie d'une revolution* translated as *A Dying Colonialism* (New York: Grove, 1964/1965), highlighted the crucial role of gender analysis and the new woman in forging an autonomous space of freedom in postcolonial Muslim societies. See also Ato Sekyi-Otu, *Fanon's Dialectic of Experience* (Cambridge: Harvard University Press, 1996), 211–35.

8. See Carl E. Pletsch, "The Three Worlds, or the Division of Social Scientific Labor, circa 1950–1975," *Comparative Studies in Society and History* 23 (October 1981): 565–90, for the best explanation of how these terms, rather than some alternative rubrics, came to define the socioeconomic gradient dividing the modern capitalist world system.

CHAPTER 4
ISLAMIC FUNDAMENTALISM

1. Fouad Ajami, "In the Pharaoh's Shadow: Religion and Authority in Egypt," in Piscatori, ed., *Islam in the Political Process*, 1983.

2. Abd al-Aziz Khayyat, Minister of Religious Endowments, the Hashemite Kingdom of Jordan, lecture delivered at Duke University on 8 October 1982.

3. *World Link* 3 (Spring 1991): 12–13. I am indebted to Dr. Paul Hoff for this reference, and for his reflections on how Islam is perceived by nonspecialists in today's world.

4. Roy Mottahedeh, "The Islamic Movement: The Case for Democratic Inclusion," *Contention* 4.3 (Spring 1995): 111.

5. For Pakistan, as for every other country considered, there are numerous dates that could be selected for mention. I provide only those that are registered most often and reverberate most widely when the subject of discussion is changes in the public sphere during the transition from anticolonial protest to postcolonial hopes merging into new points of resistance. There are many other dates to consider for the analysis of noncentrist issues crucial to civil society; some of these dates are set forth in chapter 5 for the purpose of addressing the current and future status of women in three majoritarian Muslim states—Iran, Egypt, and Pakistan.

6. My friend has asked to remain anonymous, but his sentiments are echoed by numerous Indian Muslims to the present day, as one recent account makes clear; see Rafiq Zakaria, *The Struggle within Islam* (London: Penguin, 1989), 1. Though I do not agree with the overly determined bifurcation of fundamentalism and secularism in Zakaria's sweeping account, the book does have the singular merit of presenting in lucid English both a learned Indian Muslim's view of Islamic history and a skillful weaving together of indigenous with Euro-American scholarship on that same history.

7. Hamid Enayat, *Modern Islamic Political Thought* (London: Macmillan, 1982), 102.

8. S. Barakat Ahmad, "Maududian Concept of Islamic State," *Islam and the Modern Age* 14 (November 1983): 10.

9. Mumtaz Ahmad, "Islamic Revival in Pakistan," in J. W. Bjorkman, ed., *Fundamentalism, Revivalists and Violence in South Asia* (Riverdale, Md.: The Riverdale Company, 1988), 93. Ahmad makes the analytic error of conflating the essentially nonpolitical Tablighi Jamaʿat with the very political Jamaʿat-i Islami. He also calls both groups grass-roots revivalist movements, when, in fact, neither was grass-roots or revivalist. Their appeal was urban and often elitist; their program was fidelity to scriptural norms within the modern nation-state. Despite its analytic shortfall, Ahmad's essay contains many valuable source citations.

10. Seyyed Vali Reza Nasr, *The Vanguard of the Islamic Revolution: The Jamaʿat-i Islami of Pakistan* (Berkeley: University of California Press, 1994), 59. "The Jamaʿat's rivals, from ulama parties to Israr Ahmad's Tanzim-i Islami and Tahiru'l-Qadri's Minhaju'l-Qur'an, with some changes in titles and functions, have reproduced it [the Jamaʿat's organizational model] in their own organizations." Nasr's study provides the best single overview in English of both the aims and limits of Mawdudi's organizational legacy.

11. Albert Hourani, *A History of the Arab Peoples* (Cambridge: Harvard University Press, 1991), 338, 393. Hourani, the premier Arab historian of the late twentieth century, documents this point, as so many others, with crystal clarity.

12. Adducing the significance of Nasser and his successors, Sadat and Mubarak, is a delicate task that has occupied many political scientists. For the latest effort suggesting that their achievements were more monumental than the forces constraining them, see Raymond W. Baker, *Sadat and After: Struggles for Egypt's Political Soul* (Cambridge: Harvard University Press, 1990). My approach emphasizes recurrent features of political culture rather than the psychology or mystique of particular Egyptian leaders. A boldly comprehensive study that takes account of class and economic variables in assessing the major Muslim politics of West Asia

and North Africa, including Egypt, is Alan Richards and John Waterbury, *A Political Economy of the Middle East: State, Class and Economic
Development* (Boulder: Westview Press, 1990). Especially valuable is the
authors' effort to show how the internal differentiation of the middle
class complicates any roseate picture of development in the Arab Muslim
world, as also in its Iranian and Turkish neighbors.

13. According to Joel Migdal, Nasser's was essentially a top-down
strategy of survival. Through nationalization of key industries, he precluded the development of centrifugal economic groups and structures
that were necessary for the long-range viability of the Egyptian economy.
The virtue of Migdal's broadly comparative study is to illustrate that the
dilemma of Nasserist overcentralization was neither his nor the Middle
East's alone; see Joel S. Migdal, *Strong Societies and Weak States: State-
Society Relations and State Capabilities in the Third World* (Princeton:
Princeton University Press, 1988), esp. 229–32.

14. See Hourani, *Islam in European Thought*, 401–15, for an adroit
analysis of the 1967 war as the nearly inevitable outcome of a perilous
experiment with Arab socialism cast in the mold of Nasser's Egypt.

15. John Waterbury, *Hydropolitics of the Nile Valley* (Syracuse:
Syracuse University Press, 1979).

16. Morroe Berger, *Islam in Egypt; Social and Political Aspects of
Popular Religion* (New York: Cambridge University Press, 1970), 47,
quoted by Daniel Crecelius in D. E. Smith, ed., *Religion and Political
Modernization* (New Haven: Yale University Press, 1974), 90.

17. Quoted in Richard P. Mitchell, *The Society of Muslim Brothers*
(New York: Oxford University Press, 1968), 244.

18. Sayyid Qutb, *Ma'alim fi't-Tariq*, 26.

19. This detail, along with countless others, is provided in the
thoroughly sympathetic biography of Asad by Patrick Seale (see 437).
Titled *Asad: The Struggle for the Middle East* (Berkeley: University of
California Press, 1988), it is accurately called by the author himself a
"chronicle." It is a chronicle that he concludes by asking Asad how *he*
wants it to conclude. Unsurprisingly, Asad quips: "Say simply that the
struggle continues" (495).

20. The best presentation of the socioeconomic issues and class struggle evident in Hama is offered by Fred Lawson, "Social Bases for
the Hamah Revolt," *Middle East Reports in Progress (MERIP)* 12.9
(Nov.–Dec. 1982): 24–28. The alternative explanation of modern Syrian
history as a clash of competing religious ideologies has been set forth
in Umar F. Abd-Allah, *The Islamic Struggle in Syria* (Berkeley: Mizan
Press, 1983).

21. Fouad Ajami, "In the Pharaoh's Shadow," in J. Piscatori, ed.,
Islam in the Political Process, 34.

22. Thomas L. Friedman, *From Beirut to Jerusalem* (New York: Farrar Straus Giroux, 1989), 101. While this quote from Friedman is valuable, his analysis of Hama is seriously flawed by overschematization and psychological projection. Is Asad a schizophrenic three-faced Jekyll-and-Hyde, unable or unwilling to declare himself as (1) tribal leader, (2) brutal autocrat, or (3) modernizing president? Such is Friedman's cynical surmise, yet equally plausible is the opposite surmise, namely, that Asad is a wily pragmatist ruling Syria in almost the only way that one could rule a postcolonial artifice, with almost no historical tradition as a nation-state, threatened by fissiparous forces within and beyond its borders. Friedman eschews comparative analysis in order to tell a good story, but it is not the whole story, and it may cloak the long-range historical lessons emerging out of modern-day Ba'athist Syria.

23. Norma Salem, "Tunisia," in Hunter, ed., *The Politics of Islamic Revivalism*, 158. Not only for this insight but for an imaginative theoretical overview of Islamism, applying Bourdieu's categories with analytic adroitness, I am indebted to Norma Salem's chapter.

24. Norma Salem, *Habib Bourguiba, Islam and the Creation of Tunisia* (London: Croom Helm, 1984), 38.

25. Salem, "Tunisia," 154.

26. Ibid., 155, summarizing a spate of publicity and criticism that went well beyond Tunisia during the early 1960s.

27. Clement H. Moore, *Tunisia since Independence: The Dynamics of a One-Party System* (Berkeley: University of California Press, 1965), 52n.

28. Salem, "Tunisia," 155.

29. *The Economist* (13 Jan. 1996) provides the details of a rising tide of hope for Tunisian women: "A girl born today stands a 95% chance of learning to read, and is likely to live to 71—13 years longer than one born ten years ago"(41).

30. Salem, "Tunisia," 165.

31. See *North Africa News* 2/1 (Jan.–Feb. 1991): 6. While this periodical is published by North African Students for Freedom and might be expected to tilt toward extreme conclusions, in fact this is one of the rare instances where its editorials verge on the alarmist rather than the pragmatic side of predicting the unpredictable, namely, the future of Maghribi politics.

32. Susan Waltz, "Islamist Appeal in Tunisia," *Middle East Journal* 40 (Autumn 1986): 669.

33. Choueiri, *Islamic Fundamentalism*, 75.

34. Ibid., 75.

35. Dilip Hiro, *Holy Wars: The Rise of Islamic Fundamentalism* (New York: Routledge, 1989), 116.

36. Ibid., 119.

37. James P. Piscatori, "Ideological Politics in Saudi Arabia," in Piscatori, ed., *Islam in the Political Process*, 71. On Saudi foreign policy, see Cary Fraser, "In Defense of Allah's Realm: Religion and Statecraft in Saudi Foreign Policy," in a book co-edited by Piscatori and Susan H. Rudolph, *Transnational Religion & Fading States* (Boulder: Westview, 1996), 212–40. Fraser acknowledges indebtedness to Piscatori both for reviewing the above essay and for an earlier article, "Islamic Values and National Interest: The Foreign Policy of Saudi Arabia," in Adeed Dawish, ed. *Islam in Foreign Policy* (Cambridge: Cambridge University Press, 1983), 33–53. Piscatori further explores the limits of Saudi ability to outmaneuver religious opponents of the state in Dale F. Eickelman and James Piscatori, *Muslim Politics* (Princeton: Princeton University Press, 1996); espec. 157–59.]

38. Fouad Ajami, "In the Pharaoh's Shadow," in Piscatori, ed., *Islam in the Political Process*, 32, asks this question about Egypt; it applies with equal force to Saudi Arabia.

39. This ludicrous but apt anecdote comes from Olivier Roy, *The Failure of Political Islam*, trans. Carol Volk (Cambridge: Harvard University Press, 1994), 116. In general, Roy highlights the distinctions within the Islamist movements and articulates the consequences of what he terms "a new world-space," one so permeated with commercial and communicative links to the global market that "triumphant neofundamentalism will be incapable of ensuring the insularity of Islamic societies" (202). As such, his thesis has many similarities to the principal argument of this book about diversity and accommodation, though Roy's accent is concerned mainly with political currents.

40. The first chapter title is from Shireen Hunter, *The Politics of Islamic Revivalism*; the other, from Dilip Hiro, *Holy Wars*.

41. Choueiri, *Islamic Fundamentalism.*, 70.

42. Ibid., 77.

43. The stress on Carter's human rights policy is best set forth by Henry Munson, Jr., in *Islam and Revolution in the Middle East* (New Haven: Yale University Press, 1988), 126–28. The use of cassettes was reported widely in the news media at the time, though it escaped mention in many later commentaries on the Islamic revolution.

44. Ruth Ann Willner, *The Spellbinders* (New Haven: Yale University Press, 1984), 82.

45. Turner, *Marx and the End of Orientalism*, 67, and Gellner, *Conditions of Liberty*. See also this volume's introduction, note 35.

46. The best overview of the manifold economic problems facing the Islamic Republic of Iran is set forth by Hooshang Amirahmadi in *Revolution and Economic Transition*, 70–82. Amirahmadi provides a rare and

valuable class analysis of the debate on development planning, discussed more fully below.

47. For the best assessment of this volatile issue, see Shaul Bakhash, *The Reign of the Ayatollahs: Iran and the Islamic Revolution* (New York: Basic Books, 1984), 195–216. For a case study of the controversial land cultivation bill, see his "Land, Law and Social Justice in Iran," *The Middle East Journal* 43.2 (Spring 1989): 186–201.

48. For a full review of the status of minorities during the most recent phase of the Islamic Republic of Iran, see John L. Esposito and John O. Voll, *Islam and Democracy* (New York: Oxford University Press, 1997), 69–74.

49. For more on Shariʿati, see particularly Hamid Dabashi, *Theology of Discontent: The Ideological Foundation of the Islamic Revolution in Iran* (New York: New York University Press, 1993), 102–46.

50. Amirahmadi, *Revolution and Economic Transition,* 121. All the qualified brackets come from the author, except the last, which are mine.

51. Eric Hooglund, "The Pulse of Iran Today," *Middle East Insight* 11.5(July–Aug. 1995): 40–47. The quotation is adapted from p. 41, but the entire article expounds on the role of free speech and open debate in 1990s' Iran. On the special importance of Abdul Karim Sorush, see Yann Richard, "Clercs et intellectuels de la Republique islamique d'Iran," in Gilles Kepel and Yann Richard, eds., *Intellectuels et militants de l'islam contemporain* (Paris: Le Seuil, 1990), 29–70. Alas, the window of freedom has not remained untainted, or wide open: Sorush was forced to cease teaching at Tehran Unveristy after a radical theocratic faction, Ansar-i Hizbullah, staged political confrontations against him in the mid-1990s. However, he continues to argue publicly with leading officials of the Iranian government; in most other West Asian Muslim countries, with the exception of Turkey, such open debate about the nature and role of Islam would be unthinkable.

52. The immensity of the Iranian diaspora since 1978 and the significant presence of Iranians in the United States are nowhere more evident than in Los Angeles. For a marvelous pictorial overview of the many strands of the Iranian exile community in southern California, see Ron Kelley, Jonathan Friedlander, and Anita Colby, eds., *Irangeles: Iranians in Los Angeles* (Berkeley: University of California Press, 1993).

53. The quotation comes from Paul B. Henze and S. Enders Wimbush, "A New Policy for a New Middle East," *Wall Street Journal*, 31 Jan. 1997, with a sequel by Robert D. Kaplan, "Why the U.S. and Iran Will Be Friends Again," *Wall Street Journal*, 10 Feb. 1997. Despite the hopeful tone of both articles, most policy pronouncements still tend to echo the dismal logic, and bleak pessimism, of Samuel P. Huntington, *The Clash of Civilizations and the Remaking of World Order* (New York: Simon & Schuster,

1996). As I argue below, Chandra Muzaffar, a Malay intellectual, has pinpointed the solipsistic futility of Huntington's thesis with a deftness that has escaped most Washington globe watchers: they remain mired in Cold War nostalgia even while talking of a post–Cold War future.

54. Asef Bayat, "The Coming of a Post-Islamist Society," *Critique* 9 (Fall 1996): 43–52.

CHAPTER 5
THE DOUBLE BIND REVISITED

1. Sekyi-Otu, *Fanon's Dialectic of Experience*, 214.

2. Hisham Sharabi, *Neopatriarchy: A Theory of Distorted Change in Arab Society* (New York: Oxford University Press, 1988).

3. New York: Columbia University Press, 1991, esp. 142–63.

4. The one, oft noted "exception" is the Egyptian founder of the Society of Muslim Women, Zaynab al-Ghazali. Her prison memoirs have been reprinted and reprinted, yet her life as an activist abounds in contradictions, not the least of which is her self-defined independence from her husband. See Valerie J. Hoffman, "An Islamic Activist: Zaynab al-Ghazali," in Elizabeth W. Fernea, ed. *Women and the Family in the Middle East: New Voices of Change* (Austin: University of Texas Press, 1985), and Miriam Cooke, "Prisons: Women Write about Islam," *Religion and Literature* 20.1 (Spring 1988).

5. Roy, *The Failure of Political Islam*, 59.

6. Most of these figures are taken from the superb summary provided by Mahnaz Afkhami in "Iran: A Future in the Past—The Prerevolutionary Women's Movement," in Robin Morgan, ed., *Sisterhood is Global* (New York: Anchor-Doubleday, 1984), 335. No woman who writes about Iran writes in a vacuum. Afkhami has her own personal history of involvement in the events she describes: she served as secretary-general to the Women's Organization of Iran under Muhammad Reza Shah, and for some that involvement leads to accusations of class-blindness and over-reliance on state-sponsored or top-down feminism (Haideh Moghissi, review of Mahnaz Afkhami and Erika Friedl, eds., *In the Eye of the Storm: Women in Post Revolutionary Iran* [Syracuse: Syracuse University Press, 1994], in *International Journal of Middle East Studies* 28.2 [May 1996]: 293–95). But insofar as there exists a viable umbrella movement known as global feminism, Afkhami remains one of its most articulate Iranian advocates.

7. These seeming contradictions are outlined by Freda Hussain and Kamelia Radwan in "The Islamic Revolution and Women: Quest for the Quranic Model," in Freda Hussain, ed., *Muslim Women* (New York: St. Martin's Press, 1984), 48–51.

8. Motahhari, like every other figure in the inner circle of Iranian Islamic ideologues, has a contested history. Abrahamian, in particular, is dismissive of Motahhari as a thinker, labeling his critique of Marxism and his class analysis as "half-baked and third-hand conservative arguments designed to preserve the socioeconomic status quo while implicitly questioning the political power structure" (review of Dabashi, in *International Journal of Middle East Studies* 28.2 [May 1996]: 300). Yet Motahhari's range of reinterpretation is impressive, and his views on women more compelling than his digest of Marxist ideology.

9. Motahhari, *Sexual Ethics in Islam* (Muslim Student Association—Persian Speaking Group, n.d.), 33–45.

10. Ibid., 20–21.

11. Abdelwahab Bouhdiba, *Sexuality in Islam* (London: Routledge & Kegan Paul, 1985), 19.

12. For a biography of Nazira Zayn al-Din and brief excerpts from two of her writings, see Margot Badran and Miriam Cooke, eds., *Opening the Gates: A Century of Arab Feminist Writings* (London and Bloomington: Virago and Indiana University Press, 1990), 270–78.

13. Barbara F. Stowasser, "The Status of Women in Early Islam," in Hussain, ed., *Muslim Women* 37. The concluding section of Stowasser's chapter highlights Nazira Zayn al-Din's writings and their significance for reevaluating women's status in Islam.

14. For actual statistics on marriage and literacy, see the entry "Iran" in Morgan, ed., *Sisterhood Is Global*, 326. Yet these statistics, especially on literacy, are subject to challenge, and in need of upward revision. Valentine Mogadham, "Women, Work and Ideology in Post-Revolutionary Iran," Michigan State University Working Paper #170 (May 1988), 24, n. 15, cites the literacy rate of urban women as 55 percent now, which means that the figure for rural women at best hovers around 25 percent.

15. See Friedl, *Women of Deh Koh*, 110–19. In the introduction Friedl notes: "The ultimate motivation for the many suicide attempts of women in Deh Koh is quoted as a wish 'to be at rest, quiet, out of it forever.' "

16. Hussein/Radwan, "The Islamic Revolution and Women," 65.

17. Eric Hooglund, "Islamic Feminism," in *Middle East Insight* 11.5: 70–71, quotes extensively from his interview with Shala Sherkat, the editor of *Zanan*, who claims it is "the first Islamic feminist magazine in Iran." Even allowing for a self-serving dose of hyperbole, one has to underscore the significance of a widely read literary forum directed at urban professional women in 1990s' Iran. Nor is its influence limited to Iran: a recent issue of *Critique: Journal for Critical Studies of the Middle East* featured an article by the Egyptian sociologist, Asef Bayat, in which she

NOTES TO CHAPTER 5

argued that Iran may well witness the first post-Islamist society. Her evidence derives from the popularity of a new brand of Islamic modernism emerging under a self-consciously Islamic state, namely, the Islamic Republic of Iran, and among the harbingers of this change Bayat cites women advocates writing in major journals such as *Zanan*. See Asef Bayat, "The Coming of a Post-Islamist Society," *Critique* 9 (Fall 1996): 43–52.

One example supporting Bayat's optimism is the prominence recently accorded a Qum-based cleric, Mohsen Sa'idzadeh, who directly challenges the premise of Mutahhari's approach to exegesis. Instead of assuming the complementarity of rights for men and women as the axial outlook of the Qur'an, "Sa'idzadeh contends that Islam grants women the same rights as men in all matters, including the right to become leaders, both religious and political, and to serve as judges." See Ziba Mir-Hosseini, "Stretching the Limits: A Feminist Reading of the Shari'a in Post-Khomeini Iran," in Mai Yamani, ed. *Feminism & Islam: Legal and Literary Perspectives* (New York: New York University Press, 1996), 305. Mir-Hosseini's entire essay, drawing on articles from *Zanan*, reflects some of the latest and most engaging scholarly efforts to reclaim Shi'i Islam for a new generation of Iranian women.

18. Of the many, sources that could be cited, see especially Azar Tabari and Nahid Yeganeh, eds., *In the Shadow of Islam. The Woman's Movement in Iran* (London: Zed Press, 1982); Guity Nashat, *Women and Revolution in Iran* (Boulder: Westview Press, 1983); Farah Azari, ed. *Women of Iran: The Conflict with Fundamentalist Islam* (Ithaca: Ithaca Press, 1983); and Afkhami and Friedl, eds., *In the Eye of the Storm*.

19. George A. Nader, "Interview with President Ali Akbar Rafsanjani," *Middle East Insight* 11.5:14. The opposite interpretation, of course, has been offered by some Iranian women in exile; see, e.g., Haideh Moghissi, *IJMES* 28/2 [May 1996]: 293: "the clerics have tried to co-opt and silence women through various means, including a retreat from their initial exclusionary educational and employment policies and the reintroduction of pre-revolutionary Family Law under an Islamic rubric." By this reading, there are no sources of power possible for women in a patriarchal society, and so "it can hardly be said [as Erika Friedl among others has tried to say] that in the Islamic Republic of Iran, women exert much power" (295).

20. See Nemat Guenena, "The Jihad: An Islamic Alternative in Egypt," *Cairo Papers in Social Science* 8.2 (Summer 1986): 81–87.

21. Nadia Hijab, *Womanpower: The Arab Debate on Women at Work* (New York: Cambridge University Press, 1988), 81.

22. See Margot Badran, "Competing Agenda: Feminists, Islam and

the State in Nineteenth-and Twentieth-Century Egypt," in Deniz Kandiyoti, ed., *Women, Islam & the State* (Philadelphia: Temple University Press, 1991), 222–23. Badran's article provides a rare and comprehensive overview of Egyptian women's movements under the shadow of the colonial, then postcolonial, state. Also see her recent history of Muslim women and feminism in Egypt, which goes beyond any comparable study of women in a majoritarian Muslim country and sets a high standard for all future analysis of Muslim women and the state: Margot Badran, *Feminists, Islam, and Nation: Gender and the Making of Modern Egypt* (Princeton: Princeton University Press, 1995).

23. Badran, "Competing Agenda," 219.

24. Nayra Atiya, *Khul-Khaal: Five Egyptian Women Tell Their Story* (Syracuse, Syracuse University Press, 1982), viii. The statement has been modified to reflect the reality that even government employment is no longer guaranteed since 1974.

25. Ibid., xv–xvi.

26. Ayesha Jalal, "The Convenience of Subservience: Women and the State of Pakistan," in Kandiyoti, *Women, Islam, & the State*, 105.

27. Quoted in ibid., 77.

28. Miriam Habib, "Pakistani Women: A Fractured Profile," in Morgan, ed., *Sisterhood Is Global*, 531.

29. Ibid.

30. Jalal, "The Convenience of Subservience," 79.

31. Ibid., 108.

32. Tabari and Yaganeh, *In the Shadow of Islam*, 24.

33. Nawal el-Saadawi, *The Hidden Face of Eve* (Boston: Beacon, 1982), 180.

34. Hijab, *Womanpower*, 93.

CHAPTER 6
THE SHAH BANO CASE

1. The details of the court case concerning Shah Bano are summarized, or paraphrased, from the version of the judgment that appears in Asghar Ali Engineer, ed., *The Shah Bano Controversy* (Hyderabad: Orient Longman, 1987), 23–34. I also benefited from a close reading of my earlier essay on Shah Bano by Lucy Carroll Stout, herself an expert and prolific author on Muslim Personal Law in South Asia.

2. Danial Latifi, who appeared before the Supreme Court on behalf of Shah Bano, notes that of the three forms of divorce possible under Islamic law, this is the most reprehensible, even though it is still technically "allowed by the present interpretation of the Hanafi school of law," which is the school that applies for most Muslims throughout the sub-

continent. See Danial Latifi, "The Muslim Women Bill," reprinted in ibid., 104–105.

3. Madhu Kishwar, "Pro-Women or Anti-Muslim? The Furore over Muslim Personal Law," *Manushi* 32 (1986): 8.

4. Cited in Engineer, ed., *The Shah Bano Controversy*, 24.

5. For an India-specific review of how much remains to be done, merely to describe the circumstances of all women, but especially the agrarian poor, without even considering how to redress these same seemingly intractable circumstances, see Niroj Sinha, ed., *Women and Violence* (New Delhi: Vikas, 1989). Though many of these essays suffer from both lack of editing and strident advocacy, they do contain numerous insights into the actual circumstances of Muslim as well as Hindu women. For instance, Shahnaz Bano, "Violence on Women in Muslim Society: The Case of Divorced Women" (148–54), evokes the horror and desperation that a Muslim divorcee feels, not only due to rejection by her former husband, but also from the lack of sympathy or support within her agnatic family.

6. I am indebted to the excellent analysis of Muslim Personal Law that was provided by Gregory C. Koslowski in "Muslim Personal Law and Political Identity in Independent India," a paper given at the University of Iowa conference on Religion and Law in South Asia, fall 1991.

7. The relevant passage is set forth in Engineer, 24.

8. Amrita Chhachhi, "Forced Identities: The State, Communalism, Fundamentalism and Women in India," in Kandiyoti, ed., *Women, Islam and the State*, 153.

9. See Afsaneh Najmabadi, "Interview with Gayatri Spivak," *Social Text* 28. 9/3 (1991): esp. 132–34.

10. For the ideological efforts either to deny history or to retell it from a "Hindu" viewpoint, see the comprehensive study by Peter van der Veer, *Gods on Earth: The Management of Religious Experience and Identity in a North Indian Pilgrimage Centre* (London: Athlone Press, 1988). "Ayodhya's rise as a supra-regional place of pilgrimage is relatively recent. Only during the eighteenth century did Ramanandi sadhus start to build their institutions there, while many of the buildings we see today were built in the second half of the nineteenth or the first part of the twentieth century" (36). In other words, the cult of Rama at Ayodhya is more a countermemory of Hindu revivalism than a historical reflection of ancient Indian practice.

11. Quoted from Zakia Pathak and Rajeswari Sunder Rajan, " 'Shahbano,' " in Micheline Malson et al., eds., *Feminist Theory in Practice and Process* (Chicago: University of Chicago Press, 1989), 252–53. Pathak and Rajan provide a clear articulation of the several paradoxes in press coverage and subsequent ideological invocation of Shah Bano, even

though they stress one aspect of Shahbano, namely, her subjectivity, to the exclusion of other, equally salient aspects.

12. The full text of this extraordinary bill is set forth in Engineer, ed., *The Shah Bano Controversy*, 85–88.

13. For this quotation, a paraphrase of Chief Justice Chandrachud's opinion, and also for many insights into the juridical and political maneuvering that surrounded the Shah Bano case, see Ainslie T. Embree, *Utopias in Conflict: Religion and Nationalism in Modern India* (Berkeley: University of California Press, 1990), esp. 96–101. The significance of Chief Justice Chandrachud's intervention has also been discussed at length in Erin E. O'Donnell, "Muslims in Modern India and Political Identity: The Shah Bano Case (1985) and the Muslim Women (Protection of Rights on Divorce) Act (1986) and the Elite Use of Symbols," *Annals of the Southeast Conference Association for Asian Studies* 13 (17–19 Jan. 1991): 89–102.

14. The controversy is reviewed and analyzed in Embree, *Utopias in Conflict*, 107–11.

15. For the full text of Shah Bano's demurral, see Engineer, ed., *The Shah Bano Controversy*, 211.

16. For this observation I am indebted to Professor Morris H. Abrams of Cornell University. In one of several gatherings of the Fundamentalism Project, sponsored by the American Academy of Arts and Sciences, he asked: "To what extent may one fundamentalist movement be generated to oppose an inimical fundamentalism?" (Fundamentalisms Compared, Spring Conference 1991, summary notes, 12). What follows here is an attempt to respond to the pertinent question he raised, and to trace that response in the specific context of 1980s' India.

17. A full exposé of these later developments is tracked from a feminist perspective in the above cited article by Amrita Chhachhi.

18. For instance, in Engineer, ed., *The Shah Bano Controversy*, one finds numerous essays of value as well as the text of the original judgment (23–34), but no essay sets forth the Pakistani point of view. Only a brief piece critical of the Indian ulema is included in Janak Raj Rai, ed., *Shah Bano* (New Delhi: Rajiv Publications, 1986); see Rafiullah Shahab, "A Pak View of Muslim Law," 121–24.

19. It is from this South Asian perspective that Benedict Anderson's much touted thesis about nationalism as an imaginary construct, inducing cohesion where none was intrinsically available, is in need of correction: the colonial manipulation of difference persists beyond independence and often precludes the possibility of cohesion on some superseding criterion even after independence has been achieved.

20. See Gregory Koslowski, "Shah Bano's Case and Indian Politics," in Malik and Vajpeyi, eds., *Law, Politics and Society in India*, 106.

21. Richard F. Nyrop, ed., *India: A Country Study* (Washington, D.C.: Foreign Area Studies, 1985), 394–95.

22. Naila Kabeer, "The Quest for National Identity: Women, Islam and the State in Bangladesh," in Kandiyoti, ed., *Women, Islam & Society*, 123. One of the few studies of Bangladesh to appear in collective volumes on Islam, Kabeer's is the sole attempt to give voice to the condition of Bangladeshi women under the repressive Ershad regime.

23. John Burns, "Bangladesh Hopes Trial Shows a Nation of Laws," *New York Times*, 4 May 1997: 14.

24. Kabeer, "The Quest for National Identity," 128.

25. James Heitzman and Robert L. Worden, eds., *Bangladesh: A Country Study* (Washington, D.C.: Area Handbooks, 1989), 158.

26. Richard F. Nyrop, *Pakistan: A Country Study* (Washington, D.C.: Foreign Area Studies, 1984), 303. For the contention that Zia was trying to unify the laws of Pakistan, fusing Muslim law with general law, see David Pearl, *A Textbook on Muslim Personal Law*, 2d ed. (London: Croom Helm, 1987), 40, 238–45.

27. The degradation of women was also linked to the denigration of minorities, as is outlined in Esposito and Voll, *Islam and Democracy*, 112–14.

28. The Safia Bibi case, and other cases involving women tried under the Hudood Ordinance, are reviewed in Khawar Mumtaz and Farida Shaheed, eds., *Women of Pakistan: Two Steps Forward, One Step Back?* (London: Zed Press, 1987), 103–105.

29. The irony of this move has been lost on some legal scholars. David Pearl provides a detailed and seemingly comprehensive treatment of the subject, especially with reference to Pakistan and especially with reference to the post-1979 decrees of Zia. Yet nowhere does he mention the Safia Bibi case, and, in discussing another case, he observes that Aftab Hussain, then chief justice of the Federal Shariʿat Court, refused to review a case because it concerned Muslim personal law, which was "excluded from examination by the court as a result of Article 203(b) of the (Pakistani) Constitution" (*Muslim Personal Law*, and p. 114, n. 23, 244). Why the same restriction did not apply to the Safia Bibi case remains a puzzle that admits only of political expediency as its explanation.

30. While Pakistani feminism does not enjoy rural support, neither does its ideological enemy, Islamic fundamentalism. On the alienation of Pakistani villagers, male and female, from the mechanisms of Islamization, as also the scriptural claims of its urban agents, see the insightful essay by Richard Kurin, "Islamization: A View from the Countryside," in Anita Weiss, ed., *Islamic Reassertion in Pakistan: The Application of Islamic Laws in a Modern State* (Syracuse: Syracuse University Press, 1986), 115–28.

31. See, for instance, Ayesha Jalal, "The Convenience of Subservience: Women and the State of Pakistan," in Kandiyoti, ed., *Woman, Islam & Society*, esp. 103–109, and also Mumtaz and Shaheed, eds. *Women of Pakistan*, 150–60.

32. Nikki R. Keddie, "Ideology, Society and the State in Post-Colonial Muslim Societies," in Fred Halliday and Hamza Alavi, eds., *State and Ideology in the Middle East and Pakistan* (London: Macmillan, 1988), 26.

33. Aftab Hussain, chief justice of the Federal Shari'at Court during the early 1980s, is often viewed as a supporter of women's rights because of his opinion on Safia Bibi and other personal law matters. See Mumtaz and Shaheed, eds., *Women of Pakistan*, 112, n. 25 and 155.

34. The failure of Islamists to have the offensive article (203B) of the constitution deleted has been documented in Charles H. Kennedy, "Islamization and Legal Reform in Pakistan, 1979–1989," *Pacific Affairs* 63.1 (Spring 1990): 66–67. Kennedy provides a close reading of all the legal maneuvers attendant on Islamization but is content to argue a single point, to wit, that Zia's policies did not significantly alter the institutional mechanisms of statecraft in Islamabad. The inadequacy of other branches of government to provide a counterbalance to the executive is not considered, and hence the issues of concern to marginal groups, such as professional women and rural dwellers, are either downplayed or ignored.

35. See ibid., 67 for a full exposé of all the parliamentary procedures that resulted in its not so quiet demise.

36. Despite its sometimes polemical tone, Fatima Mernissi, *Le harem politique*, 1987; trans. as *The Veil and the Male Elite: A Feminist Interpretation of Women's Rights in Islam* (Reading: Addison-Wesley, 1991), makes a compelling case for the novelty of Qur'anic dicta about women. Less passionate in tone but fuller in its range of references to both Qur'anic passages and early Islamic traditions (*hadith*) about women is Barbara Stowasser, "The Status of Women in Early Islam," in Hussain, ed. *Muslim Women*, 11–43.

37. Stowasser, "The Status of Women," 30.

38. See especially his *Islam* (2d ed., Chicago: University of Chicago Press, 1979), chap. 14, and also his *Islam and Modernity: Transformation of an Intellectual Tradition* (Chicago, University of Chicago Press, 1982).

39. Muhammad Iqbal, *The Reconstruction of Religious Thought in Islam* (London, 1934; reprinted Lahore: Sh. Muhammad Ashraf, 1982), 164.

40. Jacques Waardenberg, "Muslim States, Islamic Norms and Secular Realities," ms., ca. June 1990. Waardenberg goes on to distinguish between two kinds of Islamists, the more reflective being "fundamental-

ists"; the more political, "activists." However, in what follows it is apparent that one of the defining characteristics of fundamentalists is their insistence on implementing religious ideals in the political sphere; fundamentalists are invariably political rather than reflective. It is on this crucial point, as also on the essentialist tone of his arguments about the concept of Islam, that I differ from another of Waardenberg's wide-ranging essays: "Islam as a Vehicle of Protest," in Ernest Gellner, ed., *Islamic Dilemma: Reformers, Nationalists and Industrialization. The Southern Shore of the Mediterranean* (The Hague: Mouton, 1985), 22–48.

41. On the question of counting Muslims in America, there has been more heat than light generated, especially by the telejournalist Andy Rooney. Claiming that all Islam is inherently violent, Rooney has alleged that Muslims are the fastest growing religious community in America, already surpassing Episcopalians and closing in on Methodists. Such hyperbole stokes people's fears. It needs to be deflated, as Jonathan D. Sarna has tried to do in a recent article, "The Rise of Islam in America," *Moment* (June 1991): 34–55, where he quotes the 1990 survey by Barry A. Kosmin and Jeffrey Scheckner, "Estimating the Muslim Population of the United States in 1990," City University of New York (April 1991). Its authors, after extensive research and tabulation, deduce that in 1990 the total Muslim population in America numbered 800,000 immigrants, 400,000 indigenous Muslims, and less than 100,000 students. "Certainly," they conclude, "it cannot exceed 1.5. million."

The myth of demography once exploded does not lessen the need for dealing with Muslims in a religiously plural society; it simply makes the basis for such an undertaking more realistic and, one hopes, more fruitful.

42. One of the favorite images of headline chasers combines the two groups, representing modern-day Muslim warriors as black-garbed women in *chadors* sporting guns, often in combat pose. While that makes for an electric image, it is far from the ground-level truth: Muslim military planners are less ready to admit women warriors as regular combatants than are their counterparts in the Pentagon, that bastion of patriarchal leadership for the United States armed services which, even after the superb performance of women in Operation Desert Storm in spring 1991, would not allow female officers to fly combat missions or to serve as unit commanders in the marine corps.

43. Michel Vovelle, *Ideologies and Mentalities* (Chicago: University of Chicago Press, 1990), 11.

44. See several works but most recently *Rethinking Islam: Common Questions, Uncommon Answers* (Boulder: Westview, 1994).

45. *The Second Message of Islam* (Syracuse: Syracuse University Press, 1987).

46. See particularly the detailed and valuable study of Gail Minault, *The Khilafat Movement: Religious Symbolism and Political Mobilization in India* (New York: Columbia University Press, 1982).

47. Binder, *Islamic Liberalism*, 131–46. The criticism of Hourani that begins Binder's analysis (129–30) is disingenuous, as is the omission of *Arabic Thought in the Liberal Age* from the bibliography, since Hourani opened the larger discussion of Islamic liberalism to which Binder's own book is a sequel contribution, but otherwise Binder lays out the major issues in luxuriant detail; see also Eickelman and James Piscatori, *Muslim Politics*, 52–53, for a summary of ʿAli ʿAbd ar-Raziq's provocation.

48. See *Rethinking Islam*, ca. 75.

49. Binder, *Islamic Liberalism*, 169.

CONCLUSION
CONVERGENT SIGNPOSTS

1. I am using these terms in the sense that they are introduced and refined by Marshall Hodgson, following Karl Jaspers. See *The Venture of Islam*, 1: 50–52.

2. On Motahhari's contribution to the Shi'ite reformulation of ideology, see *Defenders of God: The Fundamentalist Revolt Against the Modern Age*, 2d ed. (Columbia: University of South Carolina Press, 1995), 221–24.

3. The practical face of corporate culture is not the same as the large-scale, conceptually moribund industries focusing on the Islamization of Knowledge, including the Islamization of Economics. While one may find some Malay proponents of this approach, it remains a minor voice in Malay intellectual circles.

4. There is no space to explore the complications inherent in the formation and strategy-planning of the G-15, but suffice it to say that as of the fall 1995 meeting in Buenos Aires, Mahathir had clearly projected Malaysian participation in this body as equivalent to, or exceeding, Malaysian participation in the biennial meeting of Commonwealth heads of government.

5. *The Asian Wall Street Journal*, 10–12 November 1995: 7.

6. Chandra Muzaffar in private conversation in Penang, Malaysia, on 6 November 1995.

7. Mukhtar Abdullah, "Historical Developments of Quality and Productivity Movements: Japan vs. The West," in Alhabshi and Nik Hassen, eds., *Quality and Productivity*, 61–77.

8. Mottahedeh, "The Islamic Movement," 111. Alas, Mottahedeh's voice is scarcely heard beyond Harvard Yard, while Huntington, though also at Harvard, is trying to become the benchmark for all international

policy planning. He is often invoked, without even being cited, as in *The Economist*, where an article on Russia and China suddenly veers toward the Muslim world, noting that "in 20 or 30 years' time, a Muslim power could arise to join the ranks of world powers. There would then be half a dozen of them, including America and Europe, possibly Japan, probably Russia. Of this number, China might well reckon that the Islamic power would be the one most likely to help it counterbalance what it will see as its chief rivals, America and Europe" (*The Economist*, 26 April 1997:20). Such sabre rattling and Islam bashing is exactly what Huntington's so-called thesis promotes, but its factual basis in the lived experience of most Muslim polities, including those of Southeast Asia, is thin and vacuous.

9. R. L. Schuyler's phrase as developed by J. H. Hexter in "The Historian and His Day," *Reappraisals in History* (New York: Harper & Row, 1961), 1–13. I am indebted to Douglas Streusand for this reference and also for elaborating its significance in Islamic historiography.

10. James Fallows, *Looking at the Sun: The Rise of the New East Asian Economic and Political System* (New York: Vintage Books, 1995), 299.

11. Ibid., 308.

12. See Mahathir's statement on 45–46, paraphrased, in *Quality and Productivity*. The technical conversation has shifted from the evils of *riba*, or usury, to the benefits of *zakat*, or almsgiving, as in Nik Mustapha Nik Hassan, "Economic Significance of Zakat," in Hamiza Ibrahim and Hasnan Hakim, eds., *Quest for Excellence* (Kuala Lumpur: IKIM, 1994), 115–20. Still others, like M. Umer Chapra, try to chart a path for Islamic economic theory that goes beyond any single measure. Too often the high-level theorists substitute platitudinous generalities for specific guidelines, ignoring the very real gap between Islamic economic theory and the actual practice of Muslim banking. See, e.g., Chapra's critique of the pragmatic approach by Timur Kuran in *Islam and the Economic Challenge* (Herndon, Va.: International Institute of Islamic Thought, 1995), 225–27.

13. M. S. Dobbs-Higginson, a former chief executive officer of Merrill Lynch Asia, is unequivocal about the role of India. "The real need for Mahathir, and ASEAN, is to review the question of India's and Australasia's participation in this vision [of regional economic growth]. Pursuing it without them will, I suspect, prove unfruitful in the long run." *Asia Pacific: Its Role in the New World Disorder* (London: Mandarin, 1994), 322.

14. One of the most unabashed Malaysia boosters is John Naisbitt, who used his fellowship at the Institute for International and Strategic Studies in Kuala Lumpur to write his recent futurist book: *Megatrends*

Asia (New York: Simon & Schuster, 1996), in which he features Malaysia as trendsetter for an Asian economic boom. Like too many forecasters, his crystal ball reflects more Pollyanna than critical thinking.

15. Zam (Zainuddin Maidin), *The Other Side of Mahathir* (English trans. Kuala Lumpur: Utusan Publications & Distributors, 1994), 242–43.

16. While the basic book on this theme in a Christian context remains H. Richard Niebuhr, *Christ and Culture* (New York: Harper & Brothers, 1951), several authors have noted the tension between religion and culture in Muslim history, including Izetbegovic in his classic work, *Islam between East and West*; Vincent J. Cornell, "Towards a Cooperation among People of Different World Religions," in Yaacob and Abdul Rahman, eds. *Towards a Positive Islamic World-View*, 90–98; and, with reference to juridical norms for women, Amina Wadud-Muhsin, *Qur'an and Woman* (Selangoor: Faja Bakti Sdn. Bhd., 1992), and her excellent contribution to Norani Othman and Cecilia Ng Choon Sim, eds., *Gender, Culture and Religion* (Kuala Lumpur: Persatuan Sains Sosial Malaysia, 1995). Titled "Gender, Culture and Religion: an Islamic Perspective," it makes clear in brief strokes how "the cultural inflections of the Islamic teachings" are not the same as first principles (30–38).

17. Syed Othman Alhabshi, *Jurnal IKIM/IKIM Journal* 2.2 (1994): 8.

18. Syed Othman Alhabshi, "Mental Change to Cope 2020" *Jurnal IKIM/IKIM Journal* 1.1 (1993), which reads more like a pep talk for Mahathir's 2020 speech than a systematic analysis.

19. See the brief reference to this incident in the often helpful, always majesterial overview of Malaysian life provided by M. S. Dobbs-Higginson, *Asia Pacific*, 317.

20. Other non-Muslim, non-Malay groups had already been alert to the danger posed by increasing resort to religious rhetoric as the instrument of political jockeying in Malaysia. See *Far Eastern Economic Review*, 22 January 1987: 25. "Non-Muslims and the more secular-minded Muslims fear that Pas and Unmo, by trying to outdo each other on the Islamic chessboard . . . may have introduced or tried to introduce Islamic reforms much too fast for the party leaders themselves to cope with in terms of fulfillment of promises—and for society to absorb. Heightened expectations and unrealistic demands by radical youths are potentially fertile soil for religious tensions, especially given the moral righteousness of religious aspirations." Despite its journalese, this summary statement better catches the generational problem in Malaysia than the full-length article by Shamsul A.B., "Religion and Ethnic Politics in Malaysia: The Significance of the Islamic Resurgence Phenomenon," in Keyes, *Asian Visions of Authority*, 99–116; the latter, perhaps due to the author's in-

volvement in one branch of Islamic resurgence in Malaysia, Pusat Islam, reads too much like a bulletin board monitoring religious traffic on the peninsula. Though it cites a volume highlighting the bases for interreligious tensions in Malaysia, it undervalues the limits of Islam as a politically dominant religion, as do the coauthors of that volume, especially in their consideration of state policies toward Chinese religious practices. See Susan Ackerman and Raymond Lee, *Heaven in Transition: Non-Muslim Religious Innovation and Ethnic Identity in Malaysia* (Honolulu: University of Hawaii Press 1988), 51, 120–53.

21. Wadud-Muhsin, *Qur'an and Woman*. While it is debatable that her approach is as new as she claims, her double effort to read the Qur'an directly from a woman's viewpoint, sidestepping all medieval exegesis (largely by men), and also to "demonstrate the relevance of the Qur'an to the concerns of the modern woman" (95), has produced a book with wide-ranging application to the issue of Muslim norms.

22. A 1993 Malay-German conference, featuring a speech by Mahathir, addressed a wide range of social dimensions and uses of religion, yet it lacked a single woman contributor. See Syed Othman Alhabshi and Syed Omar Syed Agil, eds. *The Role and Influence of Religion in Society* (Kuala Lumpur: IKIM, 1994).

23. All three citations from Mahathir's speeches are indebted to Maidin, *The Other Side of Mahathir*, 138–40.

24. Jan Goodwin, *Price of Honour* (London; Warner, 1994), 205.

25. Of all the critiques of Huntington's banal, simplistic, and ahistorical thesis, the one that applies especially to Southeast Asia comes from the Islamicist Frederick Denny. Quoting from Huntington's original 1993 *Foreign Affairs* article (the 1996 book of the same title had not yet appeared), Denny notes that "Huntington speaks only of 'the crescent-shaped Islamic bloc of nations from the bulge of Africa to central Asia' (32). What about Southeast Asia, where about a fifth of the world's Muslims live? Surely the author knows about Indonesia and Malaysia. Don't they count or do they simply provide an inconvenient set of conditions contrary to his argument about the clash of civilizations?" See Frederick Denny, "American Perceptions of Islam and Muslims," in Yaacob and Abdul Rahman, eds., *Towards a Positive Islamic World-View*, 71–72.

26. Chandra Muzaffar, *Just Viewpoints* (Penang: Just World Trust, 1994), 17. There is, of course, a danger in this argument, as also in much of Muzaffar's writing, that it/he becomes susceptible to a variant of the conspiracy theory: they are all out to get us, we must resist, only resistance works, even if it brings, à la Fanon, death. Yet Muzaffar does fluctuate between an outright condemnation of others' bad faith and the advocacy of new strategies for a just use of resources on the part of dom-

inating actors (G-7 but also Scandinavian countries). See especially his *Human Rights and the New World Order*: (Penang: Just World Trust, 144–76.

27. Alhabshi and Nik Hassan eds., *Quality and Productivity*, 45.

28. Teik, Hoo Boo, *Paradoxes of Mahathirism*, 166.

29. Muzaffar, *Just Viewpoints*, 13.

30. Teik, Hoo Boo, *Paradoxes of Mahathirism* (Kuala Lumpur: Oxford University Press, 1995), 186.

31. See K. George, "Malaysia's Economic Progress: The Other Side of the Coin," *Aliran Monthly* (1995): 10–17.

32. For the range of homologies that apply to Arabic *fitna*, usually rendered into English as "sedition" or "disorder," see the lexical display mounted by E. W. Lane, *Arabic-English Lexicon* (reprinted Cambridge: Islamic Texts Society, 1974), 2:2335–36.

33. Etan Kohlberg, "The Development of the Imami Shi'i Doctrine of Jihad," *Zeitschrift der Deutschen Morganlandischen Gesellschaft* 126 (1976), 1:68. Peters (*Jihad in Mediwal and Modern Islam* [Leioten: E. J. Brill 1977]) cites Kohlberg's article in his bibliography but seems to have ignored its content otherwise.

34. The 17 November 1995 issue of the weekly political journal *Al-Hawadith*, for instance, discusses at length the Palestinian Jihad group from the West Bank. Fathi Shaqaqi, their leader in exile in Syria, was assassinated while in Malta, presumably by Israeli agents, in late October 1995, and his successor, Ramadan 'Abdallah Shalah, has vowed revenge (*intiqam*), declaring that "our jihad is not only military but also religious, for our project is the establishment of Islam." At the same time, he, a Sunni Muslim, acknowledges that he could not hope to carry on the struggle without the assistance of others, especially the Iranian-backed Hizbollah in southern Lebanon, who "provide humanitarian aid, especially for the families of martyrs" (citations from 26 November issue of *Al-Hayat*, a Saudi daily published from London, then syndicated elsewhere).

Even as the cycle of violence never stops in the Middle East, but merely spins into newer episodes of riposte or retaliation, so it is necessary to recognize its cultural limits. Details on the latest invocation of jihad are less important than the index of symbolic capital it provides to the continuous engagement with military-political jihad in West Asia, an engagement not found in Southeast Asia.

35. Fouad Ajami, "In the Pharaoh's Shadow: Religion and Authority in Egypt," in Piscatori, ed., *Islam in the Political Process*, 34.

36. See Emmanuel Sivan, "The Arab Nation-State: In Search of a Usable Past," *Middle East Review* 19.3 (Spring 1987): 29. Sivan develops his views on jihad in a subsequent article, confirming my view that the

dominant force in Muslim politics has been what he calls "adamant nation-state egotism," but unlike me, he surmises that a turn to Islamic radicalism (the term he prefers over "fundamentalism") has become pronounced and irreversible. He even predicts that "the anti-apostate (*murtadd*) Jihad is bound to be the norm towards the end of this century." But with what result, and also with what alternatives from polities put on the defensive? These are questions that beg to be answered, yet are omitted from an otherwise deft essay. See "Jihad: Text, Myth, Historical Realities," in Evelyne Patlagean and Alain Le Boulluec, eds. *Les Retours aux ecritures: Fondamentalismes presents et passes* (Peeters: Louvain-Paris, 1994), 83–99.

37. Muhammad Shahrur, *Dirasat Islamiyat Mu'asirat (fi'd-dawla wal-mujtama')* (Al-Ahali: Damascus, 1994), 341–69.

38. Morteza Motahhari, *Jihad: The Holy War of Islam and Its Legitimacy in the Quran*, trans, Mohammad S. Tawheedi (Albany, Ca.: Moslem Student Association [Persian Speaking Group], n.d.), 35.

39. Ibid., 32.

40. Ibid., 36–37.

41. Ibid., 52–53.

42. Jihad, for Shaykh Fadlallah, is directly linked to *da'wa*, and the crucial discussion of jihad in his book takes place in the subchapter titled "The Instrumentality of jihad in *Da'wa*." Since jihad, like *da'wa*, is linked to the requirements of actualizing power, its invocation becomes justified, or legalized, by the quest for power. Hence Shaykh Fadlallah declares that "the legalization of jihad emanates from the need of Islam for power" (*wa-hiya inna tashri'a 'l-jihad intalaqa min hajati 'l-Islam ila quwwat*). Yet the actual steps by which this gambit is deployed are not spelled out. See Muhammad Husayn Fadlallah, *Al-Islam wa-mantiq al-quwwat* (Beirut: Dar al-Islamiya, 1981), 204.

43. Quoted from *Sahifah-i Nur: Majmu'ah-i Rahnimud'ha-yi Imam Khomeini* (Tehran: Vizarat-i Irshad-i Islami, 1362/1983), v. 13:92–93, as cited in Heidar Ghajar Azodanloo, "Discourses of Mobilization in Post-Revolutionary Iran," (Ph.D. dissertation, University of Minnesota, 1992), 42. As a counterpoint to the narratives from Reinhold Loeffler cited in what follows, one should consult all of Azodanloo's study, but especially chapters 4 and 5 dealing with discourses of martyrdom on the battlefront, followed by strategies for consoling, as well as maintaining the loyalty, of veterans' families.

I am indebted to Professor Bruce Lincoln for providing me with a copy of Azodanloo's dissertation, completed under his supervision while he was still at the University of Minnesota.

44. Loeffler. *Islam in Practice*, 229.

45. Ibid., 235.

46. Ibid., 237.
47. Ibid., 240.
48. Eric Hoogland, "The Pulse of Iran Today," 45–46.
49. One could elaborate on the theme of striving for justice as a modern ideological appeal, exceeding its traditional formulations while still connoting jihad, to the Imami Shiʿis of Iran. For instance, the influential anti-Pahlavi pamphleteer ʿAli Shariʿati formulated an "order of unity" (*nezam-i tawhid*) that harked back to the martyrdom of Imam Hussein. Hussein's sacred sacrifice became, in Shariʿati's view, not only the historical model for continuous opposition to persistent evils, but also the existential catalyst for "striving toward justice, equity, human brotherhood, public ownership of wealth, and, most important of all, a classless society" (Ervand Abrahamian, *Iran between Two Revolutions* [Princeton: Princeton University Press, 1982]: 466).
50. Fallows, *Looking at the Sun*, 309–14.
51. Riduan Wu Chia Chung Ibn Abdallah, "The Chinese Muslims of Singapore: Their Positions and Contributions," paper delivered at a Seminar on Islam and Confucianism: Universality of Islam in Kuching, Sarawak (Malaysia), 17–18 Nov. 1995: 6–8.

Bibliography

Abd-Allah, Umar F. 1983. *The Islamic Struggle in Syria.* Berkeley: Mizan Press.

Abdullah, Mukhtar. 1995. "Historical Developments of Quality and Productivity Movements: Japan vs. the West," in Syed Othman Alhabshi and Nik Mustapha Nik Hassan, eds., *Quality and Productivity: Creating a Difference in Modern Industry and Corporations.* Kuala Lumpur: Institute of Islamic Understanding.

Abrahamian, Ervand. 1982. *Iran between Two Revolutions.* Princeton: Princeton University Press.

———1988. "Ali Shariati: Ideologue of the Iranian Revolution," in Edmund Burke, III, and Ira M. Lapidus, eds. *Islam, Politics and Social Movements.* Berkeley: University of California Press, 289–97.

———1993. *Khomeinism: Essays on the Islamic Republic.* Berkeley: University of California Press.

Ackerman, Susan, and Raymond Lee, eds. 1988. *Heaven in Transition: Non-Muslim Religious Innovation and Ethnic Identity in Malaysia.* Honolulu: University of Hawaii Press

Afkhami, Mahnaz, and Erika Friedl, eds. 1994. *In the Eye of the Storm: Women in Post-Revolutionary Iran.* Syracuse: Syracuse University Press.

Al-Azm, Sadik. 1993–94. "Islamic Fundamentalism Reconsidered: A Critical Outline of Problems, Ideas and Approaches," *South Asia Bulletin: Comparative Studies of Southern Asia, Africa and the Middle East.* Part 1, 13.1 and 2 (1993): 93–121; Part 2. 14.1 (1994): 73–98.

Alhabshi, Syed Othman, and Syed Omar Syed Agil, eds. 1994. *The Role and Influence of Religion in Society.* Kuala Lumpur: IKIM.

Alhabshi, Syed Othman, and Nik Mustapha Nik Hassan, eds. 1995. *Quality and Productivity: Creating a Difference in Modern Industry and Corporations.* Kuala Lumpur: Institute of Islamic Understanding.

Ali, Rabia, and Lawrence Lifschultz, eds. 1993. *Why Bosnia? Writings on the Balkan War.* Stoney Creek: The Pamphleteer's Press.

Al-i Ahmad, Jalal. 1984. *Occidentosis: A Plague from the West.* Trans. R. Campbell. Berkeley: Mizan Press.

Amirahmadi, Hooshang. 1990. *Revolution and Economic Transition: The Iranian Experience.* Albany, State University of New York Press.

Anderson, Benedict. 1983. *Imagined Communities: Reflections on the Origin and Spread of Nationalism.* London: Verso. Reprinted 1991.

Anderson, Lisa. 1991. "Obligation and Accountability: Islamic Politics in North Africa." *Daedalus* 120.3: 93–112.

Arkoun, Mohammed. 1987. *Rethinking Islam Today*. Georgetown: Center for Contemporary Arab Studies.

———1994. *Rethinking Islam: Common Questions, Uncommon Answers*. Boulder: Westview Press.

Armstrong, John. 1982. *Nations Before Nationalism*. Chapel Hill: University of North Carolina Press.

Atiya, Nayra. 1982. *Khul-Khaal: Five Egyptian Women Tell Their Story*. Syracuse: Syracuse University Press.

Azari, Farah, ed. 1983. *Women of Iran: The Conflict with Fundamentalist Islam*. Ithaca: Ithaca Press.

Azodanloo, Heidar Ghajar. 1992. "Discourses of Mobilization in Post-Revolutionary Iran." Ph.D. dissertation, University of Minnesota.

Badran, Margot, and Miriam Cooke, eds. 1990. *Opening the Gates: A Century of Arab Feminist Writings*. London and Bloomington: Virago and Indiana University Press.

Badran, Margot. 1995. *Feminists, Islam, and Nation: Gender and the Making of Modern Egypt*. Princeton: Princeton University Press.

Baker, Raymond W. 1990. *Sadat and After: Struggles for Egypt's Political Soul*. Cambridge: Harvard University Press.

Bakhash, Shaul. 1984. *The Reign of the Ayatollahs: Iran and the Islamic Revolution*. New York: Basic Books.

Barone, Charles A. 1985. *Marxist Thought on Imperialism: Survey and Critique*. Armonk, N.Y.: M. E. Sharpe.

Barraclough, Geoffrey, ed. 1982. *The Times Atlas of World History*. Maplewood, N.J.: Hammond.

Bill, James, and Carl Leiden. 1979. *Politics in the Middle East*. Boston: Little, Brown.

Binder, Leonard. 1988. *Islamic Liberalism*. Chicago: University of Chicago Press.

Bjorkman, J. W., ed. 1988. *Fundamentalism, Revivalists and Violence in South Asia*. Riverdale, Md.: The Riverdale Company.

Bloom, Harold. 1992. *The American Religion: The Emergence of the Post-Christian Nation*. New York: Simon & Schuster.

Bouhdiba, Abdelwahab. 1985. *Sexuality in Islam*. London: Routledge & Kegan Paul.

Brown, Norman O. 1991. *Apocalypse and/or Metamorphosis*. Berkeley: University of California Press.

Bulliet, Richard W. 1994. *Islam: The View from the Edge*. New York: Columbia University Press.

Calhoun, Craig. 1992. "Why Nationalism? Sovereignty, Self-Determination and Identity in a World-System of States." Ms.

Casanova, Jose. 1994. *Public Religions in the Modern World*. Chicago: University of Chicago Press.

Chapra, M. Umer. 1995. *Islam and the Economic Challenge*. Herndon: International Institute of Islamic Thought.

Chefdor, Monique, et al. 1986. *Modernism: Challenges and Perspectives*. Urbana: University of Illinois Press.

Choveiri, Youssef M. 1990. *Islamic Fundamentalism*. Boston: Twayne.

Cooke, Miriam. 1995. "*Ayyam min hayati*: The Prison Memoirs of a Muslim Sister." *Journal of Arabic Literature* 26.1–2.

Corm, Georges. 1988. *Fragmentation of the Middle East: The Last Thirty Years*. London: Hutchinson.

Cragg, Kenneth. 1992. *The House of Islam*. Belmont: Dickenson.

Dabashi, Hamid. 1993. *Theology of Discontent: The Ideological Foundation of the Islamic Revolution in Iran*. New York: New York University Press.

Davidson, Basil. 1992. *The Black Man's Burden: Africa and the Curse of the Nation-State*. New York: Times Books/Random House.

Dobbs-Higginson, M. S. 1994. *Asia Pacific: Its Role in the New World Disorder*. London: Mandarin.

Eickelman, Dale F. and James Piscatori. 1996. *Muslim Politics*. Princeton: Princeton University Press.

Embree, Ainslee T. 1990. *Utopias in Conflict: Religion and Nationalism in Modern India*. Berkeley: University of California Press.

Enayat, Hamid. 1982. *Modern Islamic Political Thought*. London: Macmillan.

Engineer, Ashgar Ali. ed. 1987. *The Shah Bano Controversy*. Hyderabad: Orient Longman.

Esposito, John L., and John O. Voll. 1997. *Islam and Democracy*. New York: Oxford University Press.

Fabian, Johannes. 1986. *Language and Colonial Power: The Appropriation of Swahili in the Former Belgian Congo 1880–1938*. New York: Cambridge University Press.

Fadlallah, Muhammad Husayn. 1981 *Al-Islam wa-mantiq al-quwwat* (Islam and the logic of power). Beirut: Dar al-Islamiya.

Falk, Richard. 1971. *The Endangered Planet*. New York: Vintage/Random House.

Fallows, James. 1995. *Looking at the Sun: The Rise of the New East Asian Economic and Political System*. New York: Vintage Books.

Fanon, Frantz. 1961/1963. *The Wretched of the Earth*, trans. Constance Farrington. New York: Grove Press. Reprinted 1991 by Grove Weidenfeld.

———1964/1965. *A Dying Colonialism*, trans. Haakon Chevalier. New York: Grove Press.

Feuer, Lewis S. 1975. *Ideology and the Ideologists*. New York: Harper & Row.

Fox, Richard, ed. 1990. *Nationalist Ideologies and the Production of National Cultures*. Washington, D.C.: American Anthropological Association.

Friedl, Erika. 1989. *Women of Deh Koh: Women's Lives in an Iranian Village*. Washington, D.C.: Smithsonian.

Friedman, Thomas L. 1989. *From Beirut to Jerusalem*. New York: Farrar Straus Giroux.

Fukuyama, Francis. 1992. *The End of History and The Last Man*. New York: Free Press.

Geertz, Clifford. 1968. *Islam Observed: Religious Development in Morocco and Indonesia*. Chicago: University of Chicago Press.

Gellner, Ernest. 1983. *Nations and Nationalism*. Ithaca: Cornell University Press.

———, ed. 1985. *Islamic Dilemma: Reformers, Nationalists, and Industrialization. The Southern Shore of the Mediterranean*. The Hague: Mouton.

1994. *Conditions of Liberty: Civil Society and Its Rivals*. New York: Allen Lane/The Penguin Press.

Giddens, Anthony. 1985. *The Nation-State and Violence*. Berkeley and Los Angeles: University of California Press.

Gilsenan, Michael. 1982. *Recognizing Islam: Religion and Society in the Modern Arab World*. New York: Pantheon.

Goodwin, Jan. 1994. *Price of Honour: Muslim Women Lift the Veil of Silence on the Islamic World*. London: Warner.

Goody, Jack. 1961. "Religion and Ritual: A Definition Problem." *British Journal of Sociology* 12:142–64.

Gouldner, Alvin W. 1976. *The Dialectic of Ideology and Technology*. New York: Seabury Press.

Greeley, Andrew M. 1982. *Religion: A Secular Theory*. New York: Macmillan.

Greenfeld, Liah. 1993. *Nationalism: Five Roads to Modernity*. Cambridge: Harvard University Press.

Guenena, Nemat. 1986. "The Jihad: An Islamic Alternative in Egypt." *Cairo Papers in Social Science* 8.2 (Summer).

Guha, Ranajit, ed. 1982. *Subaltern Studies*. Vol. 1. Delhi: Oxford University Press.

———1983. *Subaltern Studies*. Vol. 2. Delhi: Oxford University Press.

———1984. *Subaltern Studies*. Vol. 3. Delhi: Oxford University Press.

———1985. *Subaltern Studies*. Vol. 4. Delhi: Oxford University Press.

Gutmann, Roy. 1993. *Witness to Genocide*. New York: Macmillan.

Halliday, Fred, and Hamza Alavi, eds. 1988. *State and Ideology in the Middle East and Pakistan*. London: Macmillan.

Harrison, Christopher. 1988. *France and Islam in West Africa, 1860–1960*. New York: Cambridge University Press.

Hijab, Nadia. 1988. *Womanpower: The Arab Debate on Women at Work*. New York: Cambridge University Press.

Hiro, Dilip. 1989. *Holy Wars: The Rise of Islamic Fundamentalism*. New York: Routledge.

Hobsbawm, Eric J. 1962. *The Age of Revolution 1789–1848*. New York: Mentor.

——1991. *Nations and Nationalism since 1870*. London: Canto Press.

——1993. "The New Threat to History." *The New York Review of Books* 16 December 1993: 62–64.

Hodgson, Marshall G. S. 1979. *The Venture of Islam: Conscience and History in a World Civilization*. 3 vols. Chicago: University of Chicago Press.

——1993. *Rethinking World History*. Cambridge: Cambridge University Press.

Hollis, Martin, and Steven Lukes, eds. 1982. *Rationality and Relativism*. Cambridge: MIT Press.

Hooker, M. B., ed. 1983. *Islam in South-east Asia*. Leiden: E. J. Brill.

Horowitz, Donald L. 1985. *Ethnic Groups in Conflict*. Berkeley and Los Angeles: University of California Press.

Horton, Robin. 1967. "African Traditional Thought and Western Science." *Africa* 38:50–71, 155–87.

Hourani, Albert. 1991a. *A History of the Arab Peoples*. Cambridge: Harvard University Press.

——1991b. *Islam in European Thought*. Cambridge: Cambridge University Press.

Hunter, Shireen T., ed. 1988. *The Politics of Islamic Revivalism*. Bloomington: University of Indiana Press.

Huntington, Samuel P. 1993. "The Clash of Civilizations?" *Foreign Affairs* 72.3 (Summer): 22–49.

——1996. *The Clash of Civilizations and the Remaking of World Order*. New York: Simon & Schuster.

Hussain, Freda, ed. 1984. *Muslim Women*. New York: St. Martin's Press.

Iqbal, Allama Muhammad. 1934/1982. *The Reconstruction of Religious Thought in Islam*. Lahore: Sh. Muhammad Ashraf.

Islamoglu-Inan, Huri, ed. 1987. *The Ottoman Empire and the World-Economy*. Cambridge: Cambridge University Press.

Issawi, Charles. 1988. *The Fertile Crescent, 1800–1914: A Documentary and Economic History*. New York: Oxford.

Izetbegovic, ʿAlija ʿAli. 1984. *Islam between East and West*. Indianapolis: American Trust Publications.

Juergensmeyer, Mark. 1993. *The New Cold War? Religious Nationalism Confronts the Secular State*. Berkeley and Los Angeles: University of California Press.

Kandiyoti, Deniz, ed. 1991. *Women, Islam & the State*. Philadelphia: Temple University Press.

Kapferer, Bruce. 1991. "Nationalist Ideology and a Comparative Anthropology," *Ethnos* 54.3–4: 161–99.

Kasaba, Resat. 1988. *The Ottoman Empire and the World Economy: The Nineteenth Century*. Albany: State University of New York Press.

Kelly, Ron, Jonathan Friedlander, and Anita Colby, eds. 1993. *Irangeles: Iranians in Los Angeles*. Berkeley: University of California Press.

Kepel, Gilles, and Yann Richard, eds. 1990. *Intellectuels et militants del'islam contemporain*. Paris: Le Seuil.

Keyes, Charles F., et al. 1994. *Asian Visions of Authority: Religion and the Modern States of East and Southeast Asia*. Honolulu: University of Hawaii Press.

Khoury, Philip S., and Joseph Kostiner, eds. 1990. *Tribes and State Formation in the Middle East*. Berkeley: University of California Press.

Kliever, Lonnie D., ed. 1987. *The Terrible Meek: Religion and Revolution in Cross-Cultural Perspective*. New York: Paragon.

Kramer, Martin. 1993. "Islam versus Democracy." *Commentary* 95.1: 35–42.

Lacapra, Dominick. 1983. *Rethinking Intellectual History*. Ithaca: Cornell University Press.

Laitin, David D. 1986. *Hegemony and Culture: Politics and Religious Change among the Yoruba*. Chicago: University of Chicago Press.

Landau, Jacob. 1990. *The Politics of Pan-Islam: Ideology and Organization*. Oxford: Oxford University Press.

Lapidus, Ira M. 1988. *A History of Islamic Societies*. Cambridge: Cambridge University Press.

Laroui, Abdallah. 1976. *The Crisis of the Arab Intellectual: Traditionalism or Historicism?* Trans. Diarmid Cammell. Berkeley and Los Angeles: University of California Press.

Lawrence, Bruce B. 1989. *Defenders of God: The Fundamentalist Revolt against the Modern Age*. San Francisco: Harper & Row. (2d edition, Columbia: University of South Carolina Press, 1995.)

————1991. "The Religious Idiom of Violence: A View from Indonesia." In Mark Juergensmeyer, ed. *Violence and the Sacred in the Modern World*, a special edition of *Terrorism and Political Violence* 3.3: 82–100.

Lawson, Fred. 1982. "Social Bases for the Hamah Revolt," *Middle East Reports in Progress (MERIP)* 12.9 (Nov.–Dec.): 24–28.

———. 1987. "Muslim Fundamentalist Movements: Reflections toward a New Approach," in Barbara F. Stowassar, ed., *The Islamic Impluse.* London: Croom Helm.

Lindbeck, George A. 1984. *The Nature of Doctrine: Religion and Theology in a Postliberal Age.* Philadelphia: Westminster.

Loeffler, Reinhold. 1988. *Islam and Practice: Religious Lives in a Persian Village.* Albany: State University of New York Press.

MacLeod, Arlene. 1991. *Accommodating Protest: Working Women, the New Veiling, and Change in Cairo.* New York: Columbia University Press.

Malcolm, Noel. 1994. *Bosnia: A Short History.* New York: New York University Press.

Malson, Micheline, et al. 1989. *Feminist Theory in Practice and Process.* Chicago: University of Chicago Press.

Migdal, Joel S. 1988. *Strong Societies and Weak States: State-Society Relations and State Capabilities in the Third World.* Princeton: Princeton University Press.

Minault, Gail. 1982. *The Kilafat Movement: Religious Symbolism and Political Mobilization in India.* New York: Columbia University Press.

Moghadam, Valentine M., 1993. *Modernizing Women: Gender and Social Change in the Middle East.* Boulder: Lynne Rienner.

———. ed. 1994a. *Gender and National Identity: Women and Politics in Muslim Societies.* London: Zed Books.

———. ed. 1994b. *Identity Politics and Women: Cultural Reassertions and Feminisms in International Perspective.* Boulder: Westview Press.

Moore, Barrington, Jr. 1966. *Social Origins of Dictatorship and Democracy: Lord and Peasant in the Making of the Modern World.* Boston: Beacon Press.

Moore, Clement H. 1965. *Tunisia since Independence: The Dynamics of a One-Party System.* Berkeley: University of California Press.

Morey, Robert. 1992. *The Islamic Invasion: Confronting the World's Fastest Growing Religion.* Eugene, Ore.: Harvest House.

Morgan, Robin, ed. 1984. *Sisterhood is Global.* New York: Anchor-Doubleday.

Mortimer, Edward. 1982. *Faith and Power: The Politics of Islam.* New York: Random House.

Motahhari, Mortaza. n.d. *Sexual Ethics in Islam.* Muslim Student Association—Persian Speaking Group.

Mottahedeh, Roy P. 1995. "The Islamic Movement: The Case for Democratic Inclusion," *Contention* 4.3: 107–27.

Mottahedeh, Roy P. 1996. "The Clash of Civilizations: An Islamicist's Critique," *Harvard Middle Eastern and Islamic Review* 2.2:1–26.

Moussalli, Ahmad S. 1992. *Radical Islamic Fundamentalism: The Ideological and Political Discourse of Sayyid Qutb*. Beirut: American University of Beirut.

Mumtaz, Khawar, and Farida Shaheed, eds. 1987. *Women of Pakistan: Two Steps Forward, One Step Backward*. London: Zed Press.

Munson, Henry, Jr. 1988. *Islam and Revolution in the Middle East*. New Haven: Yale University Press.

Murphey, Rhoads. 1992. *A History of Asia*. New York: HarperCollins.

Muzaffar, Chandra. 1993. *Human Rights and the New World Order*. Penang: Just World Trust.

———. 1994. *Just Viewpoints*. Penang: Just World Trust.

Nagata, Judith. 1984. *The Reflowering of Malaysian Islam*. Vancouver: University of British Columbia Press.

Naisbitt, John. 1996. *Megatrends Asia*. New York: Simon and Schuster.

Nashat, Guity. 1983. *Women and Revolution in Iran*. Boulder: Westview Press.

Nasr, Sayyed Vali Reza. 1994. *The Vanguard of the Islamic Revolution: The Jama'at-i Islami of Pakistan*. Berkeley: University of California Press.

Niebuhr, H. Richard. 1951. *Christ and Culture*. New York: Harper & Brothers.

Ninian Smart and Peter Merkl eds. *Religion and Politics in the Modern World*. New York: New York University Press.

Othman, Norani and Cecilia Ng Choon Sim, eds. 1995. *Gender, Culture and Religion*. Kuala Lumpur: Persatuan Sains Sasial Malaysia.

Panikkar, Raimundo. 1983. "Regional Politics: The Western Dilemma," in Niniam Smart and Peter Merkl, eds., *Religion and Politics in the Modern World*. New York: New York University Press.

Patlagean, Evelyne, and Alain Le Boulluec, eds. 1994. *Les Retours aux ecritures: Fondamentalismes presents et passes*. Peeters: Louvain-Paris.

Paz, Octavio. 1985. *One Earth, Four or Five Worlds: Reflections on Contemporary History*. New York: Harcourt, Brace, Jovanovich.

Pearl, David. 1987. *A Textbook on Muslim Personal Law*. London: Croom Helm.

Perinbaum, B. Marie. 1982. *Holy Violence: The Revolutionary thought of Frantz Fanon*. Washington, D.C.: Three Continents Press.

Peters, Rudolph, 1977. *Jihad in Medieval and Modern Islam*. Leiden: E. J. Brill.

Pick, Daniel. 1993. *War Machine: The Rationalisation of Slaughter in the Modern Age*. New Haven: Yale University Press.

226

Piscatori, James, ed. 1983. *Islam in the Political Process*. Cambridge: Cambridge University Press.

———1986. *Islam in a World of Nation-States*. Cambridge: Cambridge University Press.

Pletsch, Carl E. 1981. "The Three Worlds, or the Division of Social Scientific Labor, circa 1950–1975," *Comparative Studies in Society and History* 23: (October): 565–90.

Qutb, Muhammad. 1977. *Islam: The Misunderstood Religion*. Damascus: The Holy Koran Publishing House.

Qutb, Sayyid. 1964. *Ma'alim fi't-Tariq* (Milestones on the path). Cairo: Dar ash-Shuruq.

Rahman, Fazlur. 1979. *Islam*. 2d ed. Chicago: University of Chicago Press.

———. 1982. *Islam and Modernity: Transformation of an Intellectual Tradition*. Chicago: University of Chicago Press.

Rai, Janak Raj, ed. 1986. *Shah Bano*. New Delhi: Rajiv Publications.

Richards, Alan, and John Waterbury. 1990. *A Political Economy of the Middle East: State, Class and Economic Development*. Boulder: Westview Press.

Roy, Olivier. 1994. *The Failure of Political Islam*, trans. Carol Folk. Cambridge: Harvard University Press.

Rudolph, Susan, and James Piscatori, eds. 1997. *Transnational Religion & Fading States*. Boulder: Westview Press.

Saadawi, Nawal El. 1982. *The Hidden Face of Eve*. Boston: Beacon Press.

Sabagh, George, ed. 1989. *The Modern Economic and Social History of the Middle East in Its World Context*. Cambridge: Cambridge University Press.

Sagiv, David. 1995. *Fundamentalism and Intellectuals in Egypt 1973–1993*. London: Frank Cass.

Said, Edward. 1983. "Opponents, Audiences, Constituencies and Community." In Hal Foster, ed. *The Anti-Aesthetic: Essays on Postmodern Culture*. Port Townsend, Wash.: Bay Press, 135–59.

Salame, Ghassan, ed. 1994. *Democracy without Democrats? The Renewal of Politics in the Muslim World*. London: I. B. Tauris.

Salem, Norma. 1984. *Habib Bourguiba, Islam and the Creation of Tunisia*, London: Croom Helm.

Seale, Patrick. 1988. *Asad: The Struggle for the Middle East*. Berkeley: University of California Press.

Segal, Robert. 1994. "Joachim Wach and the History of Religions." *Religious Studies Review* 20.3: 197–201.

Sekyi-Otu, Ato. 1996. *Fanon's Dialectic of Experience*. Cambridge: Harvard University Press.

227

Seligman, Adam B. 1992. *The Idea of a Civil Society.* Princeton: Princeton University Press.

Sharabi, Hisham, 1988, *Neopatriarchy: A Theory of Distorted Change in Arab Society.* New York: Oxford University Press.

Shahrur, Muhammad. 1994. *Dirasat Islamiya Mu'asira (fi'd-dawla wal-mujtamaʿ)* (Contemporary Islamic studies on the state and society). Al-Ahali: Damascus.

Sinha, Niroj, ed. 1989. *Women and Violence.* New Delhi: Vikas.

Skocpol, Theda, ed. 1984. *Vision and Method in Historical Sociology.* New York: Cambridge University Press.

Smart, Ninian, and Peter Merkl, eds. 1983. *Religion and Politics in the Modern World.* New York: New York University Press.

Smith, Anthony D. 1979. *Nationalism in the Twentieth Century.* New York: New York University Press.

Smith, Jonathan Z. 1982. *Imagining Religion: From Babylon to Jonestown.* Chicago: University of Chicago Press.

Smith, Wilfred C. 1957. *Islam in Modern History.* Princeton: Princeton University Press.

———1962. *The Meaning and End of Religion.* New York: Macmillan.

———1981. *On Understanding Islam.* Mouton: The Hague.

Snyder, Louis L. 1982. *Global Mini-Nationalisms: Autonomy or Independence.* Westport, Conn.: Westport Press.

Spivak, Gayatri Chakravorty. 1987. *In Other Worlds: Essays in Cultural Politics.* New York: Methuen.

Tabari, Azar, and Nahid Yeganeh, eds. 1982. *In the Shadow of Islam. The Woman's Movement in Iran.* London: Zed Press.

Taha, Ustad Mahmoud. 1987. *The Second Message of Islam.* Syracuse: Syracuse University Press.

Talbot, Ian. 1988. *The Punjab and the Raj, 1849–1947.* Riverdale: Riverdale Company.

Tamimi, Azzam, ed. 1993. *Power-sharing Islam?* London: Liberty for Muslim World Publications.

Teik, Hoo Boo. *Paradoxes of Mahathirism.* 1995. Kuala Lumpur: Oxford University Press.

Tibi, Bassam. 1981. *Arab Nationalism: A Critical Enquiry.* New York: St. Martin's Press. Reprinted 1990.

———1989. *The Crisis of Modern Islam: A Preindustrial Culture in the Scientific-Technological Age.* Salt Lake City: University of Utah Press.

———1990. *Islam and the Cultural Accommodation of Social Change.* Boulder: Westview Press.

Turner, Bryan. 1983. *Marx and the End of Orientalism.* London: George Allen and Unwin.

Van der Veer, Peter. 1988. *Gods on Earth: The Management of Religious Experience and Identity in a North Indian Pilgrimage Centre.* London: Athlone Press.

Van Laue, Theodore. 1987. *The World Revolution of Westernization.* New York: Oxford University Press.

Vieille, Paul, and Farhad Khosrokhavar. 1990. *Le Discours populaire de la revolution iranienne.* 2 vols. Paris: Contemporaneite.

Vovelle, Michel. 1990. *Ideologies and Mentalities.* Chicago: University of Chicago Press.

Wadud-Muhsin, Amina. *Qur'an and Woman.* 1992. Selangor Penerbit Fajar Bakti Sdn. Bhd, and Kuala Lumpur: Oxford University Press.

Waldman, Marilyn. 1987. "The Islamic World." *Encyclopaedia Britannica Macropaedia.* Chicago: Britannica Publishing, 112–33.

Wallerstein, Immanuel. 1979. *The Capitalist World-System.* Cambridge: Cambridge University Press.

Waltz, Kenneth N. 1979. *Theory of International Politics.* New York: McGraw-Hill.

Waterbury, John. 1979. *Hydropolitics of the Nile Valley.* Syracuse: Syracuse University Press.

Weiss, Anita, ed. 1986. *Islamic Reassertion in Pakistan: The Application of Islamic Laws in a Modern State.* Syracuse: Syracuse University Press.

Willner, Ruth Ann. 1984. *The Spellbinders.* New Haven: Yale University Press.

Woodward, Mark R. 1989. *Islam in Java: Normative Piety and Mysticism in the Sultanate of Yogyakarta.* Tucson: University of Arizona Press.

Yaacob, Abdul Monir, and Ahmad Faiz Abdul Rahman, eds. 1994. *Towards a Positive Islamic World-View: Malaysian and American Perspectives.* Kuala Lumpur: Institute of Islamic Understanding.

Yamani, Mai, ed. 1996. *Feminism & Islam: Legal and Literary Perspectives.* New York: New York University Press.

Young, Robert. 1990. *White Mythologies: Writing History and the West.* London and New York: Routledge.

Zakaria, Rafiq. 1989. *The Struggle within Islam.* London: Penquin.

Zam (Zainuddin Maidin). 1994. *The Other Side of Mahathir.* Eng. trans. Kuala Lumpur: Utusan Publications & Distributors.

Index

53–56; and Islam, 9–10, 68; mimetic, 47, 49; and Muslim history, 23–25; regional, 24, 25; and religion, 13–18, 25, 51–52; secular, 33, 45–50; traits of, 48
New York Times, 4
Nigeria, 33, 35, 43, 92, 160
No Revolutions thesis, 97
nomenclature, 40–41
Numeiri, General, 155
Nun, 121

oikumene (Afro-Eur-Asian), 25
oil: impact of, 51–52; and Iran, 94, 95, 98; and Muslim state formation, 27–28; and Saudi Arabia, 36–37, 86; and Syria, 72
Oman, 47, 92
Open Door (*infitah*) policy, 123
Organization for Economic Co-operation and Development (OECD), 35
Organization of Petroleum Exporting Countries (OPEC), 51, 87
Ottoman Empire, 27, 69

Padris, 43
Pakistan, 35, 36, 56–62, 92; and oil, 28; and Shah Bano case, 6; Supreme Court, 142, 143, 145, 146; women in, 125–30, 138–49
Palestinians, 92, 176–77
pan-Arabism, 52, 63
Pan-Islamism, 23–24, 26, 52
Panikkar, Raimundo, 23
Partition (of India and Pakistan), 57–58
PAS, 167
patriotism, 25
patronage, 92
Paz, Octavio, 12–13
Peasant Union, 74
Personal Status Law, 121, 123
Pick, Daniel, 13
Piscatori, James, 89
pluralism, 4, 8, 33, 150; Chinese, 158, 168. See also diversity
political participation, 38, 105
politics, 14–15; divine, 22–26
polygyny, 54, 77, 84, 117, 125, 144

postcolonialism, 10, 24–25, 68
power, 163–64
Prabhasa Malay, 184
preservations, divinely mandated, 53–54
profit, 164–65, 171
protest, 41, 49, 74, 81, 84, 110
Provisional Constitutional Order of 1981, 143

Qabus of Oman, 47
Qaddafi, Muammar, 151
Qardaha, 71
Qazi Courts, 145
Qisas and Diyat Ordinance, 144
Qunaitra, 71
Qur'an and Woman (Wadud-Muhsin), 169
Qur'an, 22, 59; and corporate culture, 161; and fundamentalism, 136; as law, 139; and myth, 154; and power, 164; and principle of abrogation, 172–73; as state constitution, 86; and women, 117, 126, 147–48, 169
Qutb, Muhammad, 21–22
Qutb, Sayyid, 22, 68, 122

radicalism. *See* fundamentalism
Rafsanjani, 100–101, 119
Rahman, Fazlur, 148
Ramadan, 77–79
rape, 144
reform and reformers, 33, 45–50, 148–49
religion, 12–20, 78; and ideology, 157, 165; Islam as, 66; as a mask, 85
revivalism, 33, 40–44, 152
Reza Shah, Mohammed, 95
Rights of Women in Islam, The (Motahhari), 115
Rushdie, Salman, 162

el-Saadawi, Nawal, 121, 128–29
Sadat, Anwar, 65–66, 122, 123, 174
Sakr, Dr. Mohamed, 54–55
Salafiya (Islamic advocacy), 45–46
Salem, Norma, 40
Sanusis, 43
Satanic Verses, The (Rushdie), 162
al-Sa'ud, 87

235